RIGHTING THE ECONOMY

RIGHTING THE ECONOMY

Towards a People's Recovery from Economic and Environmental Crisis

Edited by
MARIANNA LEITE AND MATTI KOHONEN

agenda
publishing

First published in 2024 by Agenda Publishing

Agenda Publishing Limited
PO Box 185
Newcastle upon Tyne
NE20 2DH
www.agendapub.com

ISBN 978-1-78821-686-9

British Library Cataloguing-in-Publication Data
A catalogue record for this book is available from the British Library

Typeset by Newgen Publishing UK
Printed and bound in the UK by TJ Books

CONTENTS

ACKNOWLEDGEMENTS

We would like to thank Agenda Publishing, blind reviewers, authors and critical friends who helped shape the ideas around this book, namely Caroline Othim, Caroline Dommen, Chitralekha Massey, Daria Caliguire, Denise Martínez Velez, Duma Gqubule, Emilia Reyes, Sakshi Rai and Thorsten Göbel. We are equally appreciative of the support of Kate Donald and Verónica Cadavid González during the early and late stages of this book project. This work would not have been possible without the logistical and financial support of the Financial Transparency Coalition, ACT Alliance, the Wellspring Foundation and FORGE.

FOREWORD

The Covid-19 pandemic had an indisputable negative impact on human rights worldwide. The prolonged lockdowns marked a turning point for humanity. Unfortunately, shortly after exiting the Covid-19 nightmare, there is still a clear disregard of the pandemic's harmful effects. The return to normality, ushered in by vaccines, has led to a collective amnesia of the profound inequalities that the pandemic laid bare.

During the first months of the pandemic, hospital facilities, nursing homes, prisons and educational institutions were the focus of attention. Despite this, the tragedy exacerbated society's individualistic model, in which "everyone saves themselves". In this model, the focus on rights tends to be a matter of niche interest or to be relevant solely for countries with advanced development, which can devote effort to this task. At the same time, and without empirical basis, our economic model insists that social rights have a high cost that must be carefully weighed; as if safeguarding civil and political rights were not as costly.

In this context, in an effort not to forget the pandemic's impact on the world and to highlight its effects on historically discriminated groups, the book that I present here acquires a fundamental relevance. Covid-19 will mark this generation, and changes are expected both in terms of our own understanding of social relations and wider societal dimensions – one of which is the economic.

From Chile's perspective, this takes on special significance given the current constitutional discussion. In October 2019 social protests spread throughout the country in response to an accumulated antipathy towards the economic model installed by force during the dictatorship of General Augusto Pinochet. This model, promoted by the "Chicago Boys" and with Chile as a testing ground, has been in crisis as a result of a series of events that led to citizen protest.

Today Chile awaits a new constitution, after the first proposal was rejected by the vast majority of the population in a referendum in September 2022. Paradoxically, this first proposal placed, at its heart, the guarantee of social rights through a social rule of law instead of a subsidiary state. Because of the first plebiscite's results, the discussion has changed and refocused under the slogan of pragmatism on matters of security and public order, and it is much less ambitious in its rights-based approach.

The discussion of the role of the state in the economy continues to be a pivotal topic. It is nevertheless remarkable how, in a short period of time, a medium-sized country of about 20 million inhabitants has shifted from one side of the economic debate to the other – just as humanity, engulfed by the new "normality", forgets the lessons learned from the pandemic catastrophe and presses forward on autopilot mode.

Hence the relevance of this work and the need for academia, activists and policy-makers to come together and develop a human rights approach to the global economy. This volume presents a thorough study of the theory of the relationship between economies, human rights and the international regulatory framework of financial and corporate actors; and an empirical or practical analysis of how it is possible to transform economies through the application of a rights-based lens. It is one further effort, among several others, to give space to a discussion that we have been losing sight of.

Deva and Kaur, for example, point out the draft international legally binding instrument on transnational corporations. They deepen the analysis of globalized markets and the impact that corporations generate for human rights. The gap between theory and practice, the efforts to reimagine corporate responsibility and the focus on the centrality of rights-holders in due diligence processes are key. Given the opportunity that the ongoing discussion of the adoption of the international legally binding instrument represents for multilateralism, this is highly salient.

This book also focuses on the worldwide climate emergency, which is an equivalent pandemic affecting ecosystems. The relevant chapters enable us to understand how the economy and care for the environment have been drastically shaped by a model focused on maximizing profits. Intergenerational obligations appear here as a duty that states cannot avoid, in addition to the responsibility of states to regulate companies' activities and their impact on human rights.

States play a preponderant role in generating transformative impacts. In January 2023 Chile and Colombia requested an advisory opinion from the Inter-American Court of Human Rights on the scope of the obligations under the American Convention on Human Rights in response to the climate emergency. Like this initiative, others are under way before the International Tribunal for the Law of the Sea (ITLOS) and the International Court of Justice

(ICJ), which are aimed at clarifying states' obligations in this area. There are tools at the disposal of states, and it is possible for them to act in the way that the second part of this work considers.

This volume attempts to demonstrate that a human rights-based economy is possible and profitable. The persuasiveness of this argument under the empirical description of successful models is an important contribution. De Schutter's chapter explains this very well, refuting the idea that economic growth is the tool that allows the satisfaction of economic, social and cultural rights, or poverty reduction. The author's reference to the devastating consequences of extractive-based "growth" to the ecosystem, and its subsequent instability for communities, is illuminating.

Finally, I would like to thank Marianna Leite, Matti Kohonen and their team for the invitation to present this opinion from the Global South. Chile has taken decisive steps towards caring for the environment and recognized the importance of having a feminist approach to international relations, placing the respect and promotion of human rights at its centre. Chile's turquoise and feminist foreign policy, inaugurated with the administration of President Gabriel Boric, is evidence of this commitment.[1] Books such as this one encourage those of us who work within the state apparatus to contribute more to just and sustainable societies.

Tomás Pascual Ricke
Ambassador
Director of Human Rights
Ministry of Foreign Affairs of Chile

---

1. With regard to the environment, Boric is eager to portray himself as a Latin American leader in the fight against the climate crisis. Boric advocates for a so-called "turquoise" foreign policy: a two-pronged approach based on "green" policies to combat climate change and "blue" ones aimed at protecting the oceans. See Vilchinskii (2022).

HUMAN RIGHTS ECONOMY FOR PEOPLE AND THE PLANET: FRAMING THE CONTOURS OF AN APPROACH

*Jyoti Sanghera**

The world today appears to be at the brink of a potential system collapse; the planet is literally "burning", "drowning" and "melting", and societies are in deep distress. A daily spectacle of fires, melting glaciers, flash floods, food riots, interminable fuel queues, homelessness, gruelling poverty and capsized boats overloaded with migrants plays out before our very eyes. Oxfam and others do a competent job of updating us each year in their annual reports on the pandemic of galloping poverty and inequality. The recent global figures are beyond alarming, with the richest 10 per cent owning 76 per cent of the total wealth while the poorest half has only 2 per cent.[1] And what's more, the Covid-19 pandemic delivered a bumper harvest to the top 1 per cent of the global rich who gained almost two-thirds of the newly generated wealth since 2020.[2] From our perspective as human rights advocates, the gaping chasm between the international legal order and the reality on the ground seems increasingly unbridgeable. The right to self-determination is inalienable, entitlements to all human rights are universal, without discrimination, and states have the duty to protect, as well as to meet all their commitments under international law. And yet, we have instances where international

---

* Jyoti Sanghera was one of the two founding co-chairs of the Surge Initiative of the Office of the High Commissioner for Human Rights. Currently retired, she has authored the framing reflections for this collection in order to capture the seminal experience of the Surge Initiative advanced by the OHCHR team of staff (ESCR, SDGs, partnerships and constituency-building staff at HQ, as well as several in-country staff) and consultants (economists).

1. Oxfam, "Richest 1% bag nearly twice as much wealth as the rest of the world put together over the past two years", press release, 16 January 2023; www.oxfam.org/en/press-releases/richest-1-bag-nearly-twice-much-wealth-rest-world-put-together-over-past-two-years.
2. *Ibid.*

lawyers and the international community tip-toe around critical issues as the complexities and indeterminacies of international law are used to legitimize the status quo. The system is surely tipping over the precipice.

The trajectory of this malaise is based on several years of neglect by governments to respect their human rights obligations, especially of those most *left behind*. The social contract enshrined in the Universal Declaration of Human Rights (UDHR) 75 years ago, stands largely torn and tattered today. Covid-19 exposed the shocking consequences everywhere, of chronic underinvestment in social spending – in public health, social protection and other economic and social rights. As pointed out by the UN secretary general in the midst of the pandemic, "we are in an age of unprecedented inequality, and a *new social contract* with human rights at the core, is urgently required to reset the balance".

Sadly, it took a grave global crisis like the Covid-19 pandemic to acknowledge the urgent need for a departure from the "business-as-usual" model. It became evident to many that realizing human rights is an essential lever for achieving inclusive, equitable and sustainable development. And for saving the planet. As the detrimental effects of the Covid-19 pandemic intensified with the vaccine injustice, followed by the Ukraine war and the global economic crisis, many red flags appeared. With disproportionate consequences for the most disadvantaged groups and heightened risks of social turmoil, the UN system was compelled to think differently on how to reset economies and ramp up efforts to integrate human rights in its strategies. The Office of the High Commissioner for Human Rights (OHCHR) as the custodian of international human rights mechanisms, emerged as a key player in these efforts. However, we are not alone on this path; this collection of essays reveals several co-travellers on a common journey.

It became clear to many of us at OHCHR that innovative solutions and a fresh approach that weld together human rights with economic policy-making were the need of the hour. The concept of the Human Rights Economy (HRE) grew out of this understanding. It was developed by OHCHR's Surge Initiative[3] (2019) through its work in more than 50 countries. Notably, the

---

3. OHCHR's Surge Initiative was designed to demonstrate the value of embedding human rights in development and economic policies. It was conceived in late 2019 with the aim to step up country-focused operational advice to the UN Development System on ESCRs and to integrate human rights in efforts to accelerate the SDGs' implementation. The launch of the "Decade of Action" vis-à-vis the SDGs and repurposed UN Common Country Analysis (CCA) and the UN Sustainable Development Cooperation Frameworks (UNSDCFs) were key elements in shaping the vision of the Surge Initiative. The Surge team is composed of five macroeconomists and OHCHR's ESCR and development specialists, working in geographic teams across the five regions of the globe. It filled a long-standing gap by translating human rights standards and recommendations of UN human rights mechanisms (HRMs)

HRE concept is grounded in a reliable evidence base generated through the Seeding Change projects piloted jointly by OHCHR's country presences and the Surge team at HQ in Geneva. The HRE is a transformative approach to integrating human rights principles into economic, social and environmental policies. It places the people and the planet at its core with the aim to reduce inequalities and ensure sustainable growth for the purpose of shared prosperity and the well-being of all.[4] Rooted in the HRE approach are the principles of inherent dignity and worth of every individual, and the interdependence of civil, political, economic, social and cultural rights.

OHCHR has been working over the past four years to unpack how to expand fiscal space available to governments so as to align their fiscal policies with their human rights obligations, especially on ESC rights and SDGs. Tackling the deficit in resources available to governments is one of the major challenges. Around 60 per cent of low-income countries face debt distress with debt servicing consuming as much as a quarter of government revenue in some cases.[5] Developing countries face higher costs in accessing international capital markets, creating a severe resource gap. The investment shortfall and increased needs already since 2015 have left developing countries with a $4 trillion gap in sustainable development investments.[6]

To meet these challenges concretely, OHCHR extended support to the government in Jordan for a human rights-based budget analysis to help align revenues with development priorities and to enhance accountability in resource mobilization to effectively address inequalities.[7] In the Lao People's Democratic Republic, OHCHR supported the government to finance inclusive and sustainable development, including ESC rights, amid significant foreign debt repayment linked to major investment projects. In Argentina, OHCHR examined the impact of the pandemic and austerity measures on

---

on ESCRs into country-specialized advice and policy options for Covid-19 emergency measures and long-term socioeconomic recovery. The Surge team currently includes a senior staff member for constituency building and partnerships. It is co-chaired by the Chiefs of ESCR and SDGs sections, and is located in the Development, Economic and Social Issues Branch within OHCHR.

4. United Nations Human Rights Media Centre, "Türk calls for a human right economy", 6 February 2023; www.ohchr.org/en/statements-and-speeches/2023/02/turk-calls-human-rights-economy.

5. IMF, *Crisis Upon Crisis: IMF Annual Report 2022*; www.imf.org/external/pubs/ft/ar/2022/in-focus/debt-dynamics/.

6. UN News, "Developing countries face $4 trillion investment gap in SDGs", 5 July 2023; https://news.un.org/en/story/2023/07/1138352.

7. United Nations Jordan, "Domestic resource mobilization: a human rights-based approach to tackling inequalities"; https://jordan.un.org/en/224081-domestic-resource-mobilization-human-rights-based-approach-tackling-inequalities.

selected ESC rights by analysing the country's fiscal capacity. In Colombia and Nepal, OHCHR attempted to calculate the cost of the minimum essential levels to meet the core obligations on the right to food and reproductive health, respectively, for specific groups.

These are just some examples. The Surge team looked at how debt, revenues, budgets and corruption either restrict or free up fiscal space to provide for the rights to health, social protection, food and water, etc., as well as to fulfil the SDGs. The concrete evidence gathered also assisted in monitoring economic realities and shifts so as to signal risks or early warning triggers in relation to prevention. This innovative work by OHCHR at the country level has opened doors to new partnerships with UN agencies, governments, international financial institutions (IFIs) and, importantly, to a host of CSOs and INGOs. My opening remarks on the Surge experience are in recognition of this partnership and to support our collective efforts to drill deeper into the HRE concept in order to operationalize it in our respective work.

Despite being an essential lever to realizing the 2030 Agenda, the International Covenant on ESCR (ICESCR) has remained largely untapped by the UN development system. The covenant's Guidance underscores the obligation to ensure the "minimum essential levels" of ESC rights by allocating the "maximum available resources" to prevent "retrogression" or to "progressively" realize ESCRs. This guidance and recommendations are not consistently leveraged in engagement with governments on resource generation and budget allocation for social spending or to achieve SDG targets. Similarly, recommendations by the various human rights mechanisms are unevenly incorporated by governments and UN entities in country strategies on financing for development. By introducing country-specific, specialized economic expertise, albeit limited on account of capacity, OHCHR began the journey to redress this gap and to incrementally add flesh onto the bones of the HRE approach.

RE-IMAGINING THE ECONOMY FOR ECONOMIC AND SOCIAL RIGHTS, AND DEVELOPMENT

The Covid-19 multi-level crisis has depleted government revenues resulting in many instances, in negative economic growth. The challenge to mobilize resources for social spending in the short and long term is immense, especially in low-income countries. Under international human rights law, states are duty-bound to guarantee the "minimum essential levels" of health, social protection, nutrition and food security, water and sanitation, housing, education for all people, particularly in times of crisis. Even developing countries with inadequate resources are required to mobilize "maximum available resources"[8] to introduce low-cost and targeted programmes to assist those most in need.

Ensuring minimum essential levels of ESC rights requires analysis and policy advice such as ring-fencing social spending during economic downturns; implementing counter-cyclical fiscal policies to avoid retrogression in ESC rights; ensuring that other pressing obligations, such as servicing of debt, do not take precedence over social spending; reallocating public expenditure (e.g. redirecting resources from defence); expanding the tax base and introducing progressive fiscal policies; tackling illicit financial flows and corruption; ensuring that limited resources are used efficiently, effectively and equitably; reviewing IFIs financing and conditionalities to assess how these can support the minimum core obligations of states on the entire gamut of ESC rights. Advice on budget transparency has been key to fostering accountability by OHCHR.

KEY ELEMENTS OF THE HUMAN RIGHTS ECONOMY

• A Human Rights Economy is an economic framework that aims at enhancing promotion and respect for human rights of all, without discrimination, by facilitating sustainable development, people-centred economic policies for ESCRs and a commitment to a safe and healthy environment. It also centres the right to development and international solidarity for the common good.

• It is based on authoritative and doctrinal human rights principles of the UDHR, the human rights mechanisms and other instruments of international law held to be binding on states, international financial bodies including financial institutions.

• It approaches data collection and data disaggregation with the objective of considering every rights-holder worthy of being counted and to be

---

8. The challenge to mobilize resources for social spending in the short and longer term is immense, especially in low- and middle-income countries. Under international human rights law, states are duty-bound to guarantee the minimum essential levels of the enjoyment of the rights to health, social protection, nutrition and food security, water and sanitation, housing, and education for all people, even in times of crisis; see CESCR General Comment 24 on "State obligations under the International Covenant on Economic, Social and Cultural Rights in the context of business activities" that notes that "[t]he obligation to fulfil requires States parties to take necessary steps, to the maximum of their available resources, to facilitate and promote the enjoyment of Covenant rights, and, in certain cases, to directly provide goods and services essential to such enjoyment. Discharging such duties may require the mobilization of resources by the State, including by enforcing progressive taxation schemes." (para 23, E/C.12/GC/24).

included as a participant without discrimination in programmes aimed at the realization of ESC rights. It focuses in particular on including those left behind and those made invisible. It prioritzes economic growth which goes beyond GDP.

- It prioritizes special temporary measures and affirmative action for those left behind to address discrimination, and to right the wrongs which have produced historical disadvantage.
- It prioritizes the inclusion of all those discriminated on the basis of gender, sexual orientation, race, religion, class, age, differently-abled and migration status. It centres the intersectionality approach to multiple and persistent forms of discrimination as its core analytical category for the purpose of economic planning from below. It eschews a welfare perspective and aims to reverse the top-down approach in policies and programmes.
- It prioritizes budget decisions aimed at adequate and effective public investments on ESCRs and reduction of inequalities within and between countries.
- It aims to build sound social protection systems that are adaptive to economic shocks, social and political upheavals, climate-related disasters and diseases including to support resilience, well-being and stability.
- It aims to expand fiscal space to ensure that states meet their core obligations on minimum essential levels of ESCR by ring-fencing and/or increasing social spending during economic downturns by mobilizing the maximum available resources. Reviewing of IFI financing and conditionalities to assess how these can support human rights obligations of states to ESC rights is a key element of HRE.
- It aims to enshrine human rights in business, trade and industrial policies to promote sustainable consumption and productions patterns, accountability via impact assessments, enduring dispute resolutions, and progressive supply chains which benefit consumers and producers.
- It aims to foster care and support economies by targeted investments.

WHAT CHANGES ARE NEEDED?

Global actions are crucial to advance human rights economies, as the current international financial architecture was designed with scant consideration to climate risks and the alarming levels of social and economic inequalities today. Low- and middle-income countries should have access to higher volumes of unconditional funding and concessional loans with favourable terms. High-income countries need to commit to providing least-developed countries with a percentage of their gross national income as official development assistance.

International financial institutions must treat states' human rights obligations as binding parameters and integrate human rights into their diagnostic tools, policy advice and measurements. Debt sustainability analysis should include the potential impact on the ESC rights and SDGs, as retrogression may signal social unrest. Countries should not be penalized with sanctions for prioritizing social spending over debt servicing. Nations affected by environmental degradation and climate change should receive increased financing for mitigation, adaptation, loss and damage, biodiversity and pollution remediation.

International tax cooperation needs to address tax avoidance, evasion and illicit financial flows, particularly from multinational companies, to create more fiscal space for human rights and the SDGs. Progressive taxation of wealth and income at the national level should be supported. A new global tax architecture should be guided by greater tax transparency and information sharing, involving low- and middle-income countries as equal stakeholders in tax governance debates and rule-making processes.

WHAT COMES NEXT?

The blended nature of all rights requires a blended approach to advance and promote the inclusion of policy decisions, narrative changes and social trends that are informed primarily by the protection of human rights. Increased dialogue, communication and conversation about what HRE means in different contexts. We need to escalate our efforts for:

- Creation of space for a wider audiences and participants ranging from youth, civil society, political leaders, social influencers, and more, and to share stories, perspectives, strategies and ideas in order to own the concept and approach of the HRE, and make it real;
- Increased dialogue, communication and conversation about what an HRE means in different contexts;
- Sharing of tools and frameworks with local communities to best implement elements of HRE in the ways most meaningful, participatory and impactful.

We will know we are on the right track when *no one gets left behind and the privileges of some are transformed into rights for all.*

CONTRIBUTORS

Kate Bayliss is a Research Associate with the Department of Economics, SOAS University of London.

Magalí Brosio is a doctoral researcher in the Law School, University of Birmingham.

Edurne Cárdenas is an Argentinean lawyer and feminist activist.

Center for Economic and Social Rights is an international non-governmental organization that seeks to harness the power of human rights to inspire fairer and more sustainable economies.

Olivier De Schutter is United Nations Special Rapporteur on Extreme Poverty and Human Rights and Professor of Law at the Université catholique de Louvain and at Sciences Po.

Surya Deva is a Professor at the Macquarie Law School, Director of the Centre for Environmental Law, Macquarie University, and United Nations Special Rapporteur on the Right to Development.

Jasmine Gideon is Reader in Gender, Health and International Development, Birkbeck University of London.

Harpreet Kaur is Business and Human Rights Specialist, Asia-Pacific Regional Centre, United Nations Development Programme.

Matti Kohonen is Executive Director of the Financial Transparency Coalition.

Marianna Leite is ACT Alliance's Global Advocacy and Development Policy Manager.

Bhumika Muchhala is a Senior Advisor at the Third World Network (TWN) and a doctoral researcher at the New School, New York.

Rafael Quintero Godinez is Lecturer in Law at Birmingham City University.

Kári Hólmar Ragnarsson is Assistant Professor in the Faculty of Law, University of Iceland.

Asha Ramgobin is Executive Director of Human Rights Development Initiative and extraordinary lecturer at the Centre for Human Rights, and affiliated to the African Tax Institute, at the University of Pretoria.

Pedro Rossi is a Professor at the Institute of Economics, University of Campinas.

Celine Tan is Professor of International Economic Law, University of Warwick.

Attiya Waris is a Professor at the University of Nairobi and United Nations Independent Expert on foreign debt, other international financial obligations and human rights.

Ilcheong Yi is Senior Research Coordinator at the United Nations Research Institute for Social Development.

CHAPTER 1

INTRODUCTION: WHAT IT MEANS TO "RIGHT THE ECONOMY" AND WHY WE NEED TO DO IT NOW

Marianna Leite and Matti Kohonen

RIGHTS-BASED ECONOMIES: DISRUPTING NEOLIBERALISM

After the onset of the Covid-19 pandemic and the economic devastation it has wrought, it became evident to a far larger group of people that many prevailing economic systems and policies were largely disconnected from any productive social function and were, in fact, working in opposition to the needs of communities contending with extreme social and economic inequality, climate catastrophe, corporate abuses and a lack of justice. Fundamentally, Covid-19 laid bare the vulnerability of our institutions and exposed the underlying weakness of neoliberal economic policies, calling for a reckoning (Ahmed *et al.* 2022).[1]

Neoliberalism has failed people and the planet. Neoliberalism is, as we understand it, a political project that represents the continuity of an exclusive way of policy-making and implementation, run by an elite (Harvey 2005). Neoliberalism is based on the myth that the economic market has the power and ability to regulate itself and correct related distortions without much, if any, state intervention. It pursues endless growth and profit and relies on tools such as programmatic targeting, austerity and retrenchment (Boesten 2007). Neoliberal economic models and neoclassical economics clash with a rights-based, feminist and sustainability vision (Winch, Forkert & Davison 2019). Under neoliberalism there is no space for human rights, whether civil and

---

1. In January 2022 an Oxfam International report indicated that "[t]he wealth of the world's 10 richest men has doubled since the pandemic began. The incomes of 99% of humanity are worse off because of Covid-19. Widening economic, gender, and racial inequalities – as well as the inequality that exists between countries – are tearing our world apart. This is not by chance, but choice: 'economic violence' is perpetrated when structural policy choices are made for the richest and most powerful people." (Ahmed *et al.* 2022: 2).

political – or, indeed, social, economic and cultural rights – as they are all secondary to the proposed virtues of a self-regulating market, which exists only by virtue of the fact that states use their legislative and regulatory powers on behalf of large corporations. This was evident in the context of the Covid-19 vaccine distribution[2] between countries in the Global North and the Global South.[3]

Governments in the Global North also protect the interests of the multinational companies that are headquartered there and are often owned and financed via tax havens (Leite & Kohonen 2019). This dynamic reinforces a neocolonial cycle of North–South exploitation and is reflected in the pattern of extractivism and exploitation that fuels the climate crisis (Cirefice & Sullivan 2019). Youth in these and other communities struggle to find meaningful livelihoods because of the lack of public investment, incomes or employment prospects (Sukarieh & Tannock 2008).

Neoliberalism may well be increasingly intellectually discredited now, including by institutions such as the International Monetary Fund (IMF) (Ostry, Loungani & Furceri 2016), which has questioned some of its merits, but it is still the defining discourse behind the institutional architecture of global economic and financial governance. Rising to dominance in the 1980s and 1990s, neoliberalism was reinforced through the formalized Washington Consensus (Fine, Lapavitsas & Pincus 2001; Harvey 2006; Meier 2010) and the creation of the World Trade Organization (WTO) in 1995.[4] However, neoliberalism's "project" can be traced back to the 1920s (Fine, Lapavitsas & Pincus 2001; Harvey 2006). After the introduction of neoliberalism as an ideology, the role of the welfare state as a promoter of well-being to its population was replaced by an enabling, rather directive, government in search of good business (Dean 2002; Harvey 2006). In this sense, neoliberal purists may argue that the role of the state is to create and preserve an institutional framework appropriate to such practices (Harvey 2006). Limited government intervention and the diffusion of independent regulatory agencies with the purpose of liberalizing and privatizing utilities and trade are inherent to neoliberalism (Hall, Massey & Rustin 2013).

However, the pandemic also elevated the narrative of alternative economies as well as the role of governments in responding to the needs of

---

2. See ACT Alliance (2021).
3. We rely on critical legal theory, post-colonial theory and the work of Boaventura de Sousa Santos (2014), who defines the Global South as a metaphor for the human suffering caused by capitalism and colonialism on the global level, as well as for the resistance to overcoming or minimizing such suffering. It is, therefore, an anti-capitalist, anti-colonialist, anti-patriarchal and anti-imperialist definition of the South. It is not a geographical term but, rather, a basis for understanding the changes occurring and needed in our societies. This, he argues, is fundamental for cognitive justice.
4. See www.wto.org/english/thewto_e/history_e/history_e.htm.

people in times of crisis. For instance, multiple cities are implementing proposals such as those promoted by the Wellbeing Economy Alliance and the Doughnut Economy. Both are initiatives that promote alternative economic models, focusing on local-level solutions and changing the dominant narratives.[5] Meanwhile, Chile has declared itself as the country where the neoliberal economic model died, aiming to create a welfare-state-led economy.[6] In South Africa, a universal basic income (UBI) is gaining ground, building on the Covid-19 relief grants made to households during the pandemic (Sadiq & du Preez 2021). In the United States, there is talk of reversing the racial capitalism and supporting the care economy through initiatives such as Baby Bonds (Hamilton 2022). The search for alternative economic organizations and activities at various levels and sectors across the world, well documented by the UN Inter-Agency Task Force on Social Solidarity Economy's (TFSSE's) *Encyclopedia of the Social and Solidarity Economy*, also reflects this trend (Yi 2023). There is talk of a pandemic treaty at the World Health Organization (WHO) to overturn the rigid policy on the trade-related intellectual property rights (TRIPS) that deepened the vaccine apartheid.

Proposed transformations are often not systemic in nature, and do not tackle institutions that govern the global economy. For instance, Nancy Fraser (2022: xiv) defines capitalism as a "cannibalistic"

> societal order that empowers a profit-driven economy to prey on extra-economic support it needs to function – wealth expropriated from nature and subject peoples; multiple forms of care work, chronically undervalued when not wholly disavowed; public goods and public powers, which capital both requires and tries to curtail; the energy and creativity of working people.

Similarly, Hickel (2020) sees capitalism as an expansionist model that fails to tackle the main problem of distribution created by production and surplus at a global scale. To overcome the pitfalls of neoliberal capitalism, nonhegemonic narratives need to propose a more attractive alternative, which also tackles these more systemic levels of power.

EMERGENCE OF A RIGHTS-BASED ECONOMY

This book systematizes academic and practitioners' analyses and experiences on the topic, and draws from different epistemologies, literatures and case

---

5. See more at https://weall.org/hubs.
6. See *The Economist* (2021).

studies, outlined by the book itself and elsewhere. We intend to flesh out what a Rights-Based Economy (RBE) or economies would look like and the tools and actions – economic, legal, environmental and social – that will be needed to achieve them.

In our view, the purpose of a Rights-Based Economy is to guarantee the material, social and environmental conditions necessary for all people to live with dignity on a flourishing planet. It is based on a holistic understanding of human well-being and supported by the widely agreed framework of values and obligations enshrined in international human rights law. It is an umbrella term that aims to enable plural alternative economic models that promote the realization of human rights. It demands action to redistribute resources, remedy inequalities and rebalance power in our economies. This means that it uses the international human rights framework as a basis and a litmus test for the development and monitoring of economic policies and structures.

By using "righting the economy" as a term, we mean the utilization of human rights norms, principles, institutions and legal frameworks based on human rights, such as constitutions and laws, to bring about and enable a Rights-Based Economy. This process of "righting" is necessarily a disruptive process relating to powerful actors, norms and institutions that constitute the economy, but it is also a process that provides the possibility of reassembling the economy on the basis of human rights. Thus, the process of righting the economy is one of constant disruption and reassemblage.

In the sphere of civil society, the field has been opened up by groups focusing on social and economic rights, such as the Center for Economic and Social Rights (CESR), founded in 1993, in analysing the human rights impacts of access to food, water, sanitation and healthcare – arguing that economic policies such as sanctions harm the enjoyment of human rights. This stands in juxtaposition to the Vienna Declaration and Programme of Action, which considers that all human rights are equally important – i.e. they are interrelated, indivisible and interdependent.

Historically, in academia and in policy, there has been a bias towards the human rights field being defined by civil and political rights as the primary (at times the only) concern, actively making it harder for social and economic rights to be widely recognized in public as human rights at all (Tyson & Said 1993). This disguises the fact that international human rights law (IHRL) is far from static. IHRL is being constantly developed and shaped by legal opinions, recommendations, jurisprudence and scholarship. It is plural in terms of its origins and viewpoints. Moreover, the potential for human rights norms, principles and obligations to shape economies has not been fully explored. Traditionally, human rights have been seen by scholars and practitioners as external to economies (De Witte 2009). Human rights are then perceived as a tool that can be used to handle the distortions caused by neoliberalism

(De Witte 2009), or – worse – they are a "handmaiden" to neoliberalism (Moyn 2018).

Rarely have human rights been seen as a fundamental axis and principled approach to (re)shaping neoliberalism to avoid these distortions (Balakrishnan & Elson 2011a). This is evident in the volume edited by Molyneux and Razavi (2002), which brings a gender lens and multicultural dimension to discussions around the social effects of economic policies and their ability to facilitate or deter the realization of human rights. In their discussion of the gender implications of the orthodox macroeconomic agenda, they argue that neoliberalism is the direct opposite of the realization of women's human rights. Their case studies demonstrate that a "wide gulf remained between the articulation of global principles and their application in many national settings", particularly across economic policies (Molyneux & Razavi 2002: 3).

The different chapters of this book argue that a separation between different human rights is an outdated vision of the problem. We build upon the view that human rights are the dominant moral framework of our time, or the *"lingua franca* of justice" (Barclay 2018). There is strong consensus that economic systems and decisions have clear moral and ethical implications. However, until recently, human rights and economics were not often spoken about in the same breath (Osborne 2021). Slowly, this has started to change. Increasingly, human rights actors, including the United Nations' Office of the High Commissioner for Human Rights (OHCHR), are calling for a shift towards a "rights-based" or "Human Rights Economy".[7] Likewise, human rights monitoring mechanisms are building up a steady stream of recommendations and jurisprudence on economic policy.[8]

Most of the theoretical work thus far connecting rights and the economy has focused on the state's role in providing adequate financing for public services as a way to realize social and economic rights that often depend on financial resources. This is the subject of human rights scholarship (De Schutter 2019) and where the rights-based approach to the economy finds its roots. It is grounded in the analysis of government budgets and policies aimed at promoting social and economic rights. It also links closely with

---

7. See, for instance, Bachelet (2021).
8. Following a joint submission and accompanying factsheet on the extra-territorial effects of Swiss-facilitated tax abuse – prepared by CESR with Alliance Sud, the Global Justice Clinic of NYU Law School, Public Eye and the Tax Justice Network (TJN) – the UN committee mandated to oversee compliance with the Convention on the Elimination of All Forms of Discrimination Against Women (CEDAW) expressed concern in November 2016 at the potentially negative impact of Switzerland's financial secrecy and corporate tax policies on the ability of other states, particularly those already short of revenue, to mobilize the maximum available resources for the fulfilment of women's rights (see http://cesr.org/sites/default/files/downloads/Switzerland_CEDAW_Submission_TaxFinance_1mar2016.pdf).

the 2030 Agenda for Sustainable Development, which, although less bind-ing, more time-bound and in many ways less ambitious than the human rights framework, spells out the primacy of social development over profit and prosperity by highlighting inequalities and the ecological crisis (United Nations General Assembly [UNGA] 2015a). Civil society groups have called for a radical rethink of economic models in the wake of the Sustainable Development Goals (SDGs) in terms of mobilizing more public resources through a "fiscal revolution" (CESR & Christian Aid 2014).

A small but growing body of research also addresses the broader economic and regulatory institutions needed to enable such a Rights-Based Economy and focus on the revenue-raising side of fiscal policy or the issue of "fiscal space" from a human rights perspective (Saiz 2021). This research includes rethinking tax systems to promote rights (see Avi-Yonah & Mazzoni 2019 and Chapter 5); ways to deal with both private debt and sovereign debt crisis;[9] global tax abuse by the wealthy and large corporations;[10] creating shared pools of collectively managed investment capital including local development funds; and cooperative and mutual banking to circulate capital to socially and environmentally useful objectives, while regulating private enterprises in such a way through mandatory disclosure and access to remedy that prevents them from doing harm to local communities in business and human rights legislation.[11]

Meanwhile, feminist economists and scholars such as Berik and Kongar (2021), Berik and van der Meulen Rodgers (2009) and Seguino (2019), and practitioners such as members of the UK Gender and Development Network[12] and the Association for Women's Rights in Development,[13] have written about the macro-, meso- and micro-level components needed for the delivery of successful feminist economic systems, with reference to women's human rights. In the African context, both the Afrifem Macroeconomics Collective (Nawi Collective), launched in 2020 to analyse macroeconomic policies from a feminist angle looking at feminist macroeconomic aspects of debt (Sibeko 2022), and FEMNET have looked at the feminist macroeco-nomic implications of the African Continental Free Trade Area (Kelleher 2021). In addition, many in academia have called for the often invisible and undervalued care economy to be taken into account in creating feminist macroeconomic policies (Capraro & Rhodes 2017).

---

9. See, for instance, the CESR's "key concept" series on sovereign debt and human rights (www. cesr.org/key-concepts) and Institute for Economic Justice, CESR and SECTION27 (2021).
10. See Alliance Sud *et al.* (2016).
11. See, for instance, Initiative for Human Rights in Fiscal Policy (2021).
12. For more, see https://gadnetwork.org.
13. For more, see www.awid.org/priority-areas/building-feminist-economies.

Balakrishnan, Heintz and Elson (2016) argue that economic policies must be developed and guided from the perspective of key principles, such as the progressive realization of human rights and the use of the maximum available resources. The authors observe that the human rights approach constitutes an alternative evaluative and ethical framework for assessing economic policies and outcomes. However, such alternative evaluative frameworks, such as the OPERA framework (outcomes, policy efforts, resources and assessment) developed by CESR, or indeed other frameworks that use human rights principles as a guide in analysing economic policies, often become ineffective because of the inherent secrecy and lack of public participation in economic policy-making, especially when it comes to relationships between states and corporations. This has led to calls for public transparency and accountability in terms of corporate activities (Financial Transparency Coalition [FTC] 2017), such as disclosure of the taxes paid, contracts for extractive industries, and parliamentary and public accountability for negotiation of international treaties. Similarly, the book by McNaughton, Frey and Porter (2021) looks at the past four decades of neoliberal economic policies through the lens of existing international human rights treaties. This work focuses on existing empirical research into economic inequalities and specific geographic case studies in Canada and the United States, which look at the potential of emerging human rights rules in setting standards (McNaughton, Frey & Porter 2021).

The above-mentioned literature demonstrates that neoliberal policies based on mainstream neoclassical economics are often in conflict with existing state obligations and the full and effective realization of human rights. This is because "[n]eoliberalism is premised on the freedom of contract as the most basic value. Namely, under neoliberal policies, human rights are constrained to negative liberties, that is 'rights are primarily protections against state interference'" (Molyneux & Razavi 2002: 8) not the realization of rights by the state. However, as Balakrishnan and Elson (2011b: 2) rightly note, "neoclassical economics is not the only kind of economics". Neoclassical economics, characterized by the "marginalist revolution" of the late nineteenth century, marked a shift towards price formation in markets and utility maximization (Slater & Tonkiss 2001: ch. 1).

Historically, alternatives to neoclassical economics have existed and continue to exist. Gunnar and Alva Myrdal, whose work laid the foundations for Nordic welfare states from the 1930s onwards, argued that social protection and women's liberation would be critical for a more thriving economy and society overall (Myrdal 1945, 1978). In the context of postwar Britain, T. H. Marshall (1950) argued that social citizenship is part of the evolution of rights, and states should continue to expand rights to tackle inequality, building on the proposal for the establishment of the British welfare state as described in the Beveridge Report (Beveridge 1942). However, the concept of social citizenship was hugely criticized by neoliberal scholars at the time and thereafter (Bulmer & Rees 2016). Amartya Sen's capabilities approach is also a relevant precedent, as it asserts that civil and political freedoms cannot be practised without social and economic rights being guaranteed. Economic decisions should be aimed at the full flourishing of human capabilities and potential (Sen 2000). Together with related work by Martha Nussbaum (1999, 2003), this has led to alternative metrics being developed to gross domestic product (GDP), and the much wider well-being economy approach that is linked to it. The critique of the growth theory (Solow 1956) at the heart of neoclassical economics was developed by a range of ecological economists since the Club of Rome (Meadows *et al.* 1972), and other foundations of ecological approaches to the economy have criticized the reliance on endless growth.

We build on this often contradictory relationship between neoliberalism, neoclassical economics and human rights. Critical legal scholars have argued that rights claims work against radical social transformation by enshrining tenets of bourgeois individualism whereas feminist moral theorists contend that a focus on responsibilities would be preferable to one focusing on rights (Harvey 2006; Moyn 2014; Marks 2011). Authors such as David Harvey (2006: 169) state that human rights have also been used to legitimize neoliberal policies, which undermines any democratic attempts to openly deconstruct and challenge these same policies and the symbolic meanings associated with them. Human rights can be instrumentalized as a "smoke screen" that cloaks the neoliberal "gap between rhetoric (for the benefit of all) and realization (for the benefit of a small ruling class), increase over space and time". Samuel Moyn (2014) explains that international human rights law and the neoliberal phenomenon are too easily conflated. Susan Marks (2011) rightly notes that the way in which human rights law is constituted does not allow for the sort of structural critique eventually needed to target neoliberalism's pitfalls. Although the human rights revolution and the victory of market fundamentalism have been simultaneous, "it is far too soon – analytically in the one case and historically in the other – to sign on to either the Marxist or mainstream position about the relationship between human rights and neoliberalism" (Moyn 2014: 147–8).

THE WAY FORWARD: WHY A RIGHTS-BASED ECONOMY?

This compendium contributes to existing discussions around a Rights-Based Economy or rights-enabling economies. The chapters, written by activists and scholars from the Global North and the Global South, present a myriad of views and perspectives in terms of the purpose of the RBE and what it should look like. Rather than pushing for homogeneity, this book embraces the beauty behind heterogeneous framings, examples and contexts. Thus, we think, plurality is key in shattering orthodox economic myths and fostering a rights-based approach to heterodox economics. All chapters follow somewhat the same thread: the need to disrupt the neoliberal status quo and the importance of fomenting alternative economic policies and models that are aligned and, therefore, enable the realization of human rights.

A Rights-Based Economy enables us to test and analyse economic policies from the perspective of human rights. It is normative by nature and aims to address normative challenges and pitfalls. We are, therefore, proposing to use Balakrishnan and Elson's (2011a) framework to analyse other countries, but also go beyond by providing a litmus test to determine the minimum threshold of human rights enabling economic policies. The analysis recognizes that the litmus test depends on which human right we are evaluating. For instance, some alternative models may be more conducive to economic, social and cultural rights, but other models may be more conducive to civil and political rights. These three tests are major elements that create a thread across the different chapters of this book. To this, we add the concept of the enabling state, which is seen as important in providing the supportive institutional, legal, financial and other aspects that allow for alternative economies to flourish.

We recognize that some proponents (and critics) of a rights-based economic model allege or suggest that embracing this degree of normativity both necessitates human rights manifestly renouncing the alleged political impartiality of international human rights law and/or embracing a far more overtly "socialist" approach to human rights. Although we do not delve into this discussion, we assert that the RBE, as we conceptualize it, goes beyond the polarization between right-wing and left-wing politics. That is, by urging states and policy-makers to "right the economy", we are implying that the economy needs to be put back to "right" or "on a track" that actually serves and is in the benefit of all.

In this sense, the Rights-Based (Enabling) Economy is a normative orientation. It is plural in nature. It is a set of economic alternatives with a social proposition and ethical parameters, focusing on organizing the economy in terms of the social relationships and the realization of human rights. Economics, in the neoclassical tradition, focuses on efficiency, maximizing utility (on a social satisfaction measure) and superimposing all else so as to maximize "social utility", and therefore not on realizing human rights. It is bereft of any normative/ethical orientation and, as a result, is conducive to the violation of human rights. For example, the efficient allocation of resources, and an "optimum equilibrium" in the housing market, can leave millions of people homeless. The RBE attempts to solve parts of these ethical dilemmas faced by economists and policy-makers. It instils a sense of hope and enables systematic learning and constant dialogue. This attempt, we believe, is a reflection of human rights as a project and a natural progression for the study and praxis related to the intersection between human rights and the economy.

OUTLINE OF THE BOOK

The book is divided into two sections: Part I, "Framing the Economy", which is devoted to academic theory and analysis touching on the link between economics/economies, human rights and international frameworks regulating financial and corporate actors; and Part II, "Transforming the Economy", devoted to examples of decolonial and post-colonial economies, alternative economic analyses, models and approaches demonstrating what plural and rights-based approaches to economic models look like (or could look like) in reality. This book can be used by practitioners, academics and policy-makers alike, and may be a useful tool in informing and analysing policy approaches related to the Covid-19 recovery and post-recovery.

Part I gives an overview of human rights standards and principles, and how they can be used in framing economic practice, and presents a critical analysis of international frameworks regulating financial and corporate actors. It also examines how human rights should be used as an overarching framework to guide new economic models and proposals for changing global norms. Chapter 2, by Olivier De Schutter, looks at post-growth economics and the future of welfare as a way to challenge growth as one of the tenets of neoliberalism. Chapter 3 focuses on the work of the Center for Economic and Social Rights on the Rights-Based Economy and the role of social movements in pushing this agenda forward. Chapter 4, by Surya Deva and Harpreet Kaur, delves into the role of voluntary and binding business and human rights (BHR) rules in promoting a human-rights-centred-economy. Chapter 5, by Attiya Waris, covers the role of international financial institutions (IFIs) in promoting a Rights-Based Economy and proposes a new global fiscal architecture using a human rights lens. Chapter 6, by Pedro Rossi, scrutinizes macroeconomic policies from a rights-based lens as a way to propose solutions to decolonial and post-colonial economies. Chapter 7, by Celine Tan and Rafael Quintero-Godinez, analyses international economic law and trade regulation from the perspective of international development financing policy and governance.

Part II looks at what it takes to transform the economy, or perhaps to foment alternative and rights-based economic models, by looking at examples and concrete cases of transforming the economy or approaches that are fundamental for the promotion of the RBE. Chapter 8, by Asha Ramgobin, focuses on illicit financial flows (IFFs), tax havens and the role of the African Commission on Human and Peoples' Rights in fighting illicit financial flows. Chapter 9, by Ilcheong Yi, systematizes the information related to the Alternative Economies for Transformation programme of the United Nations Research Institute for Social Development (UNRISD) and its contribution to discussions around alternative economic models that are viable, egalitarian and ecologically sound. Chapter 10, by Kári Hólmar Ragnarsson, analyses the use of judicial remedies as a way to fight the commodification of social goods in post-2008 austerity in Europe. Chapter 11, by Jasmine Gideon and Kate Bayliss, evaluates the rights-based approach to health systems, in particular the dynamics between human rights, public–private partnerships (PPPs) and the link to new economic models. Chapter 12, by Magalí Brosio and Edurne Cárdenas, examines whether the Argentinian response to Covid-19 was sensitive to the rights of women and people with diverse sexual orientation and gender identities. Chapter 13, by Bhumika Muchhala, touches upon the New Green Deal through the lens of human rights and gender equality. Chapter 14 concludes by reflecting the role of disruption and reassemblage in promoting a human rights-based economy and the importance of the RBE in enabling plural and decolonial economic models.

This compendium builds on the work developed by other experts cited herein as well as other authors critiquing capitalist/neoliberal economic models. The different contributions also critically analyse economic alternatives to enquire if they truly promote a positive transformation and represent a material change to people's lives.

PART I

FRAMING THE ECONOMY

CHAPTER 2

TOWARDS A RIGHTS-BASED ECONOMY: POST-GROWTH ECONOMICS AND THE FUTURE OF WELFARE

Olivier De Schutter

INTRODUCTION

A new body of scholarship is emerging, under the banner of a "Rights-Based Economy" (RBE). An important part of its agenda is to seek to ensure that macroeconomic and fiscal policies support the realization of human rights. For some, it is the opposite of austerity: it consists of increasing the purchasing power of the poor and ensuring that labour receives a larger proportion of the value created in the economy, with the benefits of growth being spread more equally. For others, we need to go beyond Keynesian recipes and invent a post-growth economy. In this chapter, I try to show how human rights offers a way beyond that opposition, which often makes it difficult to forge alliances across different components of the progressive camp.

In a paper exploring the positions of the United Nations' Committee on Economic, Social and Cultural Rights (CESCR), Petel and Vander Putten (2021) note that the committee remains wedded to economic growth as a means to ensure the progressive realization of these rights. This should not come as a surprise. The idea that the realization of economic and social rights and poverty reduction require economic growth seems intuitive. It fits neatly within mainstream macroeconomic debates between the fiscally conservative, often found to the right of the political spectrum, and those, coming more often from the left, who argue for demand-driven solutions. For the former group, fiscal consolidation is a precondition for sustainable economic growth over the long term. For the latter, austerity kills growth. It is only by raising the incomes of lower-income earners and the middle class that output will be stimulated to increase and investors to invest. Both agree that growth is needed but disagree on the best way to achieve it.

The reign of this orthodoxy can be readily explained. To redistribute wealth and thus alleviate poverty, there must first be wealth created to redistribute.

Moreover, growth is generally seen to hold the promise of employment creation, since poverty cannot be tackled by social protection alone but requires the active population to be provided with jobs – allowing, in turn, for their income from work to be taxed and their social contributions to finance insurance schemes.

This is conventional wisdom. The 2030 Agenda for Sustainable Development confirms the attractiveness of growth as a means, if not the means, to overcome our predicament (UNGA 2015a).[1] Indeed, the idea is so well established that any suggestion that poverty reduction could be achieved without growth is immediately denounced as eccentric to the extreme.

This conviction is profoundly disabling. It restricts the imagination, discouraging the search for solutions beyond growth. Indeed, in the current context, with a number of factors – both structural and more conjunctural – impeding the ability of economies to achieve growth, it is tempting to believe that there is nothing more we can do, in the short term at least, than to put all our energy into trying to relaunch growth, whatever the human and ecological costs. Here, I offer five objections to relying on economic growth as a tool to fully realize economic and social rights. Each of the following sections is dedicated to a single objection. The last section provides a brief conclusion.

FALSE UNIVERSALITY

Perhaps most striking about pro-growth arguments is the contrast between the universality of the prescription and the specificity of each region. Growth is said to be the remedy for all, as if the needs of rich countries were the same as those of poor countries.

Both the nature of economic growth and its desirability itself should depend on the circumstances of each country. As a universal recipe for poverty reduction, it is barely plausible.

Such universalistic approaches also hide important questions of equity. For instance, we cannot ignore the fact that the rise in consumption is still largely dominated by Organisation for Economic Co-operation and Development (OECD) countries, whereas most of the population growth since the 1950s has been in non-OECD countries. In other words, growth in relatively poor countries can be plausibly presented as a means to provide opportunities for

---

1. Under Sustainable Development Goal (SDG) 8, which relates to decent work and economic growth, Target 8.1 is to "sustain per capita economic growth in accordance with national circumstances and, in particular, at least 7 per cent gross domestic product growth per annum in the least developed countries" (UNGA 2015a: 19). The associated indicator (8.1.1) is the annual growth rate of real GDP per capita.

a fast-growing workforce and allow households to achieve standards of living that bring them closer to those of the richer populations of the Global North. Even so, neither of these justifications holds for countries that are already rich.

In higher-income countries, growth has chiefly allowed already rich populations to become richer still, and to create the impression that all groups within those populations will one day be able to mimic the lifestyles of the wealthiest segments among them.

The sole excuse for growth as a remedy for all regions is that how a region fares has significant impact on other trading regions. Stagnation or recession in advanced economies means fewer opportunities for economies in poorer regions to make progress, when this progress relies on the possibility of exporting to consumers of rich countries who have a superior ability to pay. The proper answer, however, is not to pursue more growth in rich countries; instead it is to promote more regional integration and South–South trade, rather than insisting on global integration and long supply chains, and to encourage the achievement of progress by stimulating domestic demand and by raising living standards for people in poverty in the Global South rather than by pushing for producers from less developed regions to serve the high-value markets of the Global North.

THE LIMITS OF GROWTH

As a means to improve well-being, growth also promises more than it can deliver.

The promise of growth is that, by increasing production, the needs of all members of society will gradually be met. This approach is overly optimistic. As Richard Easterlin has noted, increases in gross domestic product have been disconnected from improvements in subjective well-being in the advanced economies since the early 1970s. Beyond a certain point of material opulence and comfort across society, additional improvements do not contribute to the betterment of subjective perceptions of well-being, or what most people call "happiness" (Easterlin 1995; Layard 2005).

GDP growth provides only an indication about the wealth created in the economy as a whole. It is silent about how such wealth is distributed. However, the staggering rise of inequalities in all societies since the mid-1980s[2] has resulted in a situation in which the increment of GDP is entirely unrelated to citizens' everyday lived experience. If it is not combined with a reduction in inequalities, GDP growth bears little or no relationship to the

---

2. Among many other publications raising the alarm about the rise of inequalities, see Stiglitz (2013), OECD (2011) and Reich (2012).

17

improvement of their social position, compared to that of others (Laurent & Le Cacheux 2015: 23–5).

Growth fails its promises as it also brings dissatisfaction and new desires even when achieving material opulence. This is true for the subjective feeling of happiness, but it is equally true for poverty as social exclusion. An overall improvement in access to material goods or services will not remedy social exclusion if social expectations rise even more rapidly.

This is the counter-productivity of growth in the fight against modern poverty.[3] The more certain items are produced at scale and enjoyed by a larger part of the population, the more they become indispensable for all. Not being able to access those items leads to feelings of exclusion.

John Maynard Keynes distinguished two classes among the needs of human beings, namely "those needs which are absolute in the sense that we feel them whatever the situation of our fellow human beings may be, and those which are relative only in that their satisfaction lifts us above, makes us feel superior to, our fellows". He remarked that the "relative" needs "may indeed be insatiable; for the higher the general level the higher still are they" (Keynes 1932: 365–6). This results in the "dependence effect": production is ostensibly meant to satisfy pre-existing needs, although in fact it creates new needs. What was once the privilege of a happy few becomes a legitimate expectation for all to acquire and enjoy (Galbraith 1958: ch. 11).

This is why the persistence of wealth and income inequalities largely cancel out the positive impacts on well-being that are expected to derive from an increase in GDP. In response to the invitation of the then French president Nicolas Sarkozy to work on new indicators of well-being, the Stiglitz Commission on the Measurement of Economic Performance and Social Progress noted that the failure to value the reduction of inequality appropriately in our classic measures of progress could explain, in part, the gap between official statistics focusing on the aggregate level of performance of the economy and the subjective perception of well-being (Stiglitz, Sen & Fitoussi 2009: 8).

Even if a particular individual's situation improves in absolute terms, but remains stagnant (or falls) in relation to other members of society, that individual may experience a loss in well-being that the increased purchasing power, and thus the improvement in material conditions, may not compensate for. This explains the paradox highlighted by Easterlin: one reason why GDP growth in high-income countries has become unrelated to measures of subjective well-being may be that, unless it is combined with greater equality,

---

3. The notion of counter-productivity is borrowed from Ivan Illich, but it is expanded here beyond the areas (education, health and mobility) to which Illich sought to apply it; see Illich (1971, 1975).

income growth is a "zero-sum game". Growth in average incomes that leaves people wide apart from one another hardly satisfies their desire to compare favourably to those around them, and so gains in life satisfaction are, at best, minimal (Jackson 2017: 57; Wilkinson & Pickett 2018: 226). The only gain, in fact, is in what some have called the "tunnel effect", whereby some people experience an increase in "happiness" from seeing others around them in wealthier positions and anticipating one day joining them.[4] But this would barely compensate for the social comparisons and dissatisfaction brought about by inequality.

This is why people care not only about absolute income but also about relative income. If they want to be able to acquire what will allow them to distinguish themselves from their fellow citizens, they will have to be richer than them (Hirsch 1977: 36). Indeed, as general affluence increases, larger portions of households' budgets go to the acquisition of goods that are positional in nature. Once a large part of the population has access to such goods, the reward disappears (Brighouse & Swift 2006: 471–9).

The limits of growth are becoming increasingly clear. The long-held belief that the flourishing of each member of society depends on the constant expansion of the possibilities of material consumption is now less plausible than ever (Layard 2005; Scitovsky 1992). On the contrary, by increasing social expectations, the rise of overall affluence within a society may in fact turn out to increase modern poverty.

Therefore, it is high time that we launch a debate on the orthodox view that well-being correlates to opportunities for material consumption. In advanced societies we should seek to identify sources of subjective well-being and instruments to fight against social exclusion that do not require the further pursuit of growth. This is more urgent as the world comes to understand that the infinite pursuit of growth is entirely incompatible with the limited biocapacity of our planet.

THE EARTH'S BOUNDARIES

Environmental destruction and poverty

Although the orthodoxy presents growth as the precondition for poverty alleviation wherever poverty persists, the destruction of the ecosystems that

---

4. The expression was coined by Albert Hirschman and Michael Rothschild, who draw on this image: even when stuck in the traffic, a car driver may experience some solace from finding that the lane next to his or hers is moving forward. To this driver, the fact that others are moving is perceived as an indication that he or she too, in time, will benefit from the general progress (Hirschman & Rothschild 1973).

growth necessarily entails is the most significant threat to people in poverty worldwide. This is another source of the counter-productivity of growth.

The rise of mass consumption society and globalization have resulted in the "Great Acceleration" (Steffen *et al.* 2015).[5] People in poverty (minority groups are over-represented) have benefited to a certain extent from the lowering of the prices of consumer items. They have also been disproportionately affected by the negative impacts of this acceleration.

People in poverty are the most immediately and seriously affected by environmental degradation. They are the first victims of air pollution,[6] because they generally live closer to the sources of pollution (Lucas *et al.* 2004) and because they live in small, overcrowded dwellings that are more difficult to ventilate properly (Service for the Fight against Poverty, Precarity and Social Exclusion [Belgium] 2019: 13). They are the most at risk from landslides or flooding, because they are forced to live wherever they can afford housing (Bullard *et al.* 2007; Morello-Frosh, Pastor & Sadd 2001; Schweitzer & Zhou 2010). They are also more dependent on ecosystems for their livelihoods (Suich, Howe & Mace 2015). People in poverty, including 476 million Indigenous peoples (International Labour Organization [ILO] 2017), are also the most affected by climate disruptions (UNGA 2019a).

The unfulfilled promise of "green growth"

Some would argue that growth does not necessarily have to lead us to cross planetary boundaries (Rockström *et al.* 2009; Steffen *et al.* 2015). "Green growth" promises economic growth combined with a reduction of its ecological footprint. The "green economy", we are told, will arguably contribute to the eradication of poverty while "maintaining the healthy functioning of the Earth's ecosystems" (UN 2012: 10, para. 56).

These objectives are certainly worth supporting. But is green growth truly achievable? The data suggest not. In a review of the empirical evidence, Hickel and Kallis (2019) note that, through most of the twentieth century, resource use increased at a slower pace than GDP. The relative decoupling between economic growth and resource use was possible because of efficient

---

5. The expression "Great Acceleration" was initially put forward in 2004, to link socio-economic trends, such as the rise of income per capita or the growth of the volumes of international trade and investment, to Earth system indicators, such as the erosion of biodiversity, the concentration of greenhouse gases in the atmosphere or the extraction of mineral resources (Steffen *et al.* 2015).

6. In the United Kingdom, people living in the 10 per cent of the country characterized as the most deprived regions faced 41 per cent higher levels of concentration of nitrous oxide from industrial activity and transport (Lucas *et al.* 2004).

technologies and a certain dematerialization of the economy. Yet, apart from the fact that this improvement did not last, it is not absolute decoupling.

It has sometimes been alleged that European countries, at least, have achieved such absolute decoupling. This is a myth. The impression of absolute decoupling is created when considering domestic material consumption alone. However, once the resource use implied in imports is taken into account, the myth dissolves (Wiedmann *et al.* 2013; Ahmad & Wyckoff 2003).[7] Europe has outsourced many of the resource-intensive production modes required to cater to the lifestyles that Europeans continue to entertain. This is also true for greenhouse gas (GHG) emissions (Le Quéré *et al.* 2019).

Even the gradual shift from manufacturing to services does not provide solace. Although the provision of services is sometimes perceived as resulting in a "dematerialization" of growth, reducing the "throughput" of wealth creation, in fact it requires significant resource-intensive infrastructure and materials. This, combined with the increased levels of consumption favoured by income growth stimulated by a service-based economy, in reality wipes out any apparent benefits that might result from the shift to services (Kallis 2017). Moreover, the resource extraction required for a service-based economy, as with industry in general, is increasingly energy-intensive over time, because the first resources to be exploited are those that are the easiest and cheapest to extract.

To assess the credibility of the discourse around "green growth", researchers from the European Environmental Bureau (EEB) systematically searched for evidence of "decoupling", with regard both to resource use and its impacts (including GHG emissions and biodiversity loss). The research concludes that there is no concrete evidence of an absolute, permanent decoupling of environmental pressures from economic growth, as it has been mainly temporary and limited in space (Parrique *et al.* 2019).

From overconsumption to the norm of sufficiency

Consumption is the main factor driving the growth of CO_2 emissions, the use of raw materials, air pollution, biodiversity loss, nitrogen emissions and the overuse of scarce water and energy (Xiao *et al.* 2019). Hence, the highest impacts come from the most affluent households or individuals.

---

7. On the importance of distinguishing consumption-based carbon emissions (taking into account emissions embodied in imports) and production-based (territorial) carbon emissions, see Wiedmann *et al.* (2013), Ahmad and Wyckoff (2003) and Wilting and Vringer (2009).

Technology, however much it is cleaner and greener, has not been able to compensate for the rise in consumption. In 2019 the "Scientists' warning on affluence" summarized the evidence: "[G]lobally, burgeoning consumption has diminished or cancelled out any gains brought about by technological change aimed at reducing environmental impact" (Wiedmann *et al.* 2020: 3107). The EEB (Parrique *et al.* 2019: 3) concludes from the empirical evidence reviewed that, in addition to increasing efficiency, there should be a focus on sufficiency by scaling down economic production and consumption to enable a good life within the planet's ecological limits.

What does "sufficiency" mean? It means lifestyle changes that allow for basic needs to be satisfied but without overconsumption. It also means shifting business models from individual ownership to shared services and items, in which firms are interested in repairing items for a longer lifespan; repairing, reusing and recycling items at the end of their life cycle. It means promoting activities that are less energy- and resource-consuming.

The choice for sufficiency-driven lifestyle changes derives from the fundamental question neglected today by societies: what do we mean by a good life, and how can we get there? Advertising fuels popular culture's belief that material consumption is the main source of happiness (Dittmar 2007a, 2007b). This neglects true sources of subjective well-being that are positively correlated with low environmental impact (Csikszentmihalyi 1997; Csikszentmihalyi, Graef & McManama Gianinno 2014; Isham, Gatersleben & Jackson 2019). Similarly, plant-based and seasonal diets and physical activity as a substitute for driving are good both for the planet and for the health of the individual.

The alignment between the well-being of the individual and the broader societal interest in the promotion of such lifestyles is an opportunity. It avoids the perspective of "sustainable lifestyles" as a form of sacrifice or renouncement. Indeed, although they are traditionally seen as limiting individual freedoms, lifestyle changes that are based on a norm of sufficiency can be reconceived as an act of autonomy, if agreed to through democratic self-determination. They are an escape from the pressures of social comparison and the manufacturing of desires by the marketing efforts of firms.

Such lifestyle changes guided by the norm of sufficiency would aim to replicate, to a certain extent, what people in poverty do – not out of choice, but out of necessity. Low-income households are the real experts in how to save energy, minimize the use of water or lengthen the life of consumer items by sharing, reusing and repairing. The experience of people in poverty presents a strong argument for improving their participation in the collective effort towards the definition of sustainable consumption at the local level (Service for the Fight against Poverty, Precarity and Social Exclusion [Belgium] 2019). Such participation would ensure that the decisions around sustainable consumption consider the specific circumstances of low-income households, as they are more effective because they are better informed but also perceived as legitimate.

THE BROKEN COMPASS

The quest for growth also leads policy-making to be distorted in favour of instruments that maximize efficiency gains and monetary value, undermining other values, and they may actually end up worsening inequalities and poverty.

This can be seen both in the reliance on economic globalization as a source of growth and, at the domestic level, in the commodification of ever more spheres of life in the never-ending search for opportunities to create value. Such strategies put efficiency above resilience and the search for profits above the search for equality. They transform the world and people into resources to exploit. They contribute to the counter-productivity of growth.

Globalization: maximizing efficiency gains through trade and investment

In the name of stimulating growth, many countries have been encouraged to open themselves up to trade and foreign investment. They have been advised to lower import and export tariffs and to enter into free trade agreements. They have been told to create a "business-friendly" environment to attract foreign investment.

The assumption underlying trade liberalization is that each jurisdiction will specialize in certain lines of production that correspond to its "comparative advantage". The idea makes intuitive sense: the deepening of the international division of labour should allow efficiency gains that all countries could potentially benefit from, since goods and services will be provided at a lower cost, and therefore be more affordable for consumers.

This reasoning neglects a number of considerations. First, what you specialize in matters. It is not the same to specialize in the exploitation of mineral resources or in the production of raw agricultural materials, which many low-income countries do, as it is to specialize in the production of manufactured goods or in the delivery of services – with higher opportunities for increasing value through technological advances. Eduardo Galeano expresses this with admirable concision in the opening words of *Open Veins of Latin America*: "The division of labour among nations is that some specialize in winning and others in losing" (Galeano 1971: 1). This was at the heart of the "structuralist approach" promoted by Raúl Prebisch and others on the continent.

Second, the process of deep restructuring and specialization in economies often results in disproportionate disruptions for impoverished societies. In low-income countries, peasants cultivating small plots of land primarily to feed their communities are gradually marginalized, as they have been forced to compete against farmers located in rich countries who are far better equipped to achieve economies of scale and to produce large volumes of commodities, and who, moreover, are often heavily subsidized by taxpayers' money. In high-income countries, it is low-skilled workers who are the most affected. The outsourcing of production to low-wage countries has increased inequalities in these countries (Milanovic 2016). Economic globalization also explains the success of populist parties, which can easily prey upon the discontent created by the disruptions and attract voters by invoking the nostalgia of peaceful and harmonious societies, undisturbed by foreign competition.

The assumption behind investment liberalization is equally questionable. According to the mainstream narrative, foreign investment will supposedly benefit the local economy by accelerating technology transfers, creating jobs, improving access to global networks of production and distribution and leading to the emergence of supply chains to serve the needs of the investor. Furthermore, the public purse would benefit from taxes on the profits made by the foreign investors.

In practice, such linkages to the host economy are largely nullified by the very strategies countries put in place to favour investment. States compete with one another to attract investors. They provide "tax holidays" and show greater tolerance for transnational corporations' schemes to reduce their tax liability. They rush into investment treaties that bar them from imposing "performance standards" on foreign investors. Moreover, states agree to extended protections of intellectual property rights that are obstacles to the aspired technology transfers.

Such extended privileges granted to investors not only significantly diminish the benefits to the host country, they also fail to actually increase the levels of investment, because almost all countries end up providing a comparable standard of protection (De Schutter, Swinnen & Wouters 2012). The inter-jurisdictional competition to attract investors becomes a game in which all countries end up losing: the more investors can choose where to build production plants, the less states can, in fact, ensure that the public interest is served.

Creating value by commodifying life

Stimulating growth has also meant accelerating the commodification of life (see also Chapters 10, 11 and 14). Robert Heilbroner (1985: 60) notes that capital expansion requires a daily examination to expand the possibilities for accumulation, bringing concerns from the private household into the world of business. He sees this commodification of life as a major source of growth in advanced economies.

As the market logic expands its reach to colonize new spheres of life to respond to demand, the world and its people are transformed into resources to exploit, for the sake of increasing profits.

Economists rely on three arguments to defend this evolution. First, they suggest that economic incentives may be the most effective means of encouraging sustainable behaviour. Second, they consider that prohibiting certain transactions would be paternalistic, violating the right of each individual to choose. Third, they argue that exchanges that are by definition mutually beneficial increase overall utility.

We may however be paying a very high price, as societies, by accepting the gradual expansion of the market logic into spheres such as intimate relationships or the fight for a clean and healthy environment, which hitherto had been governed by norms other than by the ability to pay.

The one positive contribution of this deployment of the logic of capitalism, of course, is that many activities that were performed by women, in the form of unremunerated and unrecognized work within the household, can now be outsourced to the market. But that is a pyrrhic victory; the commodification of life may, in fact, have provided a convenient pretext to delay the real redistribution of gender roles, and, despite their massive entry into paid employment, women continue to shoulder most of the burden of household and care responsibilities.

THE STATE–MARKET DUOPOLY AND THE CAPTURE OF DEMOCRACY

The counter-productivity of growth is also manifest in the narrowing of democracy that results from the quest for growth. In the conventional approach to combating poverty, the need to increase monetary wealth calls for a close alliance between the state and the market, between the government and the entrepreneurial class. To the extent that the state depends on economic prosperity to finance its redistributive policies and to ensure its popular legitimacy, it must ensure that markets can operate within a regulatory and economic framework that maximizes their ability to create wealth – investing in infrastructure, guaranteeing freedom of enterprise and acting as a lender of last resort to rescue enterprises that are "too big to fail". This is the "glass ceiling" facing any state looking to change the course of its development: it has become a "state imperative" to facilitate capital accumulation and growth (Hausknost 2020).

Two consequences have followed. First, the state–market condominium that emerges is one that narrows down the space for the "commons" to exist, let alone to prosper and expand. Throughout the twentieth century this space, in which communities democratically govern certain resources or institutions, has either been privatized (with a view to maximizing profits) or bureaucratized (and co-opted within the state apparatus). As a result, democratic life has been impoverished, often to be reduced to the ritual of elections.

While the state has been democratized, society has been de-democratized. Citizens are asked to choose, through elections, who will make decisions on their behalf; nevertheless, they have also been asked to renounce deciding for themselves. The current revival of the idea of the "commons", beyond the state–market duopoly, is a "counter-movement". It is a reaction against this trend. It illustrates the growing impatience with the current alliance between government and business interests (Ostrom 1980).

The second consequence of this alliance between the state and vested economic interests is that policy-making has been systematically skewed in favour of the most powerful corporations. Their success has less to do with corruption or lobbying than with their ability to present themselves as the champions of economies of scale, of efficiency gains through the segmentation of the production process across jurisdictions and of the control of worldwide logistical networks. Mass consumption requires mass production. The emptying out of democratic politics has often been the price to pay for both.

This rise in the political influence of dominant economic actors has gone hand in hand with the weakening ability of people in poverty to be heard in democratic processes. In fact, the more affluent a society becomes, the less people in poverty will have a say in how decisions are made. The reason is mathematical: the fewer they are, the less people in poverty count as a constituency politicians cannot afford to ignore. Moreover, people in poverty are less well organized and have fewer resources than other social groups to influence decision-making. They also vote less (Ignatieff 2000: 92). The very fact that poverty has declined removes the issue from the agenda of mainstream politics, and the remaining islands of poverty appear even more difficult to address.

The capture of democracy is an obstacle to the adoption of policies that redistribute wealth and income. However, it is also a problem for the transformation of societies into low-carbon societies that halt the erosion of biodiversity. As Joachim Spangenberg (2014) remarks, the current version of liberal democracy restricts full participation in environmental matters. A strongly sustainable society will need to extend the current democratic domain.

Democracy should be deepened in two directions. Direct participation, in particular by people in poverty, should be encouraged. In addition, a democratic requirement should extend to new areas, particularly firms, from where it has, until now, been excluded. Indeed, only by such a deepening of democracy will it be possible to move to more sustainable lifestyles in ways that will be perceived as legitimate and the result of self-determination. This will be more effective than when such lifestyle changes are imposed by technocratic fiats or through the use of economic incentives, however "smart" such incentives may be.

CONCLUSION

Economic growth, as measured by increases in GDP, is unable to deliver on its promises. It barely contributes to the improvement of well-being. It is hardly reconcilable with sustainability objectives, and it skews policy- and decision-making in favour of economic elites. How, then, can we explain its persistent hold on the imagination of policy-makers?

The first reason has already been noted. Growth cannot be endorsed as a universal prescription and certainly should not guide policies in the Global North. Yet it is still a meaningful objective for lower-income countries, which have to urgently improve the prospects of their populations – including their material standard of living.

The second reason is that almost all countries face high levels of public debt. This limits their ability to provide basic services to their population and strengthen social protection. Since the debt will be even more expensive to pay back if the economy stagnates or, even worse, falls into a recession, it is often argued that the reigniting of growth is the condition for any poverty reduction policy, whatever precise form it takes.

However, this argument underestimates the large panoply of tools that states have to maintain public debt within acceptable limits – acceptable, that is, to the creditors whom they need to borrow from during economic downturns. More could be done to fight against aggressive tax optimization strategies by transnational firms – including by improved international cooperation to reduce tax competition – and to combat tax evasion. Another avenue would be the introduction of new, welfare-enhancing taxes, such as a tax on unhealthy foods.

Equally, considerable revenues could be collected by introducing or raising wealth taxes or inheritances when they are low or even non-existent. Indeed, wealth concentration is today, even more so than in the past, largely the result of intergenerational transfers such as inheritance and gifts (Feiveson & Sabelhaus 2018). Increasing taxes on inheritance would therefore be a coherent way of tackling wealth inequalities. However, only 24 out of 37 OECD countries tax inheritance, estate or gifts across generations; and the levies are typically very low, accounting for only 0.5 per cent of total tax revenues on average for the 24 countries concerned (OECD 2021).[8]

Similarly, a carbon tax would not only increase state revenue; it would also encourage the changes needed in investment, production and consumption patterns, and support technological innovations that can decrease future abatement costs. Yet carbon taxes are not solely a means to accelerate the ecological transformation, and to increase state revenues; they can also contribute to poverty reduction, provided the revenues raised are used to support low-income households (Kenert *et al.* 2018). The experiences of Sweden, and of the Canadian provinces of British Columbia and Alberta, demonstrate that this is feasible.

The third and most immediate reason why economic growth continues to provide the compass for public policy is political. Growth has the unique virtue of bridging views from across both the left and the right. Progressive politicians can accept renouncing the radical vision of redistribution on a large scale against the promise of a steady improvement of the living conditions of low-income groups. Conservatives are also ready to compromise, as they see sharing the benefits of growth as a substitute for broader social transformations based on redistribution that would threaten the vested economic interests on which they depend.

The task ahead is to move away from this gridlock and expand the toolbox for the realization of economic and social rights. Some scholars have started this journey, searching for "preventative, relational, low-resource models of welfare provisioning" (Walker, Druckman & Jackson 2021: 9; see also Zimmermann & Graziano 2020). As Max Koch (2021: 9) notes, the task ahead is not just to identify a set of policy proposals, such as wealth taxes, caps on income or the reduction of working time, that might contribute to this redefinition of welfare; it also entails moving beyond discrete policy suggestions to develop models of how these may reinforce each other in a new virtuous policy circle. This is where the proposals for an RBE come into place.

---

8. There are important differences between countries. In the United States, only 0.2 per cent of estates are subject to inheritance taxes, and parents may transfer up to $11 million to their children exempt of taxes, whereas the figures are 48 per cent and $17,000 for the "Region of Brussels – Capital" in Belgium (OECD 2021).

CHAPTER 3

THE CENTER FOR ECONOMIC AND SOCIAL RIGHTS' JOURNEY TO ADVANCE A RIGHTS-BASED ECONOMY

Center for Economic and Social Rights[1]

INTRODUCTION

The Covid-19 pandemic, combined with the climate crisis, reignited a discussion on the urgent need to transform the economy in a way for it to work both for people and the planet. The consequences of the above-mentioned crises led to hopes[2] that governments would finally undertake much-needed reforms to global economic governance. These hopes have not been realized – at least, not yet. The world is currently facing what economic historians refer to as polycrisis, namely "multiple crises … where the whole is even more dangerous than the sum of the parts" (Tooze 2022). The polycrisis includes rising global inequality, debt distress and political polarization; a worsening hunger crisis; the ongoing consequences of the Covid-19 pandemic; and a closing window of opportunity to prevent the worst impacts of global warming.

Several alternative models have been put forward, and platforms have been created to foster dialogue (Kothari *et al.* 2019),[3] such as the one led by the Global Tapestry of Alternatives.[4] A common thread is the understanding that

---

1. The Center for Economic and Social Rights would like to thank the Rosa-Luxemburg-Stiftung New York Office, with support from the German Ministry for Economic Cooperation and Development, for its funding in 2022 for CESR's work to advance a Rights-Based Economy. CESR also thanks and acknowledges the contributions of the following current and former staff members and fellows: Meghna Abraham, Kate Donald, Allison Corkery, Alina Saba, Ohene Ampofo-Anti and Manny Zhang.
2. See the series "Up close: imagining our post-pandemic futures" on OpenGlobalRights: www.openglobalrights.org/up-close/pandemic-futures/#up-close.
3. It encompasses a variety of visions of alternatives from "community economies" to "eco-Swaraj" or "radical ecological democracy" (Kothari *et al.* 2019).
4. The Global Tapestry of Alternatives (GTA) is an initiative seeking to create solidarity networks and strategic alliances between all these alternatives at local, regional and global levels; see https://globaltapestryofalternatives.org.

the neoliberal economic model, which has dominated the economic policy landscape for the last four decades, has only further entrenched poverty and increased inequalities while fuelling the existential threat of climate change. There is a growing recognition of the need of a new model, system or social contract to tackle the intersecting and compounding crises that the world faces today. However, and as discussed later, there is mixed and patchy political support for these alternatives and divergence in emphasis on the critical elements of a new model across NGOs and social movements. The human rights framework also continues to be marginal to debates about economic alternatives, with some key exceptions.

This chapter summarize the efforts of the Center for Economic and Social Rights in articulating and catalysing a Rights-Based Economy. It explains CESR's vision for this area of work, and discusses a few alternative economic models that are gaining traction and the convergences and divergences that exist between them and an RBE. It concludes with a brief description of CESR's plans to take this work forward with social movements.

CESR'S EFFORTS TO ARTICULATE AND CATALYSE A RIGHTS-BASED ECONOMY

Origin of the work on the RBE

Towards the end of 2019 CESR embarked on its first major organizational strategic planning process. The process came at an auspicious time, with a number of internal and external shifts posing new opportunities to advance the organization's mission, while also raising pivotal questions about the "Why?" and "How?" of its work. The central aim was to systematize and build up the organization's work on socio-economic inequality.

The strategy design process involved a mix of internal reflection, external consultation and board engagement. CESR sought to identify where the organization's unique thematic and methodological expertise could be most usefully focused to best serve collective efforts for change within and beyond the human rights field. Trends that were identified as having a bearing on the organization's strategy included debates about the failures of neoliberalism, the rise of authoritarianism, the corporate capture of spaces related to public goods, concerns around the climate crisis, declining multilateralism and geopolitical shifts and growing civil unrest (CESR 2020).

There was broad agreement that human rights activism has generally played a peripheral role in promoting economic and climate justice.

The human rights field had not been able to translate these issues into a new agenda for advocacy. Reasons for these issues not gaining traction included (a) fragmentation and silos; (b) the abstraction of human rights discussions, which fails to connect with people's lived experiences of grievances; (c) an unclear vision of how to change away from capitalism/neoliberalism; (d) fears/risk of wider human rights work being overshadowed by the work connected only to the emerging economic justice field; and (e) the weakening influence of "traditional" advocacy approaches and the acceptance of human rights norms.

Despite pessimism about the working methods and assumptions surrounding their effectiveness, activist interviewees expressed a sense of utility and relevance in terms of a human rights framework for advancing economic and social justice. To facilitate systemic thinking, multiple interviewees highlighted, human rights could help "to delineate what the role of a strong and effective state is in delivering on the public interest" (CESR 2020: 4).

Other interviewees flagged the rise of new challenges, such as "pushing activists to be really creative in terms of what's effective [and] where to put their energies" and "the sense that there are real moments of opportunity to align with movements that have a progressive vision of justice". Groups suggested a gendered lens to macroeconomic policy and prioritizing economic justice in "recognition that we need structural transformation of systems oppressing women, including neoliberalism" (CESR 2020: 5).

A broad consensus emerged around centring on "the unjust distribution of resources and power" as the overarching problem. At the same time, the need to foreground one or two issues over the three years of the strategy was recognized. The changed landscape trigged by the global Covid-19 pandemic and the threat of economic meltdown were key factors in this regard. Economic measures that would have been unthinkable months earlier were now on the table, with growing calls for a "just recovery" to "build back better". But, as per CESR's analysis, policy-makers were unlikely to deliver on these calls without active, cross-movement mobilization. As the consultation process had highlighted, a list of policy demands, alone, would not be enough to inspire mobilization across fields (CESR 2020).

As one of the relatively few civil society actors working on the relationship between human rights and the economy, CESR viewed elaborating the idea of an RBE as an opportunity to fill a gap and add unique value to collective efforts. The RBE frame was built on the organization's long-standing work on fiscal policy. It also created space to address other redistributive and pre-distributive policies critical to tackling inequality and the unjust distribution of resources. Consistent with the organization's bridge-building role, it also offered opportunities to forge broader alliances with progressive development coalitions, including Christian Aid, whose campaign on economic justice was set to be launched in December 2020.[5]

CESR'S VISION AND WORK TO ADVANCE AN RBE

CESR's vision for an RBE is set out in a joint publication released with Christian Aid in October 2020. The vision is based on a holistic understanding of human well-being and supported by the widely agreed framework of values and obligations of human rights. It seeks to "guarantee the material, social and environmental conditions necessary for all people to live with dignity on a flourishing planet" (Donald *et al.* 2020: 2). It calls for redistributive and non-retrogressive economic policies and the transformation of economic governance at the local, regional and global levels.

As per CESR's and Christian Aid's blueprint, the RBE consists of five key pillars: (a) guaranteeing dignity and well-being for all, at all stages of life; (b) pursuing substantive equality; (c) tackling power imbalances in the economy; (d) working in harmony with nature; and (e) democratizing and decolonizing the global economy (Donald *et al.* 2020).

To translate the RBE values in practice, CESR and Christian Aid believed in its operationalization through policy measures. They envisaged the following areas of policy intervention to demonstrate how the end vision of an RBE could be achieved: universal social protection systems; equitable labour and wage policies; rights-based public services; progressive and redistributive tax policies; better corporate regulations and governance; and improved global economic governance (Donald *et al.* 2020).

In 2022 CESR focused on creating knowledge, resources and shifting narratives around rights and the economy. In addition, there is ongoing work around building the RBE Blueprint with the objective of fleshing out the RBE vision through broader collaboration and lesson learning from various movements (CESR 2022). Likewise, CESR worked with partners in Latin America and the Caribbean, as part of the Initiative for Human Rights Principles in Fiscal Policy, on developing the Principles for Human Rights in Fiscal Policy (Initiative for Human Rights Principles in Fiscal Policy 2021), which distil key human rights principles applicable to tax and budget policies to help design rights-based economic policies.

By explaining how human rights should inform fiscal policy, the Principles for Human Rights in Fiscal Policy also shine a light on why certain types of tax policies are inconsistent with human rights (Initiative for Human Rights

---

5. In the event, the campaign was not launched in that form, as with the advent of Covid-19 the campaign focused on debt justice as a specific area of economic justice.

Principles in Fiscal Policy 2021). For instance, tax havens and the opacity that accompanies them, regressive taxes, low to non-existent corporate taxes, illicit financial flows, transfer pricing and a whole raft of other phenomena ultimately fall foul of human rights principles. Moreover, the international solidarity that is required to enable the realization of economic, social and cultural rights for all, and the urgency of tackling the climate crisis, mean that states must be mindful of how their domestic policies impact the enjoyment of rights by people outside their country (Initiative for Human Rights Principles in Fiscal Policy 2021).

The purpose and object of fiscal policy should be to act as a tool to redistribute wealth and resources, tackle structural and intersectional discrimination and allocate the maximum available resources to the realization of rights, such as the rights to health, education and social security. The Principles for Human Rights in Fiscal Policy require states to create a participatory and transparent tax system, which enables the participation of marginalized groups such as women, LGBTQ+ persons, Indigenous peoples and racially marginalized groups (Initiative for Human Rights Principles in Fiscal Policy 2021).

This work on tax justice has become more relevant than ever before, in light of the UN General Assembly opening the door for the development of a United Nations tax convention (UNGA 2023a) and the many flaws of the OECD's global tax agreement. CESR and its partners have argued that the global tax system must make the realization of the full range of human rights (civil, political, economic, social, cultural and environmental) its explicit purpose (CESR *et al.* 2022). Moreover, international taxation must tackle inequality within and between states and redistribute wealth and resources. A key aspect of this must be to ensure effective global cooperation in fighting illicit financial flows. This would entail, among other things, a rights-aligned global financial architecture, to bring an end to tax havens, transfer pricing, trade mis-invoicing and the opacity that accompanies these policies. Instead, corporations must be taxed fairly (with a global minimum tax rate of 25 per cent or higher) and there must also be more equitable allocation of taxing rights to countries in the Global South, transparency, country-by-country reporting and a beneficial ownership registry.

The Principles for Human Rights in Fiscal Policy have been widely referenced in both the human rights and fiscal justice sector, including by the UN independent expert on foreign debt (UNGA 2023: para. 23). CESR has also produced reports, briefs and submissions to UN human rights bodies arguing for the need to reform the current economic model. These engagements have contributed to greater recognition of the RBE by UN human rights bodies. The RBE is also referenced by the United Nations Research Institute for Social Development in its flagship report (UNRISD 2022: 277), described as being "based on a holistic understanding of human well-being and ... supported by the widely agreed framework of values and obligations of human rights".

ALTERNATIVE MODELS THAT APPEAR TO BE GAINING MORE TRACTION

CESR is researching and analysing various alternative models, ranging from those put forward by institutions and think tanks to those being advanced by social movements and engaging with these actors (Ampofo-Anti & Donald 2022; Ampofo-Anti & Saba 2022). A few of the models that appear to have more broad-based support are discussed briefly below.

Degrowth

As mentioned in the previous chapter by Olivier De Schutter, the degrowth movement calls for an equitable downscaling of production and consumption with the aim of achieving social justice and ecological sustainability (Hickel 2020).

Some political parties, mostly in southern Europe, have started to adopt degrowth-oriented or degrowth-compatible policy proposals. Policies advocated by degrowth supporters (Asara 2021) include "resource caps, redistributive taxation and wealth or income caps, universal basic income, working time reduction and work sharing, as well as the relocalization of economic activities, decommodification of the main economic sectors, and strengthening of public ownership".

Degrowth is gaining traction beyond academic circles, albeit with divergence about what it entails (see Chapter 6). For instance, the Red Deal proposed by the Red Nation – a coalition of Indigenous and other activists in the United States advocating for Indigenous liberation – is an example of an alternative vision for society. Described as a degrowth agenda, it has more of a decolonial vision in essence (Progressive International 2021; Tyberg 2020). Moreover, a report on the eighth International Degrowth Conference highlights that "academic political ecology" proposals are considerably different from and far less radical than those popular movements representing marginalized groups (Boston 2021). Moving forward, the degrowth movement/network/community could benefit from strengthened relationships with allied "research and activist communities like the ones of feminism, environmental justice, political ecology, ecological economics, post-extractivism, anti-racism, commons, decoloniality, post-development and economic and environmental history" (Demaria 2018).

Global Public Investment (GPI)

The concept of GPI has been championed by the Expert Working Group (EWG) on GPI. It aims to reshape the existing international concessional public finance system. GPI proposes a fundamental shift from the traditional donor–recipient paradigm towards a common framework, within which all countries contribute (according to their capacity), all receive benefits and all decide how the money is spent via a constituency-based model (Expert Working Group on Global Public Investment 2022). Factors beyond gross domestic product per capita would be considered in assessing countries' contributions and receipts. GPI contributions would be channelled through existing regional funding infrastructure (Equal International 2022). Proponents of GPI argue that this framework will lead to additional and better-quality grant financing for public goods and other development priorities. Consistent with human rights principles, it aims for representative decision-making with a meaningful institutionalized role for civil society.

GPI principles are gaining traction in policy-making, advocacy and scholarly communities, mostly on pandemic preparedness and response, and climate finance. Crucial to the success of GPI is country buy-in, as much of its advocacy appears to be targeted at governments and multilateral institutions. As recognized in the EWG (2022) and Equal International (2022) reports, further work needs to be done to flesh out GPI's technical and political case. For the GPI funding model to work, it must also be accompanied by political and economic efforts such as redistributing wealth and ending tax abuses.

Eco-social contract

Calls for economic transformation have included the redefinition of a new social contract between people, governments and the environment. The concept of an "eco-social contract" is an example. It responds to the failure of the global economic model to account for the planet's natural boundaries, seeking to spur the transformation of economies and societies to halt climate change and environmental destruction.

In November 2021 UNRISD and the Green Economy Coalition (GEC) launched a global research and action network to support the creation of an eco-social contract. In October 2022 UNRISD defined its vision for an eco-social contract and a paradigm shift in state–market–society–nature relations. The flagship report presents seven principles for building a new eco-social contract. These include guaranteeing human rights for all, which requires bringing in those who have been left out of previous social contracts, such as women, Indigenous peoples, informal workers and migrants. A new eco-social contract must also go hand in hand with a new fiscal contract that raises sufficient resources for climate action and SDG implementation, and must be based on new forms of solidarity. UNRISD (2022) proposes three mutually reinforcing pillars for a new eco-social implementation: transforming economic systems; implementing universal social policies; and strengthening solidarity and multilateralism across the globe.

Many different proposals for economic and social reform have been framed through the prism of building a new social contract. These are being advocated by people's movements such as Fridays for Future and Extinction Rebellion, the UN secretary general, the World Economic Forum and the business sector. UNRISD's recommendations find common ground with other proposals for structural reform, including the RBE, notably in its focus on rejuvenating the role of the state in economic development and bringing into social contracts an ecological dimension alongside the social dimension. Nepal's recent political developments, with its 2015 constitution, and the new constitutions that were negotiated by left-wing governments in Bolivia and Ecuador, incorporating Indigenous visions such as *buen vivir*, are seen as examples of renegotiating new eco-social contracts.

As highlighted in Chapter 14, *buen vivir* means "living well" or the "good life" in Spanish. It is a developmental pathway or way of being, which is recognized in diverse forms among Indigenous communities in Latin America. *Buen vivir* recognizes humanity's interdependence with nature and emphasizes that the only way to achieve true well-being is through living in harmony with nature. According to *buen vivir*, enhancing human well-being and flourishing cannot be achieved by creating maximum individual freedom but, rather, through maintaining the well-being of one's community. It has a holistic view of "the community", which incorporates Mother Earth and the entire Earth community. *Buen vivir* is inherently decolonial in its nature, as it places emphasis on restoring the dignity and autonomy of Indigenous communities, their values and their ways of life.

Buen vivir is at times couched in the language of rights and at other times not. Most notably, in Ecuador's constitution, *buen vivir* marries economic, social and cultural rights with rights for nature (holding on its own terms). There is much that other alternative economic models could learn from *buen vivir*'s fluidity and capacity to capture unique forms of Indigenous cosmology.

Social and solidarity economy (SSE)

Detailed further in Chapter 9, proponents of an SSE argue that the traditional economy could be reformed towards more social and egalitarian ends if the third sector is given appropriate support, including legal and policy reforms.

The SSE has a potentially important role to play in reorienting economies and societies towards a new eco-social contract. Institutionalizing collective action and promoting environmentally and socially sustainable production, exchange and consumption aims to realize emancipatory purposes within economic spheres and the wider political economy, and rebalance economic, social and environmental objectives.

Feminist care economy

The importance of feminist care economies is touched on in Chapters 12 and 13. A caring economy "prioritizes care of one another and the environment in which we live ... everyone gives and receives care on the basis of their capacities and needs" (Women's Budget Group [WBG] 2020).

WBG's recent report *Creating a Care Economy: A Call to Action* identifies the care economy's three central pillars: gender equality, well-being and sustainability (WBG 2020). A care economy calls for social and physical infrastructure investment and transforms the worlds of paid and unpaid care work. This would be achieved by ensuring universal childcare provision from the age of six months and upwards, by increasing investment in healthcare and raising the salaries of nurses and addressing violence against women and girls (VAWG). In addition, a care economy would require implementing paid care leave while ensuring equity and parental leave entitlements, so as to improve the burden of caregiving between men and women.

A care economy requires a social security system. It would be built around economic and fiscal reforms, such as progressive taxation and redistribution, as well as the adoption of targets directly related to gender equality, well-being and sustainability. As such, the report (WBG 2022: 75) calls upon states to reallocate spending "from military and defence spending to care services, and from polluting industries to green industries".

OVERLAPS AND DIVERGENCES BETWEEN ALTERNATIVES MODELS AND HUMAN RIGHTS

There is a significant overlap between the guiding principles and policy proposals associated with some of the discussed alternatives models and the RBE, with differences in perspective regarding aims, strategies and priorities. The RBE demands a state's active role in the economy by regulating the conduct of businesses and other private actors and directing public investment towards essential infrastructure, goods and services. Likewise, proposals for a new eco-social contract have highlighted the importance of redefining the role of the state in economic development.

The RBE also draws from *buen vivir*, the well-being economy, the feminist economy, the caring economy, degrowth and more. It has also been inspired by Indigenous cosmologies to recognize the interdependence of human beings with the natural world, and the need for a shift to a vision of the economy based on this interdependence and respect for nature and planetary boundaries, rather than extraction. In so far as the GPI proposal seeks to shift the governance of international public finance to a more democratic model, it aligns with the RBE's pillar on transforming institutions and systems of global economic governance to dismantle asymmetries (Yamin & Curtain 2022). The RBE also aligns with degrowth and the emphasis on the need to dismantle the colonial nature of the global economy, whereby countries in the Global North continue to extract from the Global South in various ways. The RBE concept is inclusive and pluralistic and does not propose to "crowd out" other progressive alternative visions but, rather, to learn from them and build on them.

The RBE aims to bring the rights framework to the fora, as it is grounded in human rights standards and principles, as outlined in the Universal Declaration of Human Rights, international and regional human rights treaties and other instruments. Taken together, these international human rights embrace concepts such as human dignity, substantive equality and states' obligation to devote their maximum available resources to the progressive realization of economic, social, cultural and environmental rights. The focus on extraterritorial obligations is also a key tool for addressing the responsibilities of governments to ensure that resources are redistributed for the fulfilment of rights everywhere and to dismantle the colonial nature of the global economy. The RBE proposes that human rights can not only inform a new vision of the economy but guide the decisions taken to get there and advance movements' struggles.

Many of the alternative economic models allude to policy proposals that are consistent with what CESR would define as rights-aligned demands. Many of these models offer powerful arguments as to why the neoliberal status quo has gone awry. For instance, like degrowth, instead of using rights language to frame their demands, they focus on seeking legitimate and just ways for the economic system to operate.

Other proposals among movements and civil society, such as the Red Deal, call for intersectional or decolonized modes of organizing the economy. At their core, these proposals seek to disrupt and dismantle oppressive social hierarchies rooted in colonialism, patriarchy and related forms of oppression, which persist despite their nominal abolition. The power of these proposals is that they reveal the truth that mere legal or political declarations of the end of "slavery" or "segregation" or "apartheid" do not necessarily translate into a new lived experience for marginalized groups. By focusing on the need to reform broader systems and structures at both local and global levels, these proposals lay bare what lies at the heart of inequality, poverty and the unjust distribution of wealth and resources.

However, what is arguably absent from these proposals is the need to acknowledge that, historically, decolonization and human rights have not always been in contestation. In many ways the anti-colonial and anti-apartheid struggles were grounded in a notion of reconceptualizing the "human" part of human rights. This is because substantive equality, the principle that undergirds the entire concept of human rights, would ring hollow without a complete eradication of the structures, systems and policies that sustain disadvantage based on race or other grounds. Rights, therefore, are sites of contestation that do not have inherent meaning. Advocates and activists can give flesh and bone to human rights concepts of dignity and equality and provide a meaning that speaks to the lived experiences of so many (Cachalia 2018: 375).

For this reason, and in this sense, the RBE expressly endorses decolonization as a requirement for the realization of human rights. The human rights principles of dignity, equality and participatory democracy imply the RBE's support of decolonial demands for reparations (including climate reparations), calling for a fundamental overhaul of global economic governance institutions and providing meaningful space for Indigenous and subaltern ways of being.

TAKING THIS WORK FORWARD

CESR reached out to various stakeholders to contribute to building the RBE blueprint. The aim was to gather perceptions of an RBE and thoughts, pieces of work, artwork or visions that could inspire the design of a new economy. In their view, the RBE is an area in which human rights play a central role, is based on the value of equity, puts people over profit and is inclusive and accountable. The survey also revealed that the work of many stakeholders aligns with the five pillars of RBE, specifically the work on dismantling power imbalances in the economy, decolonizing and democratizing the global economy, pursuing substantive equality and working in harmony with nature (CESR 2022).

Based on CESR's engagement with various stakeholders, it has also identified the following challenges: mixed political support for overturning neoliberalism; the top-down approach of many alternative economic models; and the multiplicity of narratives and silos.

First, there are political parties, particularly those with an environmental focus or on the left of the political spectrum, that are willing to challenge aspects of the neoliberal economic model. This is manifested in a focus on green new deals, attempts to reduce consumption and dependence on a fossil-fuel-based economy, challenges to austerity policies and privatization of public services, support for a care economy, and so on. The election of progressive governments in Latin America has also led to an impetus for more comprehensive reforms. However, some elements of the opposition in a few countries are based on other geopolitical factors (e.g. support for increased public investment to reduce the dependence on Chinese supply chains). This leads in some cases to patchy policies and responses rather than a comprehensive rejection of the neoliberal economic model. Social movements have a major role in being able to build on and amplify these progressive trends to push through more comprehensive reforms.

Second, it is important that any economic alternatives build on the lived experiences of people and on the demands of social movements that have pushed for these reforms for decades. It is therefore a concern that many prominent economic alternatives, no matter how well intentioned and reasoned they might be, are being articulated in a top-down manner and being primarily discussed within academic, policy, NGO and UN circles in the Global North. It is key that any discussion of alternatives build on those articulated by movements and that bridges are built between academic and policy-led processes and these social movements.

Third, there are multiple alternatives that have already been articulated with different areas of emphasis by various NGOs and movements, which makes it challenging to agree a set of common principles that can be advanced across movements. There is also a reticence about the value of human rights in some movements, primarily because of a sense that the international human rights movement has been slow and shamefully late in tacking big structural issues around inequality and colonization. It is essential that any attempts to define the RBE allow for a multiplicity of perspectives and tackle these concerns head-on. In this regard, the silos between different movements, even though there has been progress in many countries and on many issues, continue to be a challenge. There are also numerous windows of opportunity in the political area because of the push by developing countries to rebalance power and resources within global economic governance through initiatives such as the Loss and Damage Fund and discussions on a potential UN tax treaty. Effective cross-movement approaches and collaboration are essential to be able to leverage these opportunities to push through reforms that go to the heart of the model, rather than achieve merely superficial changes in each area.

Future CESR activities around the RBE will focus on developing this work as a platform to identify areas of synergy and convergence between alternative visions. The CESR plans to increase its engagement and outreach to various movements in order to jointly identify and build on shared priorities in terms of critical reforms to global financial architecture and the economic system. The blueprint survey and this outreach to partners indicated considerable interest in convening around core areas and themes, which will allow dialogues between movements, NGOs, think tanks and academics focusing on alternative models. There is a general need to build dialogues across themes to break down silos and create more bridges between social movements working on human rights, climate change, gender equality, tax justice, debt justice and social justice. This is essential to amplify advocacy and campaigning efforts to a scale at which transformative agendas can be rapidly progressed for how societies can be organized and resources distributed in them so as to achieve rights for all.

CHAPTER 4

BUSINESS AND HUMAN RIGHTS: FROM "TOKENISM" TO "CENTRING" RIGHTS AND RIGHTS-HOLDERS

Surya Deva and Harpreet Kaur

INTRODUCTION

Corporations are a key driver of the free market economy in a globalized world. Because of their omnipresent role in today's economy, people have become fully dependent on corporations. They "determine what we eat, what we watch, what we wear, where we work, and what we do" (Bakan 2004: 5). Corporations – more precisely, the tiny percentage of people heading such corporations – are also the key beneficiary of the current free market economy. To illustrate, over the last ten years "the richest 1% of humanity has captured more than half of all new global wealth. Since 2020, … this wealth grab by the super-rich has accelerated, and the richest 1% have captured almost two-thirds of all new wealth" (Oxfam International 2023: 8).

Even when people may seem to be benefiting from globalized free markets, they are, in essence, at the service of corporations. For example, although global supply chains may offer a variety of cheap products and create employment in developing countries, they are also sites of exploitation of workers and outsourcing of environmental pollution to the Global South. In the name of freedom, convenience and flexibility, gig workers have bartered their employee status and all related benefits under labour laws. Similarly, people using free internet are (un)consciously becoming subjects of unconscionable data mining.

In parallel – as well as in response – to the rise in corporate power and wealth, there has been the growth of business and human rights (BHR) as a distinct field, with its own set of standards articulating human rights responsibilities of corporations. The United Nations Guiding Principles on Business and Human Rights (UNGPs) have become the posterchild of the BHR field. The UNGPs envisage all business enterprises respecting all internationally recognized human rights. They also prescribe human rights due diligence (HRDD) as the primary tool to "know and show" how corporations respect human rights (UN HRC 2011b). This voluntary responsibility to conduct regular HRDD is increasingly hardening into a legal obligation, primarily as a result of the emergence of mandatory HRDD laws in Europe (European Coalition for Corporate Justice 2022). The most recent addition to this trend is the draft proposal of the Corporate Sustainability Due Diligence Directive (CSDDD), released in February 2022 (European Parliament 2022). This hardening of the responsibility to conduct HRDD has received mixed response from states and corporations: although some states and corporations have offered public support for such a move (Business and Human Rights Resource Centre [BHRRC] n.d.), others have resisted the legalization efforts or tried to dilute the scope and ambit of these measures.[1]

How does the corporate responsibility to respect human rights under international BHR standards sit with growing economic inequalities? Is HRDD – as the main tool offered by the UNGPs – fit for the purpose of harnessing the potential of corporations to create a human-rights-based economy? This chapter critically analyses the UNGPs' theoretical underpinnings and HRDD. We contend that both the corporate responsibility to respect human rights and HRDD as a process to discharge this responsibility should be reimagined in order to recognize the centrality of rights and rights-holders. The chapter problematizes theories of embedded liberalism and polycentric governance in the context of the UNGPs. Then we contrast the theory and practice of HRDD with the help of two case studies. Following this, the chapter reimagines what the HRDD should look like to support a Rights-Based Economy. We offer brief concluding thoughts in the final section.

EMBEDDED LIBERALISM AND POLYCENTRIC GOVERNANCE IN THE NEOLIBERAL MARKET ECONOMY

The UNGPs are underpinned by John Ruggie's theory of embedded liberalism (Ruggie 1982).[2] He argues that "markets work optimally only if they are embedded within broader social and legal norms, rules, and institutional practices" (Ruggie 2013: 172). Such embedding should provide a pathway to overcome key global governance challenges reflected in the BHR field – that

1. See Global Policy Forum (www.globalpolicy.org/en/publication/copy-paste-method) and Friends of the Earth Europe *et al.* (https://corporateeurope.org/sites/default/files/2022-06/INSIDE%20JOB%20How%20business%20lobbyists%20used%20the%20Commission%27s%20scrutiny%20procedures.pdf).
2. Ruggie (1982) developed the theory of embedded liberalism in his seminal article "International regimes, transactions, and change: embedded liberalism in the postwar economic order". In the specific BHR context, see Abdelal & Ruggie (2009) and Ruggie (2020).

is, "the widening gaps between the scope and impact of economic forces and actors, and the capacity of societies to manage their adverse consequences" (Ruggie 2014: 6).

Polycentric governance provides another theoretical foundation to the UNGPs, because the "state by itself cannot do all the heavy lifting required to meet most pressing societal challenges" (Ruggie 2014: 8). The UNGPs, therefore, rely on three distinct but complementary governance systems that shape corporate conduct: the traditional system of public law and governance at the national, regional and international levels; the system of civil governance involving stakeholders concerned about adverse effects of business conduct; and the corporate governance system, which internalizes elements of the other two systems and adopts various risk management strategies and policies (Ruggie 2020: 73).

It is arguable that polycentric governance is essential to achieve the embedding of liberal values in the market because non-state actors occupy a central role in the neoliberal market economy. However, this may also be part of the problem, in that businesses may embed human rights in their global operations on terms that preserve their interests (Birchall 2021; Wettstein 2021). We problematize the normative operationalization of embedded liberalism and polycentric governance in the UNGPs as well as the corporate practice of such embedding.

First, we contend that the UNGPs aim for a softer embedding of human rights in the market only because the responsibility is not legally binding and thus may not ensure that human rights trump profit considerations in the free market economy. Moreover, the responsibility is merely to "do no harm". This negative responsibility entails taking positive steps to avoid adverse human rights impacts. However, businesses are not expected to protect or promote human rights. This, again, is a serious lacuna in a free market economy in which corporations perform all-pervasive activities and states are increasingly outsourcing the delivery of many public services to corporations (Bilchitz 2021).

Second, the main tool proposed by the UNGPs to meet the corporate responsibility to respect human rights under Pillar II (i.e. HRDD) is process-oriented. Shifting the focus away from achieving tangible outcomes means that human rights abuses may continue to coexist with businesses conducting HRDD. The HRDD process, at least in its mainstream conceptualization, is perhaps not meant to address inherently exploitative business models or systemic problems with the free market economy.[3] In other words, the over-reliance on the HRDD process is a normatively unsound recipe to disrupt the

---

3. Birchall (2019) argues for an expansive interpretation of adverse human rights impacts under the UNGPs. But such an interpretation will perhaps make it impossible for corporations ever to act in line with Pillar II of the UNGPs (Deva 2021).

neoliberal economic order – or even embed human rights in free markets, for that matter.[4]

Third, the UNGPs do not confront and address power imbalances between rights-holders and corporations, despite "the inequalities and disparities of power and wealth that are a key characteristic of the contemporary global economy" (Brinks *et al.* 2021: 1–4). David Birchall (2021) analyses corporate power over human rights in four settings: power over individuals, power over materialities, power over institutions and power over knowledge. The UNGPs do not seem to challenge corporate power in any of these settings. In fact, even human rights experts engaged by corporations to conduct HRDD, who confer a certain level of legitimacy to corporate actions (McVey 2022), may inadvertently entrench further the power imbalances between rights-holders and corporations.

Fourth, although the conceptualization of HRDD under the UNGPs is conscious of the vulnerability of rights-holders,[5] it does not do much to adequately address the various vulnerabilities of communities related to information, expertise, economic dependence, resources and historical injustices that exist on the ground. Because of these multiple vulnerabilities, rights-holders are "constantly susceptible to harm" (Peroni & Timmer 2013: 1058). At the same time, rights-holders and communities also have agency to determine the type of economic development or activities that are good for them. However, the HRDD process does not recognize their agency. Rather, rights-holders and communities are merely to be consulted (Ruggie, Rees & Davis 2021) [6]– often in a passive manner – in the HRDD process led and controlled by corporations.

Fifth, current practices in the BHR field tend to show that corporations are embedding human rights values in a free market economy only at a superficial level. Such embedding often occurs on exploitative terms set by neoliberal means of production. HRDD is based on due diligence practices known to corporations (Ruggie, Rees & Davis 2021),[7] which tend to focus on identifying, preventing and mitigating risks to corporations. Although the

---

4. For a detailed critique, see Deva (2023a).
5. Principle 18 of the UNGPs requires "meaningful consultation with potentially affected groups and other relevant stakeholders". Moreover, the UNGPs also encourage business enterprises to "pay special attention to any particular human rights impacts on individuals from groups or populations that may be at heightened risk of vulnerability or marginalization" (UN HRC 2011b: commentary to Principle 18 and commentary to Principle 20).
6. Ruggie, Rees and Davis (2021: 187, emphasis in original) note that "consultation with *these* stakeholders – to understand their views and experiences so these can be factored into business decisions and actions – ... is essential to the construct of HRDD".
7. "The construct of HRDD was deliberately adapted from other due diligence processes traditionally familiar to business (legal, financial, technical)" (Ruggie, Rees & Davis 2021: 186).

HRDD seeks to shift this narrative about risks and turns attention to risks to people (Ruggie, Rees & Davis 2021),[8] such a desired change is not happening in practice. Consequently, development projects continue to go ahead with minor tweaks with no serious attempt to address the genuine human rights concerns of rights-holders. It is arguable that such a deficient execution of HRDD is shaped by some of the normative shortcomings inherent in the HRDD process articulated by the UNGPs.

In short, HRDD as a polycentric governance tool is failing to embed human rights values in the conduct of most corporations in the neoliberal market economy. We show this below with the help of two case studies.

THE THEORY AND PRACTICE OF HRDD

The UNGPs propose HRDD as the main tool for business enterprises to "know and show" that they respect human rights (Ruggie, Rees & Davis 2021: 185). HRDD is a four-step process: identify and assess any actual or potential adverse human rights impacts; take appropriate action by integrating the findings from impact assessments; track the effectiveness of their response; and communicate externally how adverse impacts are being addressed (UNGPs, note 5, Principles 18–21). Since risks may change over time, HRDD is envisaged as an ongoing process. Conducting HRDD should enable corporations to identify, prevent, mitigate and account for how they address adverse human rights impacts. HRDD differs from transaction-based due diligence undertaken by corporations, and hence the UNGPs expect "meaningful consultation with potentially affected groups and other relevant stakeholders" (UNGPs, Principle 18). If such consultation is not possible, corporations "should consider reasonable alternatives such as consulting credible, independent expert resources, including human rights defenders and others from civil society" (UNGPs, Commentary to Principle 18).

Despite a detailed articulation of HRDD steps, there are "significant divergences among scholars and stakeholders in their understanding of the concept and, importantly, its relationship, if any, with legal liability" (Quijano & Lopez 2021: 241). More critically, since HRDD under Pillar II is "rooted in a transnational social norm" (Ruggie & Sherman 2017: 923) and is not obligatory, a great majority of corporations are not yet conducting HRDD or just paying lip service to it. A 2018 report of the UN Working Group on business and human rights concluded that "the majority of business enterprises around the world remain unaware, unable or unwilling to implement human rights

---

8. "HRDD places the focus specifically on those people whose basic dignity and equality are at risk of harm" (Ruggie, Rees & Davis 2021: 186).

due diligence as required of them in order to meet their responsibility to respect human rights" (UNWG 2018: 24, para. 92). This position is confirmed by other studies and indicators (McCorquodale & Nolan 2021: 465–7). For example, in the 2020 *Corporate Human Rights Benchmark* (CHRB), 46.2 per cent of 229 assessed corporations from five different sectors did not score any points for HRDD (World Benchmarking Alliance [WBA] 2020: 3). Moreover, most of the corporations captured in the 2022 report "are taking a hands-off approach to human rights in their supply chains" (WBA 2022: 4).

It is this significant gap between corporates' commitment to embrace the UNGPs and their failure to conduct HRDD in practice that has led to the push for making HRDD obligatory at national, regional and international levels. In addition to mandatory HRDD laws in five European states – the French Duty of Vigilance 2017, the Dutch Child Labour Due Diligence Act 2019, the Swiss Due Diligence Legislation 2021, the German Law on Supply Chain Due Diligence 2021, and the Norwegian Transparency Act 2021 – we should see the CSDDD and the proposed BHR treaty in this context.

While this hardening of soft responsibility is generally welcomed by civil society organizations (CSOs) and some businesses, it also triggers the risk of "cosmetic compliance" (Landau 2019: 221) or corporations treating HRDD as a tick-box exercise.[9] As noted above, these laws are unlikely to bring any fundamental changes to how corporations do business: the HRDD process may leave unscathed irresponsible or exploitative business models (Deva 2023: 401–4). Moreover, most mandatory HRDD laws target only those corporations that are above a certain size or that operate in a particular sector. Consequently, there is a concern that such targeted corporations may pass the burden of compliance to their business partners without providing them with adequate financial and technical support.

The two case studies discussed below also demonstrate that there is a wide gap between the theory and practice of HRDD, in that corporations continue to focus more on managing risks to themselves than addressing the adverse impacts of their business operations on people and the planet. Out of the several deficits inherent in the UNGPs and the HRDD process highlighted above, we pay special attention to power imbalances and vulnerabilities. The two cases show that having corporations in the "driving seat" for conducting HRDD is problematic, because they often do not take proactive steps to address imbalances in terms of power, information and expertise. These case studies are chosen because the corporations involved in both cases – Vale and Rio Tinto – have made a public commitment to act in line with the

---

9. In relation to the French law, Savourey and Brabant (2021: 147) note that "a number of companies still approach the vigilance plan as a tick-box exercise and are wary of transparency and stakeholder engagement".

UNGPs and have taken steps over the years to implement HRDD. Both cases relate to the extractive sector, a key site of various abuses in the BHR field, and involve communities in vulnerable positions.

Feijão Dam disaster, Brazil

On 25 January 2019 the Feijão Dam – located in the municipality of Brumadinho in the province of Minas Gerais in Brazil – collapsed, releasing 12.7 million cubic metres of mining waste (Conectas 2019). The dam contained the tailings of an iron ore mine owned by Vale. The alarm system installed by Vale in the nearby village to warn the residents of any risk did not go off (BBC News 2021). In addition to causing the death of over 270 people, the disaster caused a huge environmental crisis by releasing toxic waste from the dam, harming animal life and flora and polluting waterways (Jamasmie 2021). It is worth noting that Vale was also linked to another dam disaster three years earlier: in November 2015 a mining dam operated by Vale's subsidiary Samarco collapsed in the town of Mariana in the province of Minas Gerais (BBC News 2021).

Vale has made an explicit commitment to act in line with the UNGPs. Vale claims on its website that "Vale's Human Rights strategy and management is based on the respect, awareness and promotion of Human Rights, as well as the prevention of risks and the management of adverse impacts and Human Rights violations, and when necessary, the mitigation and remediation in Vale's activities and throughout its supply chain". The company "values engagement with stakeholders", although it is "mindful that there is still room for improvement in this process".[10]

Vale had also been a member of the UN Global Compact since 2007, and it did submit an annual communication on progress report about its implementation of the ten Global Compact principles.[11] After the Feijão Dam disaster "Vale requested to be delisted" from the Global Compact in May 2019.[12] It is worth noting that Vale had scored higher than many peer corporations on the 2018 *Corporate Human Rights Benchmark*. However, after the dam disaster the CHRB decided to exclude Vale from its 2018 benchmark rankings, as it "would not be correct for CHRB to continue to rank Vale in the higher performance bands in the wake of such a tragedy" (CHRB 2019).

---

10. See Vale, "Human rights": www.vale.com/web/esg/human-rights.
11. UN Global Compact, "Vale SA", https://unglobalcompact.org/what-is-gc/participants/2367-Vale.
12. Vale, "Vale reaffirms its commitment to the UN Global Compact Principles", www.vale.com/web/esg/un-global-compact.

This is why Rajiv Maher argues that benchmarks "are misleading in terms of human rights and corporate responsibility when considered from a rights holder perspective" (Maher 2020: 156).

How does Vale's "on paper commitment" contrast with its business practice about HRDD, especially prior to the dam disaster? A statement issued by Vale immediately after the disaster outlined several "due diligence" measures taken by the company about the dam's safety (Vale 2019).[13] However, the statement contained no reference to *human rights* due diligence or any consultations carried out with key stakeholders, including communities living close to the site. A subsequent independent committee constituted by Vale revealed that the company "knew about the facility's fragile condition since 2003" (Jamasmie 2021), thus exposing the cleavage between the company's *commitment* and *actions* to identify, prevent and mitigate adverse human rights impacts in line with the UNGPs. In fact, the committee found that Vale prioritized "regulatory compliance" over "the actual safety situation of the dam" (Müller-Hoff 2020).

Although Vale claimed to engage with stakeholders, civil society organizations alleged that HRDD was not properly conducted, especially because the renewed approval of the dam's licence "was marked by fierce opposition from representatives of civil society".[14] Despite the opposition by CSOs, the risk category of the mine was downgraded, which allowed Vale to speed up the licensing process. Moreover, CSOs had complained that the technical documents were made available only four days before the meeting (Conectas 2019). These factors seem to suggest that Vale did not take proactive steps to address power imbalances while consulting key stakeholders meaningfully. Nor did it learn any lessons from community dissatisfaction caused by the lack of participation of CSOs and the affected rights-holders in the remediation mechanism for the 2015 Mariana dam disaster (Nabuco & Aleixo 2019).

Vale's website outlines several steps that the company took after the 2019 dam disaster, such as a review of its "Global Human Rights Policy" after a public consultation, integration of a human rights lens in company policies, mandatory human rights training for employees, the inclusion of human rights violation risks in Vale's global risk management system and a commitment to perform HRDD in all Vale operations in three-year cycles.[15] However, most of these steps do not address the inherent limitations of the HRDD – that is, how to address various power imbalances and vulnerabilities. More

---

13. "The dam underwent fortnightly field inspections, all reported to the ANM (National Mining Agency) through the SIGBM (Integrated Safety Management System for Mining Dams)" (Vale 2019).
14. See https://chrgj.org/wp-content/uploads/2019/02/Allegation-to-the-Global-Compact-Dam-collapse-in-Brumadinho-11022019.pdf, p. 6.
15. Vale, "Human rights": www.vale.com/web/esg/human-rights.

critically, these steps revolve around the "do no harm" approach, instead of considering Vale's role in contributing to an inclusive and sustainable society.

Juukan Gorge destruction, Australia

In May 2020, while clearing the way for a mine expansion, "Rio Tinto set off explosives that destroyed a site sacred to the Puutu Kunti Kurrama and Pinikura people (PKKP) in Western Australia. The site included the Juukan Gorge Rock Dwellings, which have evidence of human habitation dating back 46,000 years" (Shanafelt Wong 2022). Although Rio Tinto was made aware of the Juukan Gorge's cultural and religious significance, it made no serious attempt to prevent risks of damaging the sites; for example, "three alternatives for the design of the mine that could have avoided the Juukan rock shelters were never shared with the PKKP" (Nagar 2021: 381). Under pressure from Indigenous groups, investors and the public generally, three senior Rio Tinto executives were forced to resign (Toscano 2021).

It is worth noting that Rio Tinto had acted within the law, because it had obtained a permission under Section 18 of Western Australia's Aboriginal Heritage Act 1972 to carry out explosions on the said Indigenous heritage site. However, the corporate responsibility to respect human rights under the UNGPs "exists over and above compliance with national laws and regulations protecting human rights." (UNGPs, Commentary to Principle 11). This law has been criticized for prioritizing "development and profit, often forcing Aboriginal people into agreements and gag orders" (Shanafelt Wong 2022). A federal government inquiry also found that what happened at the Juukan Gorge was reflective of "countless instances where cultural heritage has been the victim of the drive for development and commercial gain" (Allam 2021).

More critically, the permission granted by the government to Rio Tinto did not consider adequately the views of Indigenous peoples (Antar 2022).[16] Nor did Rio Tinto seek free, prior and informed consent (FPIC) from the PKKP people in line with its own "Communities and Social Performance Standard"[17] or address power imbalances within which indigenous peoples were consulted (Nagar 2021: 378–80). For example, although Rio Tinto engaged the PKPP for years, the information shared by the company during these meetings was technical, and hence these Indigenous groups never fully understood the nature and extent of the negative consequences of

---

16. "It demonstrated the almost total disregard of traditional owners as stakeholders when it comes to negotiating mining backed by government interests across Australia" (Antar 2022).
17. The PKKP want a role in decision-making, and the co-management of mining on their lands: "Put simply this means early, meaningful and ongoing engagement through all stages of mining activity" (Allam 2021).

mining on their sacred sites (Wahlquist 2020). In other words, Rio Tinto did not seem to practise the human rights standards and processes that it had committed to follow (Human Rights Law Centre 2020). It opted for a more profitable mining option, at the risk of causing irremediable damage to the Juukan Gorge.

After the destruction of the Juukan Gorge, Rio Tinto amended its website to state: "In allowing the destruction of the Juukan Gorge rock shelters to occur, we fell far short of our values as a company and breached the trust placed in us by the Traditional Owners of the lands on which we operate." Rio Tinto also committed to strengthening its "processes and approach to cultural heritage management by revising internal governance, including policies and procedures, and our practices". Moreover, it commits to obtaining FPIC from affected Indigenous peoples where its "activities may impact significant cultural heritage" and addressing "power imbalances and capacities of all parties to fully engage" with consultation processes.[18] These are important commitments. However, there is no mention of the UNGPs or HRDD on the web page about Juukan Gorge, although Rio Tinto on a separate web page declares that "commitment to human rights is core" to its values and is committed to following the UNGPs and other international standards.[19]

In November 2022 Rio Tinto reached a remedy agreement with Indigenous peoples, whereby the company will provide "financial support for the creation of the Juukan Gorge Legacy Foundation", which, "led and controlled by traditional owners, would focus on education, training opportunities and financial independence through businesses development" (Searson & Gudgeon 2022). As the terms of the agreement are confidential, it is not possible to analyse whether this agreement offers transformative remedies and addresses systemic power imbalances. From an RBE perspective, Indigenous peoples should have a right to say "No", and that "no should mean no", even if it significantly reduces corporate profits. However, as the Juukan Gorge case shows, it is suspect whether corporate-driven HRDD will be able to facilitate such an outcome.

REIMAGINING THE CORPORATE RESPONSIBILITY

We have tried to show that the leading international BHR standards, the UNGPs, are not fit for the purpose of supporting an RBE. The two case studies further demonstrate that the HRDD processes even of corporations that have a public commitment to the UNGPs were unable to identify

---

18. See Rio Tinto, "Juukan Gorge": www.riotinto.com/en/news/inquiry-into-juukan-gorge.
19. See Rio Tinto, "Human rights": www.riotinto.com/en/sustainability/human-rights.

and prevent harm to people and the planet. Therefore, this chapter makes a plea to reimagine the corporate responsibility to respect human rights as articulated under the UNGPs. Two aspects of this reimagining are noted below.

Centring rights-holders in HRDD processes

The value of HRDD to avoid causing harm to the rights-holders is suspect at both normative and practical levels (Deva 2023). One of the deficits in the potential of HRDD lies in its very architecture. Instead of putting rights-holders at the centre, HRDD puts corporations in charge of identifying, mitigating and preventing adverse human rights impacts. Corporations are of course expected to consult the relevant rights-holders. However, as shown by the cases above, consultations are on the terms, timing and narrative set by the relevant corporations. Consequently, such consultations often end up becoming a tick-box or legitimization exercise to manage risks to corporations without addressing the various power imbalances.

As a way forward to centring rights-holders, we propose that HRDD should not be conducted by businesses or consultants hired by them (Deva forthcoming). Rather, it should be carried out by rights-holders, as they are in a better position to make an informed decision about the actual or potential adverse impacts of a business activity on their rights. Rights-holders are not merely victims of corporate abuses. Rather, they have agency too, and HRDD processes should recognize this.

At the same time, there are inherent power imbalances concerning access to information, financial resources and legal expertise between rights-holders and corporations. Instead of remaining mute spectators to such power imbalances, HRDD processes should be designed to address these imbalances. With this in mind, we propose that HRDD be conducted by rights-holders. Under this model, rights-holders will not be merely consulted by business enterprises. Instead, rights-holders will design and own the entire HRDD process and invite businesses for consultation to provide input about the proposed activity or project. In practice, this would mean that workers will decide on living wages and safety conditions at work, farmers will determine whether a highway or power plant should be built on their land, and Indigenous peoples will decide whether a mining project close to a sacred lake should go ahead.

However, to address the power imbalances noted above, rights-holders should be assisted by independent CSOs, trade unions, lawyers and academia in conducting HRDD. The cost of HRDD should be borne by the relevant corporations.

Moving beyond "do no harm"

The current articulation of corporate responsibility is essentially negative in nature, even though positive steps in the form of HRDD are expected to discharge this responsibility. Although the "do no harm" approach provides a good starting point for managing the adverse impacts of corporate activities, it does not go far enough to deal with current societal challenges such as poverty and inequality. For example, in 2008 the OECD found evidence that "[i]nequality of incomes was higher in most OECD countries in the mid-2000s than in the mid-1980s" (OECD 2008a: 1). More recently, Oxfam has estimated that the "world's richest 1% have more than twice as much wealth as 6.9 billion people" (Oxfam International n.d.). The Covid-19 pandemic has exposed or exacerbated the existing inequality: the "pandemic has hurt people living in poverty far harder than the rich, and has had particularly severe impacts on women, Black people, Afro-descendants, Indigenous Peoples, and historically marginalized and oppressed communities around the world" (Berkhout *et al.* 2021: 14; see also Oxfam International 2022a).

However, inequality is not an accident.[20] Businesses actively lobby for low tax rates, minimum state regulation, diluted labour laws (including a limited role for trade unions), the creation of special economic zones and faster environmental clearance of projects. They also consciously innovate to create exploitative business models that limit risks and increase rewards. Moreover, businesses encourage states to negotiate trade and investment agreements not only to entrench their rights in such agreements but also to create a system of "privileged justice" in the form of investor–state dispute settlement (UNGA 2021a; Yilmaz Vastardis 2018). All these steps taken together create, sustain or exacerbate economic inequality at different levels in society, and, even if "respecting rights [becomes] an integral part *of* business" (Ruggie 1982: 415n10, emphasis in original) by conducting regular HRDD, economic inequality may nonetheless remain.

In other words, there are good reasons for businesses to have a responsibility to "protect" and "fulfil" human rights (Bilchitz 2010; Wettstein 2009). The limitations of the "do no harm" approach were once again exposed during the Covid-19 pandemic – whether in relation to access to vaccines, work from home mandates or workers being laid off (Deva 2021). Moreover, the acknowledgement that businesses also have a responsibility to protect and fulfil human rights should assist in resolving the uneasy relationship between Pillar II of the UNGPs and the Sustainable Development Goals (SDGs), as the

---

20. The current "inequality is the product of a flawed and exploitative economic system, which has its roots in neoliberal economics and the capture of politics by elites" (Oxfam International 2021a: 11).

latter expect businesses not to stop at causing "no harm". The SDGs envisage businesses to be an integral part of global partnerships to mobilize resources to achieve the 17 goals (UNGA 2015a). Businesses *"must contribute* to changing unsustainable consumption and production patterns, *including through the mobilization,* from all sources, *of financial and technical assistance* to strengthen developing countries' scientific, technological and innovative capacities to move towards more sustainable patterns of consumption and production" (UNGA 2015a: 12, para. 28, emphases added). Although the responsibility of businesses to respect human rights should be a starting point to contributing towards achieving the SDGs (UN OHCHR 2017), that in itself will not suffice. Ending poverty and hunger, ensuring healthy lives, achieving gender equality, reducing inequality and combating climate change will require businesses to go beyond "doing no harm".

If Vale and Rio Tinto in the two case studies discussed above had followed our reimagined conception of the corporate responsibility to respect human rights (that is, with rights-holders central to HRDD and the focus not limited to causing no harm), they would have contributed to an RBE.

CONCLUSION

It is increasingly becoming clear that the current economic model is not working for the benefit of "we, the people".[21] Stakeholder capitalism is proposed as an alternative (Schwab & Vanham 2021).[22] The UNGPs are also presented as providing a blueprint to move from "shareholder primacy towards multi-fiduciary obligations" (Ruggie, Rees & Davis 2021). However, as our brief analysis in this chapter shows, what we need is not superficial tweaks but a transformative course correction, which recognizes the centrality of both rights and rights-holders. The turn to an RBE would need to give people and the planet priority over (corporate) profits.

In this chapter, we have tried to show that neither the theoretical moorings of the UNGPs nor the conceptualizations of HRDD under Pillar II are fit for the purpose of ensuring that corporations contribute to an RBE. We have also engaged in a brief reimagining of corporate responsibility as well as HRDD, so as to harness fully the potential of corporations to contribute to a more inclusive, equitable and sustainable society.

---

21. "The very existence of booming billionaires and record profits, while most people face austerity, rising poverty and a cost-of-living crisis, is evidence of an economic system that fails to deliver for humanity" (Oxfam International 2021a: 9).
22. See also *The Economist* (2022).

CHAPTER 5

A HUMAN RIGHTS ECONOMY APPROACH AS THE BASIS FOR A GLOBAL FISCAL ARCHITECTURE

Attiya Waris[1]

INTRODUCTION

The development and enforcement of sound fiscal law and policy are essential for the realization of human rights (Kohonen, Waris & Christensen 2011: 78). Fair, just and principled use, management and distribution of public resources constitute the core of a human-rights-centred response (Waris 2013). The United Nations' Human Rights Council (HRC) has recalled the primary obligation of every state to promote people's economic, social and cultural development, acknowledging that inequality continues to increase worldwide and contributes to social exclusion and the marginalization of certain groups and individuals (UNGA 2022a: para. 5).

Unequal revenue collection within and between countries is a partial cause of uneven wealth distribution and the pervasive increase in poverty and exclusion around the world. Furthermore, states continue to face severe difficulties in properly assessing and efficiently collecting revenue. Because of this, one key area in discussing fiscal issues is the taxation of cross-border transactions. When wealthier individuals and business institutions that transact across borders are able to use the international fiscal system to their advantage, fewer resources may be available for public services and human rights. Inequality can be exacerbated by the existing international financial architecture and its weaknesses and loopholes.

---

1. This chapter draws on my report as independent expert on foreign debt and human rights on the effects of foreign debt and other related international financial obligations of states on the full enjoyment of all human rights, particularly economic, social and cultural rights (UNGA 2022). I am very grateful for the support provided by Waridah Latif in the preparation of the chapter.

The movement of money across borders when either the method of movement, its earning or its use is not legal is referred to as an illicit financial flow (IFF) (UN Economic Commission for Africa [UNECA] 2015: 9). IFFs reduce the resources countries could otherwise use to finance the protection, promotion and progressive realization of all human rights.

Although there are many different forms and definitions of illicit financial flows, tax and commercial-related IFFs – particularly those resulting from tax avoidance and evasion and the planning activities of transnational corporations, such as trade mis-invoicing, transfer pricing and the shifting of profits into or through low-tax offshore jurisdictions – are the most significant components of such flows on a global scale, resulting in significant tax revenue losses for governments around the world.

According to *The State of Tax Justice 2021*, countries lose $483 billion in revenues a year, which includes $312 billion owing to cross-border corporate tax abuse and $171 billion due to offshore tax abuse by wealthy individuals (TJN 2021: 10). Tax-related IFFs are therefore crucial, as they represent lost state revenue that could have been used to finance state activity. As noted by a previous mandate holder of the position of UN independent expert on foreign debt, other international financial obligations and human rights (hereafter UN independent expert on foreign debt), individuals and corporations hiding unreported assets abroad for tax evasion or money-laundering are, essentially, stealing from the public. The funds generated from these illegal activities should be allocated towards public service funding (UN OHCHR 2016).

Shared global concerns are corporate-tax-related IFFs by multinationals and the offshoring of wealth by high-net-worth individuals and corporations, both of which operate within the global financial system partly, if not wholly, through the formal economy. The pervasiveness of tax-related IFFs indicates fundamental deficiencies in the international, continental, regional and national tax governance architecture – concerns that could be resolved through international cooperation and assistance regarding the development and enforcement of fiscal law and policy using democratic systems. The proliferation of tax havens or secrecy jurisdictions and the industrial scale of untaxed offshore wealth sends a sign of potential political will of some governments, multilateral organizations and economic blocs. Adapting existing fiscal governance structures is being further complicated in an increasingly digitalized world.

As a result, the attempt to gear systems towards equitable tax collection (Waris & Seabrooke 2018), domestically focused and/or inwardly directed tax action and tax competition between and within countries (and groups of countries) has created fertile ground for multinational corporations and high-net-worth individuals to obfuscate their tax obligations (IMF 2022a: 9). Often, lobbying by stakeholders to ensure that systems are reviewed or reformed in their favour by increasing fiscal competition is pushing political will in that direction. As a result, numerous domestic and international compromises by states are leading to reduced resources for the funding of public services, the Sustainable Development Goals (SDGs) and implementing human rights obligations.

This chapter first contextualizes the discussion by setting out the global processes for countering IFFs. Second, it reflects on what a human-rights-focused approach to tax reform might include, and refers to calls for the creation of a global tax body and to a UN-led global tax convention. Last, the chapter offers conclusions and recommendations for states and other stakeholders.

INTERNATIONAL COMMITMENTS TO TACKLE TAX-RELATED ILLICIT FINANCIAL FLOWS

Under international human rights law, states have obligations to ensure equality and non-discrimination and to take measures to the maximum of their available resources to ensure the progressive realization of economic, social and cultural rights. Various human rights treaty bodies and mechanisms have underlined the design and implementation of fiscal and tax law and policy measures towards the realization of human rights (UN Economic and Social Council 1990). The "Guiding principles on human rights impact assessments of economic reforms" reaffirm that states ought to design and implement fiscal policy to ensure that they use the maximum available resources for this progressive realization, with a view to promoting substantive equality and non-discrimination and building a human rights economy (UN Human Rights Council 2018). In addition, guiding principles stipulate that fiscal policy should be anchored in the core democratic principles of transparency, participation and accountability in the governance of public resources (Waris 2019; Elson, Balakrishnan & Heintz 2013: 16). Fiscal policy is not enough; fiscal law, policy, regulations and guidelines need to reflect those principles at national, regional, continental and global levels.

As early as 1979 the preamble to the Convention on the Elimination of All Forms of Discrimination against Women stated that "the establishment of the new international economic order based on equity and justice will contribute significantly towards the promotion of equality between men and women".[2] Many countries fail to allocate their maximum available resources and have often taken retrogressive steps, such as lowering funding for social

---

2. See www.ohchr.org/en/instruments-mechanisms/instruments/convention-elimination-all-forms-discrimination-against-women.

services without justification or privatizing some of them – healthcare in particular. That key impediment tends to have a higher impact on women and low-income earners, deepening inequalities between and within countries and regions. A radical reassessment of the international tax architecture is indispensable for countries to ensure their exhaustion of domestic resources and commitment to fulfilling their financial obligations in line with human rights principles.

The Millennium Development Goals (MDGs) in 2000 facilitated the fiscal assessment of the most pressing human rights goals to be achieved by 2015. In 2002 the Monterrey Consensus of the International Conference on Financing for Development underlined global agreement on increasing international financial and technical cooperation for development (UN 2003: 5, para. 4); the special role of equitable and efficient tax systems and administration (UN 2003: 7, para. 15) to mobilize public resources for development policies; and the need for broader, effective and equitable participation of developing countries in decision-making and norm-setting regarding international economic and financial standards and codes (UN 2003: 19–20, paras. 57, 62). The document recognized the role of international cooperation in reducing capital flight and fighting corruption, repatriating illicit funds to source countries and eliminating money-laundering (UN 2003: 21, para. 65). It also acknowledged the importance of mobilizing domestic financial resources for development and the role of good governance, including respect for human rights (UN 2003: 6–7, paras. 10, 11).

In 2008 the Doha Declaration on Financing for Development reaffirmed the commitments of the Monterrey Consensus, giving special recognition to the draining of resources resulting from tax and IFFs more broadly. The Declaration also reiterated international commitments to fight corruption through the Stolen Asset Recovery Initiative (UN 2009: 8–10, paras. 16, 20). The Declaration stressed the need for reform of the international financial architecture, prioritizing transparency as well as the participation of developing countries and countries with economies in transition in international decision-making and norm-setting, with the involvement of the United Nations central to that undertaking (UN 2009: 25–26, para. 68).

Reaffirming and building upon those instruments, the Addis Ababa Action Agenda of the Third International Conference on Financing for Development (UNGA 2015b) called for a global framework to address the challenges, needs and aspirations for financing for development in the post-2015 period. Regarding illicit financial flows and taxation, states committed to substantially reducing IFFs by 2030, with a view towards elimination. The Agenda also laid the normative groundwork for the reform of the taxation of multinational corporations, recognizing the need to distribute tax benefits between source and destination jurisdictions, the essential roles of country-by-country reporting and the sharing of beneficial ownership information (UNGA 2015b: para. 27). Critically, state actors redoubled efforts to ensure that developing countries are not disadvantaged or excluded from international taxation norm-setting (UNGA 2015b: paras. 23, 27, 28).

In 2015 those international commitments were solidified in the 2030 Agenda for Sustainable Development (UNGA 2015a). The 2030 Agenda was aimed at anchoring a broader, human rights-based understanding of development. Goals 16 (peace, justice and strong institutions) and 17 (partnerships for the goals) are especially pertinent. Target 16.4 calls for countries to significantly reduce illicit financial and arms flows, strengthen the recovery and return of stolen assets and combat all forms of organized crime. The statistical definition of Target 16.4.1 was concluded in 2020 because of the limitations of the available data. Going forward, the analysis was limited to flows emanating from criminal activity, not only financial (including barter), over a period and across borders. Based on this dataset, the analysis is now in the pilot/testing phase. This preliminary analysis is already showing that, first, the dataset is dated and intensive; and, second, that it requires multilateral engagement and political willingness.

Relatedly, Target 17.1 mandates countries to cooperate to ensure that developing countries have the requisite capacity to mobilize domestic resources for the achievement of the 2030 Agenda. To the extent that a reform of the international tax system is needed to correct inequalities by allocating taxing rights between developed and developing countries, Goal 10 (reduce inequalities within and among countries), particularly Target 10.6 (ensure enhanced representation and voice for developing countries in decision-making in global international economic and financial institutions in order to deliver more effective, credible, accountable and legitimate institutions) is also a relevant part of the framework on international tax cooperation.

Now, only a few years remain until the 2030 deadline, with huge setbacks and little forward movement. The MDGs were not achieved in many parts of the world (Ritchie & Roser 2018). There have been global calls to embark on a fourth-round global conference on financing for development. This discussion is urgently needed, based on the multiple global crises, notably the Covid-19 pandemic and the changed context. Financing for the progressive realization of human rights seems not to be moving forward. Global inequalities are deepening, and the fiscal solutions that were being pushed seem not to have borne as much revenue as had been expected. Although conversations in the regions and in the large economic blocs have progressed, the majority of least developed countries, as well as many low- and middle-income countries, are losing ground. Several representatives of states, human rights experts and civil society organizations have indicated that there is a perception of regression with respect to the priority given to financing for human rights.

In 2015, at the Financing for Development Conference in Addis Ababa, the debates on creating a global tax body resulted in compromised support for the tax discussions that had at that time commenced at the OECD. However, the process remains incomplete, and seems to have gone forward without the much-touted inclusivity and consensus principles that were at its origin. Reasons for the lack of broad consensus included harmful neoliberal macroeconomic policies, regressive taxation, privatization, and fiscal consolidation in response to economic crises. It has often been argued that some of those previously mentioned measures were allegedly needed to improve investment or growth. However, none of those fiscal measures have led to positive results (Tax and Gender Working Group, Global Alliance for Tax Justice, cited in UNGA 2022a).

The human rights approach remains siloed from fiscal spaces. Human rights principles should be integrated into the design, development and application of international tax rules. The international tax rule-making under the governance of the OECD and its Base Erosion and Profit Shifting project largely presents a human rights lens absence. A human rights approach has been only partially reflected at the Committee of Experts on International Cooperation in Tax Matters. Fiscal legitimacy principles of transparency, accountability, responsibility, effectiveness and efficiency, as well as fairness and justice, ought to be linked to human rights principles in approaching the global fiscal system and its framework (Waris 2013). In addition, discussions on revenue generation from the digital economy remain fragmented. There are numerous ongoing actions in this field, as set out below.

INTERNATIONAL TAX REFORM AND HUMAN RIGHTS

Countries need to mobilize financing from all sources to fulfil human rights obligations and achieve the 2030 Agenda. Resources lost to tax abuse caused by deliberately, negligently or erroneously crafted fiscal law and policy could – and ought to – be reformed, reassessed and enforced with a view to protecting countries' fiscal space and shared global fiscal space so that state revenue can be collected and spent with the goal of raising living standards. Addressing tax abuse would increase the progressivity of the tax system as a whole and ensure that these funds are employed to finance public services and goods. Using the tax principle of ability to pay and equity, all taxpayers, including multinational corporations and high-net-worth individuals, should have the same tax obligations and provide the same level of transparency.

This would allow for the creation of a level playing field for all countries and their respective taxpayers. The current asymmetry of access to information and agenda-setting prevents the equitable treatment of multinational corporations, wealthy individuals and countries.

The UN Human Rights Council (2021) has recognized that tax abuse, particularly tax evasion and avoidance by corporations, contributes to the build-up of unsustainable debt. Governments facing challenges in raising domestic resources through taxation will resort to other forms of revenue collection, including external borrowing, to finance their obligations. Combating illicit financial flows in order to strengthen the capacity of states to mobilize tax resources can be a necessary complement to the various efforts required to address debt unsustainability, including much-needed structural reforms (Li 2021). In 2022 low-income countries were expected to pay $43 billion in debt servicing, an amount exceeding spending on health care, education and social protection by 171 per cent (Oxfam International 2022b: 6).

For reforming the international tax system, there are already elements in both human rights and fiscal spaces that could be examined in conjunction with the aim of ensuring adequate funding for the realization of human rights. One relevant source would be the work done over the years by the OHCHR on indicators on taxation, budgets and resources. Treaty bodies, notably the Committee on Economic, Social and Cultural Rights and the Human Rights Committee, have required states to collect disaggregated statistics and indicators, and, in some cases, have included taxation and budget analysis in their concluding observations.

Civil society contributions to this debate build upon and clarify those obligations, notably in the principles of human rights in fiscal policy (Initiative for Human Rights Principles in Fiscal Policy 2021). The principles reiterate the proactive role of states in relation to fiscal policy, ensuring that the role is directed towards the respect, protection and fulfilment of rights.

These instruments and guidelines are unambiguous in recognizing that the human rights obligations of states in relation to fiscal law and policy in general, and taxation more specifically, go beyond unilateral efforts at the domestic level. States have an extraterritorial obligation to ensure that fiscal law and policy respect and protect human rights beyond their borders and to contribute to the creation of an enabling international environment, as well as refrain from exerting undue influence on other states in ways that undermine their ability to fulfil their human rights obligations (UN independent expert on the effects of foreign debt 2018). In addition, in female-dominated areas, such as the informal economy and unpaid care work, efforts by women remain an "invisible hand" in the economic and tax system global, continental, regional and national levels. Fiscal laws and policies should not only recognize but resolve that underrepresentation (submissions by the Tax and Gender Working Group and Global Alliance for Tax Justice, cited in Waris 2022).

In the context of the OECD initiative on taxation of the digital economy in 2020, 137 members of the Inclusive Framework joined the "Statement on a two-pillar approach to address the tax challenges arising from the digitalisation of the economy" (OECD 2020). Many countries continue not to be part of the Inclusive Framework under which that agreement was conceived. The South Centre Tax Initiative pointed out that, although the decision-making process on tax purposes under the Inclusive Framework has a two-layer structure, there is a lack of transparency regarding how various country interests are balanced, owing to the "over-representation" of certain jurisdictions (South Centre 2021).

The proposal is divided into two pillars. Pillar One provides a blueprint for a formulary-based reapportionment of taxing rights between market and residence jurisdictions. Pillar Two is an agreement on minimum global corporate tax, set at 15 per cent, on all multinational enterprises with more than $750 million in global revenues. According to the IMF, Pillar One will reallocate $125 billion in profits from the largest and most profitable multinational enterprises to the market jurisdictions where those companies operate (South Centre 2021).

However, only $10 billion is expected to be reallocated to developing countries (IMF 2022a). Pillar Two raises additional challenges. A global minimum tax rate of 15 per cent is below the effective tax rate in many developing countries. For example, as statutory corporate income tax rates in Africa vary between 25 and 35 per cent, the implementation of Pillar Two would mean that countries would lose significant taxing rights (African Tax Administration Forum 2021). Developing countries and civil society organizations have called for a global effective minimum tax rate of 21 to 25 per cent, which would raise an additional $200 billion in tax revenues, compared with only $150 million according to the Pillar Two proposal (Independent Commission for the Reform of International Corporate Taxation 2021).

On 30 March 2022 a series of joint allegations letters[3] were sent by several UN mandate holders to the OECD, the presidency of the Group of 20, the executive secretariat of the Group of 77, the intergovernmental Group of 24 and the delegation of the European Union to the United Nations in Geneva. In these letters, the authors referred to information received about the two-pillar solution to address tax challenges arising from the digitalization of the economy. Concerns were raised about the scope and content of

---

3. See AL OTH 21/2022, https://spcommreports.ohchr.org/TMResultsBase/DownLoadPublic CommunicationFile?gId=27165.

the announced agreement. Among those concerns, several low- and middle-income countries consider that the agreement does not respond to their needs and would diminish their fiscal space, especially at a time when countries are seeking to recover from the crisis resulting from the Covid-19 pandemic. As of September 2023, a response had been received only from the OECD. In the response, questions over transparency regarding the rejection of alternative proposals by the Group of 24, compensation for lost revenues and safeguards to ensure the realization of economic, social and cultural rights are left unanswered (OECD 2022).

Although individual measures and policies have recently been adopted by many countries around the world in order to enhance transparency in commercial transactions and to prevent illegal financial activities, they do not meet the level of financial transparency needed. That would require the establishment of an international beneficial ownership registry that considers the human rights principles of transparency and access to information and that registers the ultimate beneficial owners of assets around the world. That could be done through the signing of an international agreement, within the framework of the United Nations, being housed in one institution. It could take the form of a contractual obligation whereby its parties are obligated to provide sufficient information about the beneficial owners of companies operating on their territory (submission by Maat,[4] cited in UNGA 2022a).

Currently, although various draft instruments guide international and regional fiscal policies, none have yet been concluded; the scope and function to enforce a fair and inclusive international fiscal framework remain elusive; and no bodies are currently actively working to align the protection of human rights with taxation, apart from the UN Committee of Experts on International Cooperation in Tax Matters, and that only to a limited extent.

INTERNATIONAL TAX GOVERNANCE

In 2014 the special rapporteur on extreme poverty and human rights produced an extensive analysis of the human rights implications of taxation policies and made recommendations for policy and legal framework reforms to address tax matters at the domestic and international levels. International tax cooperation recommendations included working towards a multilateral regime for tax transparency, the strengthening of frameworks for the automatic exchange of information, country-by-country adoption of reporting

---

4. Maat is an Egyptian civil society organization, established in 2005.

standards for transnational organizations, the establishment of national public registries to improve beneficial ownership transparency and the ensuring of the effective participation of developing countries in international forums (UN HRC 2014a).

High-net-worth individuals, informal sector actors and cross-border criminals all tend to use the same processes, procedures and systems that corporations have been using, often through enabling lawyers, banks, accountants and other mid-level service providers. In addition, the individuals who are responsible for administering `traceable and trackable systems and for lobbying are predominantly engaged in the formal economy.

States have also made commitments pertaining to the combating of IFFs and the promotion of more progressive, transparent and efficient global tax governance. In the Monterrey Consensus, countries agreed to strengthen international tax cooperation, enhance dialogue between tax authorities and greater coordination between multilateral bodies and relevant regional organizations and give special attention to the needs of developing countries and countries with economies in transition (UN 2003: 21, para. 64).

An international fiscal authority (which would include a global tax body) should promote expansion of the fiscal space by assessing the possible adverse impact on inequality, poverty and social inclusion of fiscal consolidation and spending cuts. It should also emphasize the need for the careful design of fiscal policy, in particular tax and transfers systems, to achieve equity, taking into consideration potentially harmful indirect effects, so that people living in poverty, the working poor and the near poor do not end up as net payers (UN Economic and Social Council 2019). Illicit financial flows and climate finance constitute sufficient reason to support the setting up of a fiscal authority; others focus on the need for transparency and equity in discussion spaces (submissions by Algeria and Maat, cited in UNGA 2022a).

Various organizations continue to advocate for instruments that establish inclusive and legitimate global coordination with a view to financial health and economic development (UN Economic and Social Council 2021), such as a United Nations convention to set global standards and establish an inclusive intergovernmental body on tax matters. International development cooperation can help to strengthen countries' capacities to mobilize and manage resources to promote development aims, such as the provision of quality social services, debt servicing and the promotion of economic and social rights (UN Secretary-General 2020). The report of the High Level Panel on International Financial Accountability, Transparency and Integrity for Achieving the 2030 Agenda (FACTI Panel 2021) provides a blueprint for a more inclusive financial system that is able to secure resources for the financing of the SDGs. The creation of a globally inclusive intergovernmental forum to set international tax norms is critical to resolving the shortcomings of the international tax system and upholding the legitimacy of international financial structures. Specifically, the FACTI Panel recommends that the international community make progress towards a UN-led global tax convention.

This recommendation is echoed in a report the same year by the UN secretary-general, "Our common agenda" (UN Secretary-General 2021). Reducing IFFs and tax avoidance and, more specifically, reforming international tax systems, are among the critical actions that the secretary-general argues are necessary for ushering in a sustainable recovery from the pandemic and building a renewed social contract anchored in human rights.

United Nations regional bodies have made similar proposals. In the ground-breaking 2015 report of the High-Level Panel on Illicit Financial Flows from Africa, the African Union (AU) and the UN Economic Commission for Africa, it is recommended that UN processes and frameworks should coordinate the combating of illicit financial flows (UNECA 2015). More recently, in May 2022, in the light of global crises, African ministers of finance adopted a resolution (UN Economic and Social Council 2022) calling upon the international community to undertake appropriate actions at the national, regional and global levels to ensure that IFFs are treated as a system-wide challenge at the global level and that the international community adopts a mechanism for global coordination to systematically monitor IFFs.

In 2021 the executive secretary of the United Nations Economic Committee for Latin America and the Caribbean [UNECLAC] (2021) noted that "for a reform of the global tax system to incorporate the needs of developing nations and emerging economies … the United Nations should be the main space for that discussion". The shifting of global tax norm-setting to the United Nations or an international body has also received support from states and intergovernmental groups and bodies (submission by Mauritius, cited in UNGA 2022a).

The Group of 77 and China has called for the Committee of Experts on International Cooperation in Tax Matters to be accorded the status of a United Nations intergovernmental body with experts representing their respective governments. That body could then invite the Committee to consider proposals to further international tax cooperation at the United Nations (UNGA 2021c: 6, para. 19). Within that global body, areas are already being developed on a piecemeal basis that could be consolidated. This includes the development of a global beneficial ownership registry, which already exists under the Extractive

Industries Transparency Initiative for the mining sector, and could be extended to other industries.

Beneficial ownership registry

The non-profit organization Open Ownership has developed a global registry that currently contains over 16 million beneficial ownership records from jurisdictions that publish data in their central registries.[5] It regularly imports data from the beneficial ownership registries of Denmark, Slovakia and the United Kingdom of Great Britain and Northern Ireland. A global registry can help track illicit financial flows by enabling the analysis of complex ownership structures across different jurisdictions. However, a necessary condition for a global registry is the development of robust national data housed in a place where all taxpayers feel their information is safe and protected. The complexity of the necessary reforms to achieve universal beneficial ownership data is a concept that is still in its infancy (submission by the International Secretariat of the Extractive Industries Transparency Institute, cited in UNGA 2022a).

Civil society supports the recommendation for a UN-led tax convention that is aligned with human rights and that strengthens global norms and standards on tax policy and practices, enabling governments to fulfil their human rights obligations (Ryding 2022: 6). To curb illicit financial flows and massive transfers of untaxed wealth on the part of corporations and individuals, a public global asset registry is a key component of global tax reform and an important tool in the fight against inequality (Asian Peoples' Movement on Debt and Democracy, cited in UNGA 2022a).

Regulation of enablers

The discussion around "enablers" includes the consideration that a number of professionals and enterprises are set up to assist high-net-worth individuals and companies in evading taxation. The list of enablers can be long, and may often include legal firms, accounting firms, financial advisers and services and information technology specialists. The discussion remains fraught because of self-regulation at the national, regional, continental and global levels and the lack of state monitoring and regulation in some cases. Global scandals, such as the Luxembourg Leaks, the Swiss Leaks and, most recently, the Pandora Papers, show that the enablers are the key to solving IFF facilitation.

---

5. See more at www.openownership.org/en/about/the-beneficial-ownership-leadership-group.

INTERNATIONAL TAX TREATIES IN A HUMAN RIGHTS CONTEXT

In recent years there have been several discussions and proposals to address the limitations and challenges of the global tax system in a more comprehensive and multilateral way. In 2019 the Group of African States supported the call for a United Nations tax convention (UNGA 2019b). This policy position was also supported by the Conference of African Ministers of Finance, Planning and Economic Development in 2022 (Etter-Phoya 2022). In 2021 the South Centre proposed the creation of a United Nations framework convention on tax cooperation, which would take the form of a conference of the parties, granting mandates to existing international tax governance forum, such as the Committee of Experts on International Cooperation in Tax Matters, the Inclusive Forum and the Global Forum on Transparency and Exchange of Information for Tax Purposes (Muheet Chowdhary & Picciotto 2021: 2). In addition to creating a global tax governance structure in which all countries can participate on an equal footing, protecting their national sovereignty, the framework convention would expand the scope of the OECD/ G20 forums by recognizing mandates from all countries that are parties to the United Nations system (IMF 2022a).

Civil society organizations have also made important contributions in that regard. The European Network on Debt and Development and the Global Alliance for Tax Justice produced recommendations for a United Nations tax convention that would be underpinned by government commitments and obligations with respect to human rights, SDGs and the key principles of substantive equality, transparency, participation and public accountability (Ryding 2022: 7). Accordingly, the convention would differ from the UN framework convention on tax cooperation in that it links human rights with taxation, the promotion of policy coherence and the need to ensure that global tax standards promote progressive tax systems. In both proposals, incorporating linkages to states' human rights obligations – maximum available resources, non-discrimination and extraterritorial obligations – could guide decision-making on tax matters. A convention would be designed to gradually replace the incoherent and highly complex network of bilateral and multilateral tax treaties and agreements, with a view to introducing one coherent overall global framework. That would increase the effectiveness of the global tax system, remove opportunities for international tax-dodging and ensure the suitability of certain provisions within international tax agreements for each state impacted by the agreement (Waris & Oyare 2021).

Critically, under that model, countries would not be forced to accept controversial dispute resolution mechanisms. Instead, the convention would have a strong focus on dispute prevention. In addition, states would have to exercise due diligence to minimize the risk of human rights violations through the adoption and operation of bilateral investment treaties and free trade agreements. This would foreclose the danger of compensating foreign investors for having adopted necessary fiscal, financial and debt resolution measures or policies designed to respond to changing circumstances, such as financial crises, new scientific findings or public demand for laws of general application. Individuals and groups should reclaim their democratic right to participate in decision-making in the determination of governmental budgetary, fiscal, economic, trade and social policies. They should demand the primacy of human rights over investment privileges and vindicate the social contract, as reflected in an index of public satisfaction composed of both material and non-material indicators (Waris & Oyare 2021).

Emerging issues in digital taxation highlight the need for a global approach that prioritizes the needs and sustainable development of all countries over the economic interests of a small number of nations. The objective of a global minimum tax rate is to discourage multinationals from shifting profits and tax revenues to low-tax countries and/or tax havens based on where their goods or services are sold, regardless of whether they have a physical presence in that nation. In addition, the employment of a global minimum tax allows countries to harness revenue from intellectual property and digital services that are otherwise lost in cases of profit-shifting, tax avoidance and evasion (Tang 2021).

CONCLUSION AND RECOMMENDATIONS

Many countries are facing the cumulative impacts of multiple crises, including high debt-related distress, illicit financial flows, the severe socio-economic effects of the pandemic, increased climate-related emergencies, the higher cost of living, famine and food insecurity. The ramifications are wide and deep, particularly for the populations of low- and middle-income countries. Many of the gains in poverty reduction achieved in previous decades have been lost. The average household has lost 1.5 per cent in real income as a result of price increases in corn and wheat alone (UN Global Crisis Response Group on Food, Energy and Finance 2022).

Recent estimates point to a need for $1.2 trillion per year to reduce the social protection gap in developing countries and $4.3 trillion annually to fund SDGs (UN Global Crisis Response Group on Food, Energy and Finance 2022). A worrying 60 per cent of least developed and other low-income countries are already at high risk of, or in, debt distress (UN Inter-Agency Task Force on Financing for Development 2022), meaning that "a domino effect where solvency problems create a systemic developing country debt crisis must be avoided at all costs" (UN Global Crisis Response Group on

Food, Energy and Finance 2022: 4). As a result, the fiscal space and capacity of states to respond to their populations, recover from the pandemic and honour their human rights obligations has shrunk dangerously. Warnings by the UN Global Crisis Response Group on Food, Energy and Finance (2022) about growing inflation and tightening financial conditions have called for the urgent need to ensure structural, fit-for-purpose reforms in the international financial system.

This chapter has discussed some aspects of the global tax system, its pitfalls and main characteristics, and presented arguments for combating IFFs. It has offered some thoughts about the human rights aspects that can underpin an international tax overhaul, with references to calls for the creation of a global tax body and a UN-led tax convention. Such reforms are part of a larger set of reforms at the international level that should promote a Rights-Based Economy. They must be designed and implemented with the aim of enhancing the well-being and dignity of people, particularly the most marginalized, and of ensuring that human rights obligations are at the centre of financial and fiscal decision-making. At the international level, a structural reform of the taxation system should also aim at reducing inequalities within countries and promoting a multilateral response that considers all countries on an equal footing. The reform of the global taxation system should be anchored in positive practices of international cooperation and assistance, as well as in international human rights standards and norms.

There is a need for new international fiscal norms on a clear, equitable and transparent basis so as to ensure a high standard of transparency, while incorporating the interests, concerns and needs of developing countries. These should include provisions on the "ABC of tax transparency", namely automatic information exchange, beneficial ownership transparency and public country-by-country reporting. Although a number of such systems already exist in some form, the convention would ensure one coherent global system designed to work for all countries, including developing countries.

CHAPTER 6

MACROECONOMIC POLICY AND DEVELOPMENT AGENDA FOR A RIGHTS-BASED ECONOMY

Pedro Rossi

INTRODUCTION

A Rights-Based Economy is not a natural result of market forces; it requires political intentionality and clear purposes to guide the economic organization. Thinking about an RBE is a complex and multidisciplinary task. It demands revisiting every aspect of economic relations from the perspective of rights and questioning the idea of social justice, which is implicitly present in economic theory and in the implementation of economic policy.

An RBE should not limit itself to protecting vulnerable groups in the face of market failures and undesirable social outcomes. Its purpose requires rethinking the organization of the economy as a whole and the distribution of economic resources and outputs based on normative standards offered by human rights.[1] This contrasts with the mainstream economic view, which does away with the moral dimension of the economy and reduces social organization to a calculation problem of maximizing individual utility. The efficient functioning of markets does not necessarily result in an adequate economic organization from a human rights perspective.[2]

---

1. According to CESR, the primary purpose of an RBE is "to guarantee the material, social and environmental conditions necessary for all people to live with dignity on a flourishing planet" (CESR 2020: 2).
2. "In fact, orthodox economics takes a positive approach to understanding the allocation of scarce resources, the efficiency of which is achieved, with a few exceptions, by the free operation of market mechanisms [...] The human rights approach, on the other hand, follows normative standards that establish universal rights and assumes equity of access to them. This approach stipulates *a priori* that a part of the economy should be organized in such a way as to allocate resources to guarantee human rights, unlike the positive approach to economics which, in theory, does not involve value judgment" (Rossi, David & Chaparro 2021: 6). For more analysis of the methodological aspects that disconnect the human rights approach from the orthodox economic approach, see Rossi, David and Chaparro (2021), Reddy (2011) and Branco (2009).

This chapter aims to contribute to the discussion of an RBE by bringing the macroeconomic and development dimension into focus. To this end, its first section deals with the elements of a macro policy for an RBE; among these elements are the need to rethink monetary and exchange rate policy and the use of alternative instruments to fight inflation. Additionally, it points out that the logic of fighting inflation with unemployment is contradictory with respect to human rights. This section also addresses fiscal policy, which is crucial for the construction of an RBE, as it defines priorities in the allocation of resources through public spending and taxation. Fiscal policy for an RBE should go beyond Keynesian full employment stabilization and must redefine the concept of fiscal responsibility to include human rights as a final goal.

The following section of this chapter approaches the concepts of growth and development and argues that the literature of Latin American structuralism can help with a formulation of an RBE with a decolonial perspective. An RBE should not be omitted from the discussion of the international system's power hierarchies and from the discussion about sovereignty and economic dependence on peripheral countries. In turn, for the progressive realization of rights, countries should pursue a transformation of their economic structures towards the reduction of their vulnerability to external shocks. Therefore, there is an important productive dimension in an RBE, and a material base necessary for the realization of human rights.

Finally, the last section proposes a mission-oriented approach for structuring an RBE. Social and environmental missions focused on areas such as health, education and decarbonization define the purpose of the development process and seek solutions to specific problems that prevent the full realization of rights. To this end, a variety of policy instruments can be mobilized, such as public spending and taxation, the promotion of new technologies and industrial policies and incentives for local and sustainable production, among others.

MACROECONOMIC POLICY FOR AN RBE

Monetary policy, exchange rate and inflation policy in an RBE

The impacts of monetary policy on human rights generally occur indirectly, but they are crucial for guaranteeing rights. Monetary policy is different, therefore, from fiscal policy, which directly impacts on human rights through income transfers and the provision of public services. In democratic countries, although fiscal policy decisions are defined in a budgetary process that permeates democratic instances, monetary policy is often defined in the rooms of an autonomous central bank and with little interaction with society.

Nevertheless, monetary policy affects the economy as a whole through monetary contractions and expansions, usually carried out through changes in the economy's basic interest rate, managed by the central bank. For analysis purposes, the impact of monetary policy on human rights can be divided into two: the impact on prices/inflation and the impact on employment.

Fighting inflation should be a fundamental objective of monetary policy, as it erodes the purchasing power and increases the cost of living of the population, interfering with well-being and in the realization of human rights in societies where part of the access to rights is commodified. When rights – such as housing, food, health and education, among others – become commodities, access to them is no longer universal and their price limits access.[3] Therefore, as discussed in Chapter 10, the decommodification of rights is a way to challenge the neoliberal logic and ensure an RBE.

Inflation is especially harmful to impoverished people. This is because inflation's impact is unequal on different social classes and can cause an increase in inequality, poverty and access to rights, such as the right to adequate food and access to fundamental services such as water, energy, public transport and housing. According to the Instituto de Estudios Socioeconómicos (INESC 2022: 15):

> Food inflation, for example, may violate the right to appropriate and healthy food and nutrition. Inflation of services – such as electricity and water – and goods, such as fuel and natural gas, also inhibits access to rights. For example, increasing fuel prices will increase the prices of bus tickets, which can prevent a family from going to the nearest health centre. Inflation of property prices and rentals, on the other hand, can compromise the right to housing and access to land.

In addition to this, the poorest part of the population has somewhat less ability to protect itself from inflationary processes, and less access to financial instruments that protect income and wealth from inflation. In peripheral countries, with a history of higher inflation, workers, especially informal ones, hardly have their income linked to inflation indexes. This is unlike the case of forms of capital income, such as rents paid to property owners or

---

3. This raises the issue of the growing importance of the financial sector and the financialization of human rights: "As human rights become more and more like commodities, the financial market acts as an intermediary in granting access to them" (INESC 2022: 16).

the profit of companies that operate in public concessions, which are usually contractually indexed to inflation.

Therefore, fighting inflation is a means of guaranteeing social well-being and human rights. To translate it into practice, it is necessary to preserve the national currency's stability and the population's purchasing power, especially those with the lowest income.

However, the population's purchasing power does not depend solely on inflation, which determines access to a right that has been commodified. Employment and income evolution also impact purchasing power. Thus, fighting inflation must be reconciled with a goal of full employment and it must be compatible with income growth, especially workers' salaries and the income of the poorest portion of the population.

In certain situations, an increase in interest rates slows the economy's rate of growth. It creates unemployment, which can be perceived as a violation of the right to work and a waste of productive resources. In addition, an increase in interest rates creates financial fragility, which affects indebted families, benefits lenders and other wealth holders and represents a fiscal cost for the state.[4]

Interest rate variations can also affect the availability and cost of credit to finance, for example, both production and access to food (Food and Agriculture Organization [FAO] 1999). A higher interest rate increases the cost of financing for the agricultural sectors and weakens indebted families, making them more susceptible to food and nutritional insecurity.

Fighting inflation with recession and unemployment violates the principle that monetary policy must protect purchasing power. In other words, if the main objective of monetary policy is to protect the population's purchasing power, especially its most vulnerable segment, the strategy of fighting inflation with recession and unemployment is counterproductive and inadequate from a rights-based perspective.

In this context, the pursuit of central banks for a very low rate of inflation can compromise the realization of rights: "Very low rates of inflation require high rates of interest, and this is a disincentive to investment, and leads to high unemployment, underemployment and a lack of decent work" (Balakrishnan, Elson & Patel 2010: 34).

There are different ways to reduce inflation. The monetary policy for an RBE must evaluate the composition of the inflationary process and the use of alternative instruments to combat inflation. Food inflation, for example, is undoubtedly a challenge that may require policy responses other than an

---

4. Another issue that links rights with monetary policy is the discrimination that occurs within the credit system. As pointed out by Ladd (1998) and Paixão (2017), the discrimination can be both in the access to credit and in the terms of the credit agreement.

increase in interest rates, which may have more negative consequences than benefits. This is because monetary policy does not affect most food prices, as their price depends on international markets or climatic or harvest factors. Therefore, in the face of food inflation, a contractionary monetary policy can aggravate food and nutritional security by reducing employment and income without substantially reducing food prices.

Among the instruments that can contribute to stabilizing food prices is the constitution of public food buffer stocks. As discussed by the FAO (1999) and Diaz-Bonilla (2015), governments can purchase food through a state agency at times of low prices, allowing them to build stocks when supply is abundant and reduce these stocks at times of high prices, increasing the food supply and contributing to the stabilization of food prices.

Increasing taxes on food exports and reducing taxes on specific food items are instruments that can be used to mitigate food inflation in specific situations. It is worth emphasizing the contradiction that occurs in countries that are large food exporters when, simultaneously, part of the population is starving. This contradiction of unequal economies is organized by a market logic that should not occur in an RBE.[5]

Furthermore, organizing the distribution system, creating financing mechanisms and encouraging local food production based on family farming can reduce volatility in food prices and improve access to them. The same goes for other strategic prices, such as water and energy supply. Additionally, it is necessary to bring price controls back into the discussion as auxiliary instruments in the fight against inflation.

Thus, a monetary policy for human rights must follow important principles. As proposed by INESC (2022: 4):

> [The] execution of a human rights-oriented monetary policy must comply with four broad guidelines: (i) avoid recessive monetary adjustments and exorbitant interest rate increases; (ii) promote a more equitable and fair credit system with access for everyone; (iii) use multiple instruments to combat a multi-cause inflation, coordinate monetary policy with other policies and focus primarily on protecting prices that impact the most vulnerable and public policies that ensure that rights are met; and (iv) promote a more transparent and democratic monetary policy.

---

5. It is worth noting that food-producing countries can and should protect the right to food, but this action could result, from a global point of view, in an increase in the international price of food and impacts on the enjoyment of rights elsewhere. Therefore, the issue calls for an international cooperation agenda.

Finally, the exchange rate policy is another important instrument in the fight against inflation. This is the established policy for the price of the national currency when measured in a foreign currency. The exchange rate policy has ambiguous impacts on employment and income; however, moments of exchange rate crisis or abrupt variations in the exchange rate tend to negatively impact growth and increase unemployment, which frequently occurs in peripheral countries.

Exchange rate movements affect the relative prices of goods produced domestically and those imported. Food prices are especially important, since internationally traded commodities are a core part of food systems. Thus, an exchange rate devaluation of the domestic currency in relation to an international currency makes imported food more expensive and increases the amount of domestically produced food destined for the international market, reducing the domestic supply. The same devaluation also increases the cost of imported inputs necessary for agricultural production.

Therefore, currency devaluations tend to pressure food prices and exacerbate food security problems, as well as necessary inputs for the health system and other services that guarantee the realization of rights. On the other hand, periods of strong appreciation of a currency against the international currency make imported products cheaper, harming local producers. Therefore, the exchange rate policy must be adjusted to reduce the national currency's volatility and mitigate the impact on the realization of rights. In this context, the financial regulation agenda of capital flows must be part of an RBE discussion.

Fiscal policy for an RBE

The relationship between fiscal policy and human rights is documented in works by Rossi, David and Chaparro (2021), Chaparro (2014), Balakrishnan, Elson and Patel (2010), Nolan *et al.* (2013) and UN HRC (2018) and in the Principles for Human Rights in Fiscal Policy (Initiative for Human Rights Principles in Fiscal Policy 2021).

Fiscal policy deals with managing the public budget through public spending and taxation. Rossi, David and Chaparro (2021) detail the interrelation between fiscal policy and human rights. They highlight that, on the one hand, guaranteeing human rights requires resources. Thus, fiscal policy choices have an impact on the management of rights. On the other hand, human rights principles and agreements should guide fiscal policy.

Consequently, in an RBE, human rights should be a parameter to guide fiscal policy. Fiscal policy for an RBE should go beyond the traditional Keynesian full employment goal and must include the human rights dimension through principles, such as the principle of non-regression and the guarantee of the minimum core content of economic and social rights. Likewise, the responsibility to avoid backsliding in specific social areas must complement the stabilization function of fiscal policy, which seeks to achieve a high level of resource utilization and a stable value of money. This frequently happens in times of economic crisis, but can also happen in times of growth, with full capacity utilization (Rossi, David & Chaparro 2021).

Economic crises are associated with reduced wages, impoverishment, increased unemployment and social exclusion, which constrain access to human rights. Concerning health, for example, it is precisely in times of crisis that the demand for public health services increases while the demand for private health plans and services decreases (Guidolin 2019). In short, there is no room for social spending cuts during crises; a human rights-based fiscal policy should increase resources for public health and other social areas in times of crisis and avoid fiscal austerity strategies that can contribute to human rights violations.[6]

Setbacks in guaranteeing rights can also occur outside the context of economic crises. For this reason, the stabilizing function of fiscal policy must at all times pay attention not only to the macroeconomic level, aggregate demand, employment and growth but also to inequality and the guarantee of rights. An economy at full employment that grows unevenly can harbour human rights violations associated with the right to food and access to health, education, retirement and sanitation, among others. Similarly, fiscal policy must also react to environmental setbacks by allocating the necessary resources for their remediation. As argued by CESR (2020), the Covid-19 pandemic was an exceptional moment when governments adopted emergency measures, which also provided an opportunity to rethink the role of fiscal policy in the context of a rights-based social protection system.

Thinking about fiscal rules means ensuring flexibility in fiscal policy by allowing room for discretion and reinforcing automatic stabilizers that guarantee more resources for social areas in times of greatest need. To this end, fiscal rules must have well-defined escape clauses, not only for situations of economic crises, natural disasters or other unexpected events but also in the face of changes in sentinel indicators of the guarantee of rights. These changes can be triggered when retrogressions or human rights violations are identified in specific areas. No fiscal rule should override the realization of rights.[7]

---

6. For a discussion of the impacts of fiscal consolidation in human rights, see CESR (2018), INESC, OXFAM and CESR (2018) and Dweck, Rossi and Oliveira (2020).

7. The Brazilian case of the spending ceiling is an example of a fiscal rule that defunds education, health and other social areas, as shown in Rossi and Dweck (2016). In 2016 the Brazilian government approved, through a constitutional amendment, a long-term rule that impedes the real growth of public spending and leads to a reduction in public spending as

Besides countering the effects of the cycle in the short term, the stabilizing function of fiscal policy must also ensure the sustainability of public finances in the long term. The concept of fiscal sustainability does not possess a fully agreed definition among economists, nor a precise operational application. Chalk and Helmming (2000) demonstrate how fiscal sustainability is commonly associated with public debt stabilization in the literature. Even so, they argue that the concept is also used as the ability to continue fiscal policy over time without affecting the state's solvency, which does not necessarily depend on stabilizing public debt. The fact is that there is neither an ideal number nor a reasonable technical explanation that defines an optimal or maximum level for the public debt. The analysis of international experience shows diverse levels of the ratio of debt to GDP and widely differing attitudes concerning the treatment given to the problem.

Fiscal sustainability will depend, therefore, on the specifics of each country, its taxation capability, whether or not it issues debt in its own currency and if it avoids external debt and on the relationship between fiscal policy and external stability. However, this does not mean a constraint for short-term fiscal stimulus or an impediment to expanding the social functions of nation states. The idea that money has run out is a farce.[8] In unequal societies there will always be resources that can be allocated by the state to improve the realization of rights.

Finally, there is no trade-off between fiscal responsibility and social responsibility. In fact, assuming the realization of human rights as the purpose of fiscal policy means that social responsibility is not something external but a constituent part of fiscal responsibility. Budget-balancing, debt stabilization and reductions in public spending cannot become goals in themselves. When the search for fiscal surpluses prevents the guarantee of human rights, fiscal policy becomes irresponsible. In this context, responsible fiscal policy must respect human rights, ensure full employment and seek the progressive realization of rights.

ECONOMIC DEVELOPMENT FOR AN RBE

Despite some controversy across the scholarship, this chapter contends that economic growth is not necessarily good or bad. This assessment depends on qualitative aspects.[9] The increase in the production of goods and services can

---

a proportion of GDP and human right violations, as discussed in Rossi, Dweck & Oliveira (2018). In 2020, with the pandemic, an emergency act suspended the spending ceiling and allowed for the expansion of social spending. In the following years constitutional amendments were made to "pierce the ceiling", given the unfeasibility of the rule.

8. This idea underlines the austerity discourse, as discussed by Blyth (2013).

9. For a different view, see Hickel (2020) and others from the degrowth literature.

have negative impacts by promoting unsustainable consumption patterns, increasing inequalities, social exclusion, environmental degradation, etc. The cutting down of forests can drive growth as well as security spending arising from violence and an increase in transport services because of the distance of people from their place of work. This kind of growth is associated with a loss of quality of life and, obviously, is not the growth we need.

It is worth remembering that the commodification of society also implies economic growth, since growth fundamentally captures mercantile exchanges. Therefore, substituting jobs associated with subsistence, voluntary care and community and solidarity relations with paid jobs tends to generate economic growth.

However, the problem is not about growth but about the kind of growth. In a capitalist society, especially in peripheral countries, social demands to guarantee human rights imply growth. The construction of new housing results in economic growth as well as the expansion of health services, the production of new technologies and an increase in cultural activities. It is worth noting that growth can also be compatible with environmental preservation, since the transformation needed to ensure an ecological transition and to change the energy and transport matrices generates growth and employment. This transformation requires massive investments in renewable energy, energy efficiency, public transport, railways, electric vehicles, water infrastructure and new technologies, among others.

An RBE is not about growth but rights; however, growth can result from an organized economy that guarantees the realization of rights. Furthermore, it is possible to reconcile economic growth with social transformation to tackle the multiple dimensions of inequality (social, racial, gender, regional, etc.). To enable this, it is necessary to transform social agendas into the very objective of the development process.

This chapter understands development as growth with structural transformation (Bielschowsky 2014). Transformations means change in the pattern of the economic system and its structures of demand and supply, labour market, consumption, productive structure and distribution of income and wealth. In this sense, there can be growth without development, such as when a commodity-exporting economy grows thanks to an increase in the international price of commodities but does not change its economic structures. It often happens in peripheral countries that extraordinary gains are appropriated by the elite and there are no substantive changes in the distribution of wealth, nor in the labour market or in the productive structure.

Latin American structuralism proposes an analysis of economic development based on the specificities of underdeveloped economies and the existing hierarchy in the global economy. Celso Furtado (1961, 1971) uses the term "underdeveloped countries" rather than "developing countries", since underdevelopment is not a path to development but a condition of a hierarchical global economy. Thus, it can be seen that overcoming underdevelopment has political resistance from the central countries and from national economic elites that benefit from the existing economic system.

Therefore, there is no single recipe for the development of the various countries in the system, and the recommendations associated with economic liberalism can act as traps for peripheral countries. As Robert Skidelsky (2021: 42) argues, for structuralism, free trade policy recommendations end up "locking rich and poor into their pre-existing positions in this global structure". Development, therefore, is not a natural result of market forces nor a consequence of economic opening but a political intention to be driven by society, using the state and economic policies.

Latin American structuralism can help, as a starting point, in the construction of an RBE. This is because economic structures affect the realization of human rights by influencing the distribution of income and wealth, the composition of the labour market, foreign trade, the productive structure, etc. An RBE is not a natural result of market forces; its construction requires the transformation of economic structures guided by a political project.

The distribution of income and human rights have a strong relationship. Unequal countries are those in which access to rights also occurs unevenly and the deprivation of rights is more frequent. Uprimny Yepes and Chaparro (2020) propose that, although inequality does not automatically violate human rights norms, there are strong and undeniable empirical links between high levels of inequality and disenfranchisement.

Likewise, employment, unemployment and qualitative aspects of the labour market are determinant for several human rights. In this way, a development agenda for an RBE may also include, in addition to income and wealth distribution, employment and labour market policies.

There is also a productive dimension of an RBE to be highlighted. For example, providing public universal health services requires equipment, medicines and technology. A peripheral country can import these inputs, and, for that, it needs foreign currencies. In commodity-exporting countries, obtaining these currencies depends on the price cycle and, consequently, the proper functioning of the health system. Consequently, realizing the right to health depends on an external economic circumstance.

Therefore, an RBE also involves thinking about local, domestic alternatives to provide a material basis for the realization of rights, in addition to prioritizing the use of foreign resources. Regarding this topic, the idea of socio-environmental missions can be an important instrument for thinking about an RBE.

MISSION-ORIENTED RBE

As illustrated by Mariana Mazzucato (2018), mission-oriented public policy originates from the development of technologies for specific objectives defined by the state, such as the mission of NASA's historic Apollo programme that put "man on the Moon". Adapting missions intended for defence, nuclear energy and aerospace to meet the objectives of an RBE is also possible.

Thus, socio-environmental missions point out the purposes of the development process and point to the solution of concrete human rights problems. These missions organize social resources, articulating social demands with a necessary economic, productive and technological base. In other words, socio-environmental missions reinforce the concept of planning and guidance for articulating the demand side and the productive structure.

The missions' configuration revolves around "social and environmental investment" axes. They can include urban mobility and transport, sanitation, environment and green technology, popular housing, health, education, regional development, etc. In addition, policy-makers must include transversal dimensions such as environmental, gender and racial issues in each mission.

Designing socio-environmental missions through a bottom-up process based on local experience and influenced by social movements is possible (Mazzucato 2021). By having a process based on a bottom-up approach, missions identify problems and solutions on the basis of evaluation of the characteristics of the territory, considering local and regional specificities, the demand for final goods and services and the necessary inputs for their provision. In contrast, development projects constituted "from top to bottom" are unable to deal with heterogeneity and local specificities. Hence, the concept of missions promotes the development of local cooperatives and aligns with the construction of a solidarity economy by proposing a new approach to the organization of production and labour.

A relevant case for this development model is the mission aimed at expanding and improving public health. Somehow health and development go together, as it is one of the main purposes of this process. In other words, the point of arrival of the development process must be to guarantee minimum health conditions for the entire population. Health, in a broad sense, is an aspiration towards well-being. On the one hand, health conditions depend on the development pattern, which affects health indicators through social constraints such as sanitation, nutrition, working conditions, education, etc. – also known as social determinants of health. On the other hand, investment in health brings important beneficial impacts on society, on labour productivity and thus on long-term growth and development.

As discussed in Gadelha (2022), the provision of health services moves the so-called "health economic-industrial complex" (HEIC). The HEIC articulates service provider sectors – hospitals, outpatient clinics, diagnostic and treatment services – with industrial sectors, such as the chemical and biotechnology industry. This latter industry supplies pharmaceuticals, drugs, vaccines, blood products, diagnostic reagents and equipment. It also includes the industries based on mechanics, electronics and materials, which supply mechanical and electronic equipment, prostheses and orthoses and consumables.

In this sense, a mission for public health involves the development of HEIC, which can generate jobs, income and technology, in addition to reducing the vulnerability of the system in the face of health crises such as the Covid-19 pandemic. It is not enough, therefore, just to increase public spending on health, as it can raise dependence on imports and the need for foreign currency. Building an RBE also means thinking about the economic potential of the domestic economy to produce the necessary material base to guarantee rights.

Therefore, a socio-environmental mission, and the construction of an RBE itself, must mobilize various instruments, such as public spending and investment, science and technology policy, public banks and credit policies, industrial, commercial, tax policy, among others. Furthermore, the focus of public policies must be on missions and not on specific industrial sectors.

The example of health applies to many other social fronts. A mission to decarbonize the economy, for example, is a vector of structural changes that generates jobs, growth and technology in the process of facing the climate emergency.

Finally, unlike the economic discourse that empties collective responsibilities, argues that there is no money and delegates solutions to the market, this mission-oriented development model shows that it is possible to transform economic organization, especially in peripheral countries. These countries generally do not have scarcity of resources but, rather, inequality in the distribution of resources and bad allocation of those. In conclusion, it is possible to build a new economy, based on rights and environmental protection, guided by the ethics of care, collective responsibilities and a pact of solidarity.

CHAPTER 7

FINANCIAL COMPLICITY AND HUMAN RIGHTS: EXPLORING THE LEGAL AND POLICY LANDSCAPE OF RESPONSIBILITY FOR SOVEREIGN DEBT

Celine Tan and Rafael Quintero Godinez[1]

INTRODUCTION

Sovereign financing refers to the financial resources raised by governments to fund public expenditure. It is an essential tool for contemporary governments to finance economic and social policy, as taxation and other forms of domestic resource mobilization are often insufficient to cover all public services and capital expenditure. Sovereign financing also plays a key role in overcoming temporary financial crises and providing relief from unexpected economic shocks and natural disasters. In today's globalized economy, sovereigns can access funds from a variety of sources, such as grants from official and non-governmental donors, export credits, equity investments, sovereign bonds, loans and guarantees from international financial institutions (IFIs), bilateral development finance institutions (DFIs) and private banks and insurers.

The financial obligations undertaken by sovereigns that are not direct monetary transfers, such as official development assistance (ODA) grants, are considered to form part of their sovereign debt liabilities that governments are expected to repay in accordance with the terms of the debt contract. The contracting of such debt by sovereigns can contribute towards and

---

1. This chapter is drawn from research submitted as a report to the UN independent expert on foreign debt and human rights, Juan Pablo Bohoslavsky (2014–20). We would like to thank Stephen Connelly and Juan Pablo Bohoslavsky for comments and contributions to the original report. We would also like to thank Matti Kohonen and Marianna Leite for their comments and recommendations and to Verónica Cadavid Gonzalez for her editorial work on the chapter. All errors and omissions remain our own.

facilitate serious and systematic violations of human rights (Bohoslavsky & Černič 2014; Tan 2013; Wong 2012). Legal and political institutions, such as parliaments and finance ministries, shape sovereign borrowing practices, but sovereign financing also shapes state political institutions and governments' capacity to respect, protect and fulfil human rights (Bohoslavsky & Černič 2014).

External finance to states can initiate, contribute to or compound human rights violations, both actively and by omission. Poorly contracted and badly managed sovereign finance can lead to unsustainable debt burdens and economic programming that can impact on countries' ability to meet human rights obligations to their populations (Bantekas & Lumina 2018; Bohoslavsky 2012). Sovereign debt can also be contracted for the purposes of shoring up repressive governments or maintaining authoritarian, corrupt and/or inefficient regimes. Individual projects funded by external financiers, such as IFIs, DFIs or export credit agencies (ECAs), can also lead to human rights violations (Aizawa, dos Santos & Seck 2018; Černič 2014).

This chapter examines the relationship between sovereign financing and human rights, notably the role of official sovereign financiers, in contributing to and/or sustaining the commission or perpetuation of human rights violations in the recipient states of such financing. The chapter focuses on (a) exploring the legal framework and standards applicable to attributing responsibility to sovereign financiers; and (b) examining current and potential frameworks for increasing the accountability of sovereign financiers for human rights compliance, in both national and international law. We focus specifically on the role of official sector financiers, because of the public nature of finance, which implicates the financing state as the duty bearer under international human rights law. We argue that a human rights-based approach to contracting sovereign debt and settling sovereign debt disputes is important to ensure that external finance is directed to sustainable and equitable global development.

GOVERNING REGIMES FOR SOVEREIGN FINANCING

Despite the rapid globalization of capital and financial flows, sovereign financing remains governed by a patchwork of different municipal, institutional and international laws. There is no overarching body of rules aimed at regulating sovereign borrowing or lending and no single international organization is charged with the oversight of sovereign financing (Tan 2014: 250–1). Instead, the regime of sovereign financing relies on a constellation of formal and informal rules, practices and institutions that can follow a highly regimented process.

Broadly speaking, sovereign financing can be categorized into official sector financing and private financing. The governing regime for sovereign finance will depend on the type of financing (see Figure 7.1). All sovereign finance will be executed by an agreement or contract between the financier and the sovereign entity that spells out the terms and conditions of the financing, including terms of repayment and provisions for dispute resolution and remedies for breach of contract. Beyond the immediate legal framework governing the financing contracts, whether public or private, financing to sovereigns will also be governed by the general rules that govern the financing entities themselves, whether through municipal law, including both civil and criminal; domestic or transnational regulatory regimes, including so-called "soft law" or non-binding normative standards set by official or private actors; or international law.

Focusing on official sector financing, these financing arrangements are usually governed by international law or the national law of the donor/financier state, depending on whether these are bilateral or multilateral financing arrangements (Dann & Riegner 2011; Head 2008). Official sector finance can include grants, loans, credits and guarantees from (a) *multilateral sources*, such as multilateral development banks (MDBs), IFIs, such as the IMF and the European Stabilization Mechanism (ESM), and UN agencies; and (b) *bilateral sources*, such as bilateral aid agencies (for example, the US Agency for International Development [USAID]) and direct financing for non-ODA expenditure, including military support. The export credit agencies of industrialized countries are a major source for bilateral finance

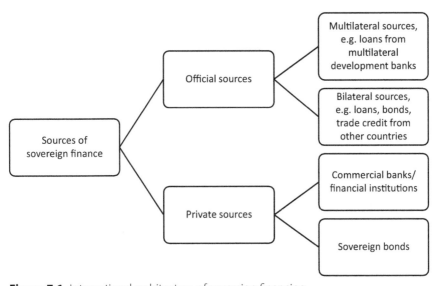

Figure 7.1 International architecture of sovereign financing

for developing countries. ECAs provide credit to domestic companies for exports or foreign investment as well as provide credit to developing countries purchasing goods and services from these companies.

Finance from multilateral sources is typically governed by international law and the internal institutional law of the MDB or IFI involved (Dann 2013: 157–217). Finance from the World Bank's International Bank for Reconstruction and Development (IRBD) and International Development Association (IDA), for example, are governed by a number of legal agreements and institutional operational policies, including the IBRD and IDA's respective articles of agreement (their governing charters), the general conditions of financing applicable to loans, credits and grants; the financing agreement of specific loans or credits; disbursement guidelines for investment project lending (when applicable) and other guidance under the World Bank's operational policy framework; and the national law of the borrower state, international law and industry or sector codes of conduct and best practices (when applicable) (Naudé Fourie 2016). Finance from the European Union is governed under the terms of the Treaty on European Union (TEU) and the Treaty on the Functioning of the European Union in relation to development cooperation matters (Dann 2013: 174–80) and EU Regulation 236/2014, which lays down the common rules and procedures for implementing the European Union's instruments for financing external action. This has a notable impact on safeguards in the European Union, as the European Investment Bank (EIB) cannot invest in jurisdictions designated as "tax havens" by the European Council's "grey list".[2]

Bilateral sources of financing – notably bilateral grants, loans and guarantees – are governed through the municipal public law of the donor/financier state, usually through enabling legislation or statutory budgetary authority or delegated powers of executive bodies (Dann 2013; Harrington & Manji 2018; Manji 2016). The United Kingdom and Canada have two of the most highly structured statutory regimes for the governance of bilateral aid. As bilateral financing is a governmental act, the mobilization and disbursement of such financing is also governed by the public law of the respective bilateral donor agencies.

Official financiers are also governed by several non-binding codes of conduct that outline different aspects of international development cooperation. For example, members of the Association of Bilateral European Development Finance Institutions (EDFI) have endorsed the EDFI principles for responsible financing of sustainable development (EDFI 2019). OECD Development Assistance Committee (DAC) member states are committed to various

---

2. The EU list of non-cooperative jurisdictions for tax purposes can be consulted at www.consilium.europa.eu/en/policies/eu-list-of-non-cooperative-jurisdictions.

political and technical agreements, such as the Paris Declaration on aid effectiveness (OECD 2005) and the follow-up Accra Agenda for Action (OECD 2008b).

Recent changes to the financing for development landscape, involving significant shifts to private sector finance, have also resulted in a plethora of new codes for official financiers engaged in private sector projects. Official financiers are routing financing through private entities within developing countries or via public–private partnerships, rather than through national governments or subnational public entities (Cotula & Tan 2018; Tan 2019; Tan & Cotula 2018). Two important codes of conduct have been established recently to govern the deployment of official finance to the mobilization of private finance (through so-called blended finance instruments): the enhanced principles on the use of blended concessional finance developed by the DFI Working Group on Blended Concessional Finance for Private Sector Projects (DFI Working Group 2017)[3] and the OECD DAC Blended Finance Principles (OECD 2018b).

In relation to sovereign debt, several initiatives have aimed at regulating sovereign borrowing and lending practices and preventing the build-up of unsustainable debt burdens, as well as laying down best practices for the resolution of sovereign debt disputes (non-binding in nature). These include "soft law" instruments, such as the Institute for International Finance's Principles for Stable Capital Flows and Fair Debt Restructuring in Emerging Markets (2004; updated 2022), the United Nations Conference on Trade and Development (UNCTAD) "Principles on responsible sovereign lending and borrowing" (UNCTAD 2012),[4] the UNCTAD Roadmap and Guide for sovereign debt workout mechanisms (UNCTAD 2015) and the UN General Assembly Resolution on Sovereign Debt Restructuring Processes (2015).[5]

None of these initiatives are binding, nor do they establish a unified framework for managing sustainable debt burdens and fair and transparent debt restructurings. Despite recurrent episodes of sovereign debt crises, the heightened potential for financial contagion and significant human rights

---

3. These principles are an updated version of the Private Sector Roundtable (2013) in terms of definitions and consistency with the new guidelines.
4. As Espósito *et al.* (2013) note, the UNCTAD Principles initiative results from a series of UN General Assembly resolutions (67/197, 67/198 and 67/199), which stressed the role of UNCTAD in promoting responsible sovereign lending and borrowing.
5. The latter, in line with the "Principles on responsible sovereign lending and borrowing", stresses that good faith, transparency, impartiality, legitimacy and sustainability are also principles to be applied to processes of sovereign debt restructuring. Although adopted by the UNGA through Resolution 69/319, six member states voted against, including the main jurisdictions for the contracting of sovereign debt (United States, United Kingdom, Germany, Canada, Japan and Israel); see https://documents-dds-ny.un.org/doc/UNDOC/GEN/N15/276/59/PDF/N1527659.pdf?OpenElement.

impacts of unsustainable debt, no formal international mechanism coordinates orderly sovereign debt workouts in the event of imminent or actual default and to restore debt-distressed states to a more sustainable fiscal position. Current debt restructuring initiatives mostly revolve around informal and voluntary negotiations between the debtor state and their creditors, mediated through IFIs, notably the IMF, and using informal and/or semi-informal groups, such as the Paris Club and creditor committees.[6]

SOVEREIGN FINANCING, FINANCIAL COMPLICITY AND HUMAN RIGHTS

The contracting of sovereign finance necessarily implicates states' human rights obligations, as it involves the exercise of public authority by both the borrower state and, in the case of the official sector financer, the creditor state (Bantekas & Lumina 2018; von Bogdandy & Goldmann 2013). Sovereign debt can undermine states' ability to meet the "reasonable minimum core of economic and social rights of its populations" (Černič 2014: 141). When states are spending large proportions of their revenues to service high debt repayments and/or when indebted states are conditioned by the terms of official financial assistance to undertake measures to reduce government expenditure, resources can and do get diverted away from public services (UN Human Rights Council 2011).

Additionally, external financing may support basic government functions, such as law enforcement, and the institutional and regulatory capacities to uphold human rights standards and prevent abuses by state and non-state actors (UN HRC 2014b: 6, para. 14; 2011a: 3, para. 3). Although these funds may not directly support surveillance or security apparatuses, they can still provide fiscal space in government budgets to strengthen coercive capacity and the clientelist networks of the regime (Bohoslavsky 2012: 67; Bohoslavsky & Esribá-Folch 2014: 22–3). This, in turn, can facilitate the containment of political protest and resistance to the regime on the funding of social and economic programmes.

In this context, the relationship between external financing, sovereign debt and human rights raises the question of financial complicity. This generally refers to situations in which the actors that are trading with, are investing in

---

6. Recent informal processes include the G20's Debt Service Suspension Initiative (DSSI), established in May 2020, whereby bilateral official creditors, through end-December 2021, suspended debt service payments from the poorest countries (73 low- and lower middle-income countries) that requested the suspension (World Bank 2022a), and the Common Framework for Debt Treatments beyond the DSSI – an agreement of the G20 and Paris Club countries to coordinate and cooperate on debt treatments for up to 73 low-income countries that are eligible for the DSSI (IMF 2021).

or are financial sponsors of human-rights-violating state actors are not the main perpetrators but are involved in the direct or indirect sustenance of the government entities or regimes engaged in the violation of human rights or international crimes (Bernaz 2014: 63). *Financial complicity* can be differentiated from *corporate complicity*, with the latter meaning direct involvement and the former alluding to the provision of capital to the perpetrator of such violations or crimes.

The issue of financial complicity is complex and necessitates a broader examination of the links that structure the international architecture of sovereign financing and the legal, regulatory and policy interactions between sovereign creditors and debtors. As many have observed, the notion of corporate accountability for human rights violations has evolved significantly over the years; however, the legal and policy tools to address financial complicity have remained underdeveloped (Bohoslavsky & Rulli 2010).

At a political and policy level, it is necessary to consider the relationship between financiers and human-rights-violating regimes at a broader macro level, taking into account the fungibility of financial resources coupled with the complexity of the contemporary global financial system. It requires mapping the interlinkages between the operations of sovereign financiers, including financial markets, and systemic human rights violations (Bohoslavsky 2012: 59). This requires a shift from viewing rights solely in terms of individual entitlements to examining the structural conditions that give rise to the perpetration of human rights violations by state and non-state actors (Dowell-Jones & Kinley 2011: 188–9).

From a legal perspective, it is necessary to establish micro-level connections between financiers and incidences of human rights abuse, linking specific violations of human rights to acts or omissions of the entity that provided or facilitated the resources to the perpetrator of such abuse (Bernaz 2014: 62). One major challenge in holding financial actors accountable is establishing a causative link between their actions or omissions and the resulting harm.

Applying human rights standards to "the operations of the financial sector is much more challenging than it is in the context of traditional providers of goods and services" because of the intermediary nature of financial actors and conventional notions of "arms-length distancing" (Roca & Manta 2010: 7). This is further complicated when considering (a) financing that is extended for general budget support or policy-based lending when resource flows cannot be directly attributed to specific projects, such as the construction of a hydroelectric dam or road network, or specified expenditure, such as military equipment; (b) the cumulative effect of sovereign liabilities on the overall sovereign debt burden (Bohoslavsky 2012; Michalowski 2007; Wong 2012); and (c) that the separate legal personality of multinational companies, the protection of the corporate veil and the creation of subsidiary companies restrict accessing redress when it comes to human rights violations (*Adams v Cape Industries plc* [1990]). This is attributable to companies' ability to distribute responsibility across different legal entities, through limited companies or subsidiary companies acting as agents in their business operations (Muchlinski 2010).

Despite these challenges, the linkages between sovereign financing and debtor and creditor states' human rights duties are clear (Scali 2022). The contracting of sovereign financing as an exercise of public authority engages a broader suite of national and international laws, which transcends "private law that views sovereign financing and debt as a series of discrete and individual legal arrangements towards one that is located in within a 'multi-dimensional' landscape of governance based on national and international public law duties paradigm" (Bantekas & Lumina 2018; von Bogdandy & Goldmann 2013). This entails more than just conformity "to a minimum of procedural and substantive standards" (von Bogdandy & Goldmann 2013) in the *ex ante* contracting of sovereign finance and the *ex post* resolution of sovereign debt disputes requiring a more holistic reorientation of the practice of sovereign financing that accounts for the fundamental character of human rights obligations (Bantekas & Lumina 2018).

OFFICIAL FINANCIERS AND COMPLICITY FOR HUMAN RIGHTS VIOLATIONS

For the most part, national and international legal systems remain ill equipped to deal with notions of accountability and complicity for human rights violations by financiers, especially from the perspective of "project affected people" or general populations "who are not in a contractual relationship with development-lending institutions" (Naudé Fourie 2016: 6).

As discussed above, official financiers' contractual obligations remain primarily with the borrowing state or, in some cases of private sector financing, with the entity that has contracted the financing or a grantee of the financing (Suzuki 2010: 83–4). Furthermore, traditional human rights law has generally approached duties as falling under the jurisdiction of the state on whose territory the human rights violations have occurred, raising the question of whether financiers can be held accountable for harms that occur outside their territory (*Azemi v Serbia* [2013], para. 41; *Banković and Others v Belgium and 16 Other States* [2001], para. 34 et seq.).

The absence of a direct relationship between the financier and the individuals or communities that have suffered harm has been a barrier to seeking greater accountability from official financiers for their acts and omissions in sustaining human-rights-violating regimes. This issue of accountability rests on two questions: (a) whether the financier can be responsible for human rights violations/harms that are facilitated by financial resources extended to the borrower; and (b), if they can be held responsible, what mechanisms are available to hold them to account for such violations, and by whom? We address these two questions in turn.

Complicity of official financiers

With respect to official financiers, in principle, they are responsible only for their acts – in this case, for providing financial resources. The perpetuation of harm, namely human rights violations, can be attributed to both the assisting and acting official financier when the assistance of the former is deemed necessary for the wrongful act to occur (International Law Commission [ILC] 2001: commentary on Article 16, para. 10).

The rules applicable to determine the complicity of states also apply to international organizations, when adding or assisting a state or another international organization in the commission of an internationally wrongful act (ILC 2011a: 66, commentary of Article 14, para. 1). The rationale behind this is that, "from the moment that [international] organizations exercise legal competencies of the same type as those of states, it seemed logical that the same consequences should attach to the actions of both one and the other" (Lanovoy 2016: 87; International Court of Justice 1949: 178).

International law (states)

The legal basis for states' financial complicity in international law is outlined in chapter IV of the Draft Articles on Responsibility of States for Internationally Wrongful Acts (DARSIWA).[7] Three articles govern this subject. Article 16 deals with situations in which one state provides aid or assistance to another with the intent of assisting the latter in committing a wrongful act. In this regard, three conditions must be met to consider that such aid or assistance materially facilitates or significantly contributes to the commission of a wrongful act.

First, the assisting or aiding state must be aware of the circumstances surrounding the wrongful act (ILC 2001, Article 16 (a)). In this context, a state providing financial assistance to another state would bear international responsibility only if it knew of the circumstances under which the other state would use its aid or assistance (ILC 2001, commentary on Article 16: para.

---

7. Chapter IV addresses not only instances of financial complicity but also any situation in which one state provides aid or assistance to another to facilitate the latter's commission of an internationally wrongful act.

4). Second, the aid or assistance must be given with the intention of actually facilitating the commission of the wrongful act. As a result, a state cannot be held liable for aiding or assisting unless the relevant state organ intended to facilitate the wrongful conduct through the aid or assistance, and the act was actually committed by the aided or assisted state (ILC 2001, commentary on Article 16: para. 5). The third condition limits aid or assistance to only those circumstances in which the aiding or assisting state is also bound by the same obligation. In other words, the aiding or assisting state should not deliberately cause another state to breach any shared obligation that applies to both of them (ILC 2001, commentary on Article 16: para. 6).

In line with these three conditions, Aust (2011: 132–47) presents two examples of financial assistance in economic cooperation that, if funding had not been cut off, could have amounted to states' complicity in aiding or assisting in the commission of an internationally wrongful act. First, Germany, Austria and Switzerland withdrew their export credit guarantees for the Ilisu Dam in southeastern Turkey after the revelation that the project had disastrous effects on human rights (including the eviction of numerous Kurds), the environment and the security and stability of the area. Second, after a new military government in Suriname was accused of committing serious human rights violations in 1982, the Netherlands ceased providing financial support for the military's upkeep.

The second provision governing complicity is Article 17. It prescribes that a state that both controls and directs another in the commission of an internationally wrongful act is held accountable for the entire act. The term "controls" refers to a situation in which a state has dominance over an internationally wrongful act – as opposed to simply exercising oversight, influence or concern. The term "directs" implies an actual direction of an operative kind, rather than just incitement or suggestion (ILC 2001, commentary on Article 17: para 7). Last, Article 18 deals with the extreme case in which one state wilfully forces another into committing an internationally prohibited act. According to Lanovoy (2016: 140), if the coerced state commits a wrongful act, the controlling state is considered responsible as the act is, in essence, the act of the controlling state.

Aid or assistance does not have to be critical to the commission of an internationally wrongful act. It is sufficient if it has a significant impact on the performance of the act (ILC 2001: commentary on Article 16, para. 6; Lanovoy 2016: 170). This is an important factor to consider, given the World Bank and IMF's comments on Article 16 of the DARSIWA. The World Bank argued that organizations that offer financial assistance typically do not take on the risk of the assistance being used to commit an international wrong. Consequently, if this risk were to be assumed, it could lead to a chilling effect on international financial institutions offering economic assistance to eligible borrowers and recipients (ILC 2011b: 115). Meanwhile, the IMF asserted that, since its financing is not aiming for a particular conduct that could significantly contribute to a state's wrongful conduct, its financial assistance is intended to support a member's economic programme addressing the balance of payment issues (ILC 2007: 22). We concur with Lanovoy that such arguments are untenable. A presumption of responsibility arises from any aid or assistance that is factually related to the main wrongful act; only the absence of knowledge of the circumstances surrounding the primary wrongful act can rebut such presumption (Lanovoy 2016: 186).

International law (international organizations)

The basis for international organizations' responsibility and financial complicity, particularly IFIs, in financing states committing human rights abuses is contested. As Bradlow and Hunter (2010: 18) point out, "It is clear that IFI operations can have profound social and environmental impacts … it is less obvious that international law offers guidance to the IFIs in understanding their responsibilities in this regard." They identify four reasons why the legal basis for IFI accountability remains unclear. First, IFIs are not signatories to human rights, social or environmental treaties, and, thus, have no formal obligation to adhere to those requirements. Second, not all the member states of IFIs are parties to such treaties, making it uncertain whether the IFIs should insist that their member states adhere to these treaty stipulations. Third, even if all member states are parties to a particular treaty, it is unclear whether the IFIs have the power to impose their interpretation of that treaty on their member states, especially when treaty interpretation is contested, or there is no authoritative interpretation. Fourth, there is no universal agreement on what constitutes applicable customary international human rights and environmental law in regard to the IFIs (Bradlow & Hunter 2010: 18–19).

Additionally, Bretton Woods institutions – the World Bank and the IMF – have traditionally claimed that the pursuit of human rights is not explicitly enshrined in their constitutive treaties and, therefore, consideration of such standards when making financial decisions may be inconsistent with their constitutional mandates (Tan 2008: 86–7). For example, in response to the letter from UN special rapporteurs De Schutter and Lumina regarding the human rights implications of the role of the World Bank in the privatization of Burundi's coffee industry, the Bank's vice president for Africa and the general counsel wrote a joint letter.[8] The letter acknowledged the connection

---

8. The letter can be viewed at https://spcommreports.ohchr.org/TMResultsBase/DownLoad File?gId=31461.

between development and human rights in the funding of projects and programmes, but stated that it must adhere to the articles of agreement vested in the Bank by its shareholders, which state explicitly that only economic considerations with a direct and obvious economic effect relevant to the Bank's work can be considered in the decisions made (Van Den Meerssche 2021: 98).

One could argue that Article 27 of the Vienna Convention on the Law of Treaties contains a first legal basis of complicity for international organizations, which provides that "a party may not invoke the provisions of its internal law as justification for its failure to perform a treaty", including the internal law of international organizations (Suzuki 2010: 78–9). This is particularly important considering that "the IMF, as a UN specialised agency[,] is bound by the general aims and principles of the UN Charter, including respect for human rights and fundamental freedoms" (Independent expert on the promotion of a democratic and equitable international order 2017: 42). Moreover, the three conditions previously mentioned concerning the responsibility of states also apply to IFIs (ILC 2001: commentary on Article 14, para. 1; UNGA 2005: 27).

In this context, the *Chixoy Dam* case before the Inter-American Commission on Human Rights and the Inter-American Court of Human Rights is a prime example of how IFIs' financial assistance can facilitate the commission of an internationally wrongful act. Here, the Global Initiative for Economic, Social, and Cultural Rights; Rights Action; and the International Human Rights Clinic at Western New England University School of Law filed an *amicus curiae* brief arguing that the World Bank and the Inter-American Development Bank should be held accountable for their complicity in human rights violations related to the Chixoy Dam project, as they should have been aware of the potential project's violation of economic, social and cultural rights of the Guatemalan people (cited in Nollkaemper *et al.* 2020).[9]

This is in line with the special report of the UN special representative for business and human rights, John Ruggie, which asserts that IFIs and private corporations must respect international human rights (UN HRC 2011b: 4, para. 6). This duty implies an obligation to refrain from formulating, adopting, funding and implementing policies and programmes that directly or indirectly contravene the enjoyment of human rights (UN HRC 2011a: 6, para. 9). In this context, Ruggie noted that the stringent IMF-mandated austerity measures had threatened the right to health (UN HRC 2011b: para. 55). As an

---

9. The Court held Guatemala responsible for its wrongful acts. However, the *amicus* brief of the petitioners was addressed neither by the Commission nor the Court. See *Case of the Río Negro Massacres v Guatemala* [2012], judgment.

example, IMF conditionalities to reduce expenditure on health by African governments have hindered their efforts to achieve universal health coverage (Stubbs *et al.* 2017: 225).

Accountability mechanisms

Despite the contested legal basis for the responsibility of official financiers, both states and international organizations, for human rights violations in recipient states, most official financiers are governed by legal and regulatory accountability systems for their financing operations. Accountability for the mobilization and use of official financing falls into two categories: internal frameworks of accountability; and external frameworks of accountability. The accountability of official financiers for human rights violations depends on how they are held accountable by these various frameworks.

Internal frameworks of accountability

International frameworks of accountability for official sovereign financiers are those mechanisms that are internal to the bilateral agency or multilateral organization. These frameworks may be mandated by external law or regulations. Even so, they are internal procedures designed to regulate the mobilization, disbursement and use of resources, and to redress and remedy actions when a party involved in the financing transaction breaches these policies or regulations. In some ways, their design has partly responded to an emerging international consensus that official financiers, especially IFIs, have a "duty of accountability" under international and/or national law. The duty's contours remain contested in theory and in practice (Naudé Fourie 2016: 4).

Although these mechanisms may not deal with human rights violations per se, these frameworks of accountability offer a certain level of oversight for the acts of the official financiers within their operational governance structures. The standards contained in these internal frameworks can serve as deterrents to the misuse or abuse of funds by the sovereign borrower and provide some measure of oversight over funds extended to sovereigns. To a limited degree, they provide access to complaints and remedies for communities that may have been adversely affected by projects funded by official financiers. At the same time, there is the question of whether official financiers have a duty or legal responsibility for the realization of human rights, as opposed to merely possessing a negative duty to refrain from complicity in human rights violations (Tan 2008: 88).

External frameworks of accountability

Although the standards enshrined in internal policies may be derived from external standards, official financiers, notably IFIs, have been very reluctant to be bound by international standards protecting human rights (Naudé Fourie 2016: 141–2; Tan 2008: 92–3). The World Bank, for example, has been quite clear about the non-legal nature of its operational policies. Its former general counsel, Ibrahim Shihata, argued that "a violation by the Bank of its policy even if established by the Inspection Panel … is not necessarily a violation of applicable law that entails liability for ensuing damages … [I]ts findings on Bank violations cannot be taken *ipso facto* as conclusive evidence against the Bank in judicial proceedings" (Naudé Fourie 2016: 141).

Beyond the institutional mechanisms for accountability, external frameworks can provide avenues for further redress and for holding official financiers to account. This includes obligations the entity has under domestic and international law and compliance with so-called "soft law" standards and codes.

An important avenue for accountability is through national legislation governing the mobilization and disbursement of development finance and recourse through public law or administrative law. As Dann (2013: 300) argues, "Decisions on ODA transfers take place mostly in the executive … that development administration is manifested as an exercise in public authority." For example, the Canadian ODA Accountability Act 2008 (Government of Canada 2008) includes provisions for parliamentary oversight of Canadian aid policy and practice. It requires the submission of annual reports to parliament indicating, among other things, the total amount of aid expenditure, a summary of activities or initiatives taken under the Act, a summary of a report on Canada's financial contributions to and decision-making activities at the World Bank and the IMF (under a separate Bretton Woods and Related Agreements Act 1985: Government of Canada 1985) and "summary of any representation made by Canadian representatives with respect to priorities and policies of the Bretton Woods Institutions" (Government of Canada 2008: sec. 5).

CONCLUSION

This chapter has examined the relationship between sovereign financing and human rights, distinctly on the legal, regulatory and policy framework under which such financing takes place. It has focused on understanding how the rules and institutions that govern sovereign financing perpetuate risks of egregious human rights violations and presented potential avenues for accounting for and remedying harms caused by such violations. From a human rights regulatory perspective, we have demonstrated that the landscape for sovereign financing remains fragmented and governed by a mix of private and public law, domestic and international, institutional law and a plethora of "soft", non-binding codes and standards and informal processes.

Sovereign financing has significant human rights implications. The alignment of sovereign borrowing and lending policies and practices with principles of human rights at both international and domestic levels is an urgent need, notably by guaranteeing accountability and remedial provisions for affected individuals and communities. In this sense, moving towards a Rights-Based Economy implies that the financier state or international organization responsible for such financing should ensure that these resources are invested and utilized in line with the fulfilment of the human rights obligations of states.

PART II

TRANSFORMING THE ECONOMY

CHAPTER 8

ILLICIT FINANCIAL FLOWS, TAX HAVENS AND THE AFRICAN COMMISSION ON HUMAN AND PEOPLES' RIGHTS

Asha Ramgobin[1]

INTRODUCTION

In 1961, four years after winning political independence for Ghana, President Kwame Nkrumah described Africa as a continent where the paradox of poverty existed amid plenty, and scarcity amid abundance (Worger, Clark & Alpers 2010: 156). He argued that true economic independence could be won only through African unity and solidarity, and saw that era as a unique moment filled with great opportunity for Africa. He believed that, individually, the independent states of Africa – some of them potentially rich, others poor – could do little for their people. Nevertheless, together, by mutual help, they could achieve much (Worger, Clark & Alpers 2010).

Nkrumah's ideas are more important today than ever. Illicit financial flows (IFFs) are eroding current advances in the rule of law, democracy, human rights, social and economic justice and – above all – African unity and solidarity. Revenue leaves Africa via both legal and illegal means, often with African states' collusion (UNECA 2015). Consequently, African states lack adequate revenue to fulfil their human rights obligations, conduct free, fair and regular elections and pursue peace, security and stability.

In 2016 the "Panama Papers" revealed that prominent political leaders, government officials, judges and people related to them from at least 16 countries in Africa were listed as shareholders, directors and beneficiaries of secret offshore shell and mailbox companies.[2] In 2017 the "Paradise Papers" presented a similar situation regarding at least ten individuals or companies

---

1. Ramgobin is undertaking her LLD with the support of SARChI and received financial assistance from the National Research Foundation (NRF) towards this research. Opinions expressed and conclusions arrived at, are those of the author and are not necessarily attributable to the NRF.
2. See www.icij.org/investigations/panama-papers. See also Mbeki (2016).

from seven countries in Africa.[3] In 2018 the revelations expanded with information from the "Mauritius leaks".[4] More recently, in 2021 the Pandora Papers revealed that nearly 50 politicians and public officials from 18 African states were connected to offshore entities.[5]

These revelations confirmed findings by the African Union High-Level Panel on IFFs regarding tax havens, financial secrecy jurisdictions and opacity on beneficial ownership of firms (UNECA 2015). The evidence presented a network of offshore accounts and complicated investment vehicles shrouded in secrecy, allowing tax avoidance and evasion. The South African president, Thabo Mbeki, contended that if not earlier, at least now, firm action from African governments and the rest of the world was essential (UNECA 2015).

It became clear that Africa's peoples have been, and continue to be, effectively deprived of their wealth by carefully and deliberately designed processes and systems that enable large corporations, several non-African states (including some with large, developed economies) and a small minority of African individuals to get rich by allowing wealth to flow freely out of Africa (Ogle 2018; Meredith 2006, 2014). Corruption perpetuates governance weaknesses, in particular enabling corruption, with officials turning a blind eye to suspicious transactions. These phenomena allow these flows to persist and have a crippling effect on human rights in Africa (UNCTAD 2020).

Since many powerful individuals are vested in maintaining the system, I turn to international human rights law and enquire how the African regional human rights system is positioned to deal with IFFs from Africa and with tax havens' laws and policies within Africa, particularly the African Charter on Human and Peoples' Rights (hereafter "the African Charter" or "the Charter") together with its treaty monitoring body: the African Commission on Human and Peoples' Rights (the "African Commission" or ACHRP).

I focus on just two of the Charter's articles, namely Article 21 and Article 29(6). Then I analyse how the African Commission has used the Charter to address IFFs while looking critically at significant missed opportunities. I conclude after proposing a special mechanism on IFFs and human rights.

AFRICAN CHARTER ON HUMAN AND PEOPLES' RIGHTS

In 1986 the African Charter on Human and Peoples' Rights entered into force (Worger, Clark & Alpers 2010). The Senegalese president, Léopold Senghor, at the Organisation of African Unity (OAU) summit in 1979 reminded the

---

3. See www.icij.org/investigations/paradise-papers.
4. See www.icij.org/investigations/mauritius-leaks/treasure-island-leak-reveals-how-mauritius-siphons-tax-from-poor-nations-to-benefit-elites.
5. See www.dw.com/en/pandora-papers-expose-african-leaders-offshore-secrets/a-59399552.

drafters of the Charter that "Africa is watching them" to ensure scrupulous respect for freedoms and rights (Heyns 2002). He emphasized that, in Africa, rights cannot be separated from obligations. The brief given to the drafters included a system of individual duties, together with individual rights, and a system of peoples' rights or group rights, together with the principle of solidarity (Murray 2004: 49–72). The Charter indeed included all these elements, and by 1999 all member states of the OAU had ratified it.[6] Today the African Charter provides a strong instrument in the human rights-based fight against IFFs.

Peoples' rights in the African Charter: a tool to combat illicit financial flows

The Charter includes the peoples' right to equality and non-domination (Article 19), solidarity and self-determination (Article 20), disposal of wealth and natural resources in the interests of the peoples of Africa (Article 21), the peoples' right to development (Article 22) and the peoples' right to peace and security (Article 23). These rights, coupled with the duty to pay tax under Article 29(6), form the human rights framework for state obligations and responsibilities of non-state actors to combat IFFs.

It is true that Africa is, in a sense, a victim of looting and that the perpetrators are mostly from outside Africa (Dean & Waris 2021; Oguttu 2011). It is also true that several African member states to the African Charter are complicit (ACHPR 2017a). The collective rights under the African Charter were specifically included because the founders knew that Africa could achieve liberation and economic independence only if all African states worked together in solidarity against colonialism and foreign economic domination (Umozurike 1997; Mutua 1995). This remains essential today. Unless African states work together in solidarity to combat the impact of neoliberalism, they will not be able to reclaim their economic autonomy.

Article 21: the right to dispose of wealth and natural resources in the exclusive interests of the people

Article 21 of the Charter centres on the *exclusive interests of the people* regarding the right to dispose of wealth and natural resources. It further creates three very specific obligations for state parties, namely (a) to promote international economic cooperation based on mutual respect, equitable exchange

---

6. Morocco withdrew from the OAU in 1984, was readmitted to its successor organization, the African Union (AU), in January 2017 and has not yet acceded to the African Charter.

and principles of international law (Article 21:3); (b) to strengthen African unity and solidarity, individually and collectively (Article 21:4); and (c) to eliminate all forms of foreign economic exploitation, particularly as practised by international monopolies (Article 21:5).

The African Commission has discussed Article 21 in the case of *Social and Economic Rights Action Centre v Nigeria* [2001], stating as follows:

> The origin of this provision may be traced to colonialism, during which the human and material resources of Africa were largely exploited for the benefit of outside powers, creating tragedy for Africans themselves, depriving them of their birthright and alienating them from the land. The aftermath of colonial exploitation has left Africa's precious resources and people still vulnerable to foreign misappropriation. The drafters of the Charter obviously wanted to remind African governments of the continent's painful legacy and restore cooperative economic development to its traditional place at the heart of African society. Governments have a duty to protect their citizens, not only through appropriate legislation and effective enforcement, but also by protecting them from damaging acts that may be perpetrated by private parties. This duty calls for positive action on the part of governments in fulfilling their obligation under human rights instruments.

The Working Group on Extractive Industries (WGEI), a special mechanism of the African Commission, has defined the content and underlying principles of Article 21 in its "State reporting guidelines" (ACHPR 2018). The choice of a state reporting guideline as the instrument is not the most appropriate for norm elaboration and to discharge the interpretative mandate of the Commission. Nevertheless, some of the conclusions reached are seeds for a potentially disruptive role as we work towards a Rights-Based Economy.

The guidelines (ACHPR 2018) stipulate that international trade and investment agreements, as well as bilateral investment agreements, must adhere to the principles of mutual respect, equitable exchange and international law. Any obligations that undermine the right of peoples to control their wealth and natural resources will not be safeguarded under Article 21(3). Consequently, existing clauses, such as those that grant foreign companies an unfair competitive advantage over local businesses engaged in the same activity, investor–state dispute settlement mechanisms excluding human rights obligations and tax incentives depriving people of their entitled benefits, should be reviewed and renegotiated.

Significantly, the 2018 guidelines boldly go further than the UN Guiding Principles on Business and Human Rights by categorically stating that non-state actors have both positive and negative *obligations*, not only a *responsibility* to respect. Their positive obligations revolve around fiscal transparency. Their negative obligations entail endeavouring to do no harm and taking appropriate steps to rectify any harm done. This ethos also permeates supply chains and proper fiscal management and compliance. The WGEI bases this finding on the lack of such obligations resulting in non-state actors operating within a human rights vacuum, wherein they may operate without observing human rights (ACHPR 2018: 37, para. 56).

State parties have the obligation to respect, protect and fulfil human rights. The state obligation to protect is of paramount importance, as IFFs are often a consequence of the actions of non-state actors. For example, in Tanzania in April 2017 the president, John Magufuli, appointed two committees of academics to investigate the contents of containers at the Acacia gold mines and at the port of Dar es Salaam. The committees confirmed the suspicion that the consignment contained eight times more gold than the company had reported – besides other rare minerals, such as iridium and ytterbium (Forstater & Readhead 2017; Els 2017). Here, the state obligation to protect includes protection of citizens from the actions of Acacia Mining, its subsidiaries, its legal advisors, its accounting officers and its auditors, if they all operated in collusion to misrepresent the quantity of gold and the types of substances under consideration.

Consequently, the obligation to protect entails enacting and enforcing laws and regulations for non-state actors that empower the state to investigate the activities of all the entities within the extractive industries supply chain, as in Tanzania's case. Further, the state bears the obligation to prosecute, if necessary, and to take proactive steps to ensure that revenues due to the state do in fact reach the state. The obligation also entails spending revenue in the people's interests.

Under Article 21(5), the duty to act in solidarity and unity in combating foreign economic domination must arguably include IFFs. The ACHPR (2018) concluded that a state party breaches this obligation when entering into agreements with other states or with investors in the extractive industries that compromise the ability of other state parties to harness the due revenues, depriving the people of their entitled benefits.

Finally, the guidelines allow individuals to invoke Article 21(4), clarifying that this article imposes an obligation on state parties vis-à-vis other African states. However, there is the qualification that the benefit of such cooperation must accrue to the people of the states, hence suggesting that citizens have the ability to demand compliance with this by their governments. It will be interesting to see the litigation arising from these provisions both within domestic tribunals and, importantly, before the African Commission.

Article 29(6): duty to pay tax

Articles 27 to 29 address individual duties in the African Charter. Importantly, Article 29(6) states that "[e]very individual has the duty to work to the best of their ability and to pay tax according to law in the interests of society".

Within African legal philosophy, an individual's rights cannot be separated from his or her duties or obligations (Mutua 1995). Justice Kéba M'Baye, a leading expert and drafter of the African Charter drafting, emphasized: "In Africa, laws and duties are regarded as being two facets of the same reality: two inseparable realities" (International Commission of Jurists 1985). African philosophy, tradition, culture, history and differing notions of the state are the roots of these rights and duties. In Dr Makau wa Mutua's opinion, the purpose behind duties in the pre-colonial period was to assist in developing social cohesiveness towards "a shared fate and common destiny" (Mutua 1995: 368), which the modern state fails to achieve. In his view, the duties listed in Articles 27 to 29 of the Charter were perhaps an attempt "to recreate the bonds that existed in the pre-colonial era among individuals and between individuals and the state" (Mutua 1995: 368).

Samuel Moyn contributes to this discussion and points to the gap in the protective framework of human rights treaties caused by the exclusion of the duties of individuals to their own states and the duties of states to one another (Moyn 2016).

Fernando del Valle and Kathryn Sikkink build on Moyn's arguments, asserting that every right has a correlating duty. Their argument regarding global inequality is particularly relevant, interlinking the right to an adequate standard of living with the duties of individuals to pay taxes. Moreover, the authors propose recovering and updating the understanding of individual duties to equip human rights with the necessary vocabulary to address critical collective policy concerns (del Valle & Sikkink 2017: 193). One of these pressing global policy concerns is the inordinately high levels of tax evasion, avoidance, profit-shifting and other fiscal machinations that reduce state revenue. They conclude by highlighting that "declarations of international rights unaccompanied by recognition of duties would make those rights no more than 'pious aspirations'" (del Valle & Sikkink 2017: 193).

Since its conception, the relationship between rights and duties has been integral to the African regional human rights system (Viljoen 2007; Mutua 1995). However, normative content is required to enable state parties to clearly understand their core obligations under this provision. Further elaboration could address the following questions.

- How is the term "individual" defined within the context of the jurisprudence of the African Commission? Does it, for example, include non-state actors and corporations? What are the implications of including non-state actors and corporations? Will that then give rise to corporates claiming other rights under the African Charter? How can these adverse consequences be mitigated?

• How is the concept of "duty" defined and understood within the context of international law and the African human rights system? Does this duty of an individual give rise to state obligations? If so, what types of obligations? What are the legal obligations of legal professionals and accountants in the context of this provision? How does this provision impact upon the rules of ethics of the legal profession and accounting professions?

• What are the obligations of state parties to each other when one state party operates as a tax haven, international financial centre or secrecy jurisdiction to the detriment of other state parties? How does this provision relate to the obligations under Articles 21(3) and (4) regarding the obligation of promoting international economic cooperation and strengthening African unity and solidarity?

As the Commission learnt about the scourge of IFFs and tax havens, the attention on duties increased, albeit marginally, particularly regarding the duty to pay tax, which falls significantly short. The African Charter is the only binding international human rights instrument containing a "duty to pay tax". Even so, there is little clarification as to its content.

A general comment can solve the clarification problem. Besides clarifying the duty to pay tax within a regional human rights instrument, which is a disruptive tool in the human rights discourse, it could contribute, more generally, to international normative standards on balancing rights and entitlements with duties and obligations. The clarity will have implications for state policy and practice. This is particularly relevant when building the social and solidarity economy contemplated for Africa (ILO 2022c). Further, the duty to pay tax exists in both the African and Inter-American regional human rights systems. A general comment would provide insights for other regional human rights systems and into the global discourse on the obligation to mobilize the maximum available resources of the International Covenant on Social, Economic and Cultural Rights.

THE AFRICAN COMMISSION'S RESPONSE TO ILLICIT FINANCIAL FLOWS

The African Commission has a supervisory mandate to protect, promote and interpret the Charter based on its Article 45 (Viljoen 2007). It has three mandates: a protective mandate, with jurisdiction over individual communications and inter-state complaints; a promotional mandate, to prepare reporting guidelines, receive periodic reports of state parties, and to provide concluding observations guiding states on corrective action; and, last, an interpretative mandate, for issuing general comments with guidance on the normative content on provisions of the Charter. The Commission may appoint special mechanisms on specific thematic areas to deepen their impact (Viljoen 2007).

As a quasi-judicial human rights treaty monitoring body, the Commission has the potential to play a disruptive role in the unjust global economic system and its enabling networks, particularly those operating on the African continent. To some extent, it has grasped the opportunities and acted accordingly. However, as presented in the analysis below, this potential has not been fully realized.

The African Commission: strategic interventions to address illicit financial flows?

In 2013 the African Commission seized an important moment by adopting Resolution 236, on illicit capital flight from Africa.

Through this resolution, the African Commission[7] made it clear that it was aware that illicit loss of revenue from both multinationals and individuals undermines a state's capacity to meet its obligations under the African Charter and to achieve its development goals. The Commission expressed concern about IFFs perpetuating a vicious cycle of poverty, malnutrition and diseases, leading to greater dependence on external aid, a "short-term, unsustainable and unreliable form of revenue".[8] The resolution highlighted that this revenue loss is possible because of the weakness of the laws with loopholes and ineffective tax collection and monitoring systems and ineffective tax collection systems. The African Commission recognized the complexity of the issue and undertook to conduct an in-depth study that would guide its future response to the various dimensions of IFFs. In the interim, it called on state parties to proactively review their tax policies and laws.

Resolution 236 was timely, and, as a first step, it set the course for a more robust approach to IFFs as human rights violations. It had the potential to be extremely disruptive, as the African Commission's plan to implement the resolution involved studying each state party's tax laws, banking laws, company laws, trust laws, international trade and investment agreements and tax agreements and making clear recommendations to each state party.[9] The

---

7. https://achpr.au.int/index.php/en/adopted-resolutions/236-resolution-illicit-capital-flight-africa-achprres236liii2013.

8. See https://achpr.au.int/index.php/en/adopted-resolutions/236-resolution-illicit-capital-flight-africa-achprres236liii2013.

9. The Human Rights Development Initiative was instituted to assist the African Commission implement this resolution, and it assisted with the development of this action plan.

planned outcome of the study would have been a set of normative stand-ards addressing many dimensions of IFFs, such as the impacts on growing distributive inequality in Africa and the concomitant power imbalances. It would lay the foundation for the Commission to invoke its promotional and interpretative mandate to address IFFs and distributive inequality as a human rights issue. In addition, it would serve as the foundation for con-cluding observations to state parties requiring corrective action; failing to do so would be a violation of a regional human rights treaty.

The African Commission did not succeed in undertaking that strategy. On the one hand, development agencies rejected all applications for financial support. On the other, certain key stakeholders expressed grave reservations about a human rights-based intervention to address IFFs. At the same time, the AU political structures in charge of appointing commissioners recalled the two commissioners who had championed Resolution 236.

Among multiple possible explanations, many development agencies desired the appearance of addressing the issue but hesitated to support a potentially disruptive initiative. Fragmented positions could be discerned within certain embassies. Some individuals within the development cooper-ation division, for example, might have similar priorities, and even enthu-siasm, to address the root causes of poverty and inequality that lie embedded within an unjust economic order. However, the trade and investment division, and even the peace and security division, of the same government might have conflicting priorities. Consequently, we see imbalanced bilateral agreements, tax treaties and other policies perpetuating the system facilitating IFFs.

The response of key stakeholders within civil society could be simple and classic gatekeeping: jostling for limited funding and jealously guarding territory without any further underlying motive. It could be a result of the ideology that views human rights-based approaches as part of a neoliberal agenda, with indi-vidual civil rights and entitlements at the centre and economic and social rights at the periphery.[10] Moyn (2018) describes a historic emphasis on status equality at the expense of distributive inequality, with the age of human rights also being the age of the victory of the rich. Maybe these ideas influenced the attitude of civil society organizations. They were misdirected, as this was a strategy rooted within a human rights charter that was designed for distributive equality and to be disruptive of the unfair global economic order.

The African Union has a history of interfering in the independence of the Commission, which it continues to do (Viljoen 2007; Human Rights Watch

---

10. This is particularly prevalent when considering competing rights, such as the conflict between the right to privacy when juxtaposed against the need for public registries that contain beneficial ownership disclosures. See European Court of Justice in Joined Cases C-37/20 of Luxembourg Business Registers and C-601/20 of Sovim.

2019a). Whenever it feels that the Commission is "overreaching", subtle or aggressive steps are taken, such as reining in the Commission's budget or replacing commissioners. Sadly, the net effect is the African Commission's relegation of the continental fight against IFFs to the sidelines. Since then, all work on IFFs has been delegated to two special mechanisms: the Working Group on Extractive Industries and the Working Group on Economic, Social and Cultural Rights (WG-ECOSOC).

The Commission has adopted Resolution 367 (ACHPR 2017b) in connection with the extractive industries sector, which, without using the terminology as such, touches on notions of beneficial ownership disclosure, country-by-country reporting and the automatic exchange of information, and, as mentioned above, has proposed a potentially important regional mechanism to fight illicit financial flows.

The few other steps taken by the African Commission can all be characterized as weak and ineffectual, and more akin to those steps that civil society organizations could take. Instead, the African Commission has sidestepped the robust platforms and opportunities laid out before it as a treaty-monitoring body.

Missed opportunities for norm elaboration on illicit financial flows as a human rights violation

The African Commission missed several opportunities to join the fight against IFFs by using one of the strongest weapons in Africa's arsenal: the African Charter. I can exemplify it with two such situations. First, there is the Commission's response to Mauritius, both regarding the revelations in the Paradise Papers and to its periodic report. Second, there is the Commission's weak advocacy of its findings in the 2018 "State reporting guidelines".

Concluding observations and recommendations on the periodic report submitted by Mauritius and the December 2017 press statement on the Paradise Papers

In the "Concluding observations and recommendations" to Mauritius (ACHPR 2017c), the Commission notes the growing inequality in Mauritius as a factor restricting the enjoyment of rights, and the lack of information in the periodic report about laws and policies aiming to ensure that multinationals are taxed for activities undertaken in Mauritius. Unfortunately, there is no reference to either of these two pertinent issues in their final recommendations to the state. The Commission missed an opportunity to assist

Mauritius in reviewing its role in relation to other African state parties' ability to mobilize tax revenue.

Instead, on 12 December 2017 the WGEI addressed all these issues in a press statement in response to the revelations in the "Paradise Papers" (ACHPR 2017a).[11] It expressed particular concern about state parties operating as tax havens and highlighted the use of shell companies in Mauritius and the Seychelles.

The conditions were ideal for the African Commission to adopt a country resolution and attach it to its report to the African Union. If the African Commission had adopted a country resolution or issued a formal communiqué or *note verbale* addressing the state parties, namely Mauritius and the Seychelles, it may have increased the likelihood of eliciting a response and reactions from both governments and the African Union. As it is, the press statement failed to receive either coverage by any major media house or a public response from the two states in word or deed. In their study on the implementation of findings of the African Commission, after looking at state responses to country resolutions, Murray and Long conclude that country resolutions served a quasi-protective function, carried significant political weight and had persuasive or moral force (Murray & Long 2015). They also suggest that the African Commission ought to use and refer to its own findings to consolidate their value and thereby advocate for better use of the findings – another unfortunate missed opportunity.

Implementation of the fiscal reporting requirements in the 2018 "State reporting guidelines"

Part III of the 2018 guidelines deals with the fiscal regulation of the extractives sector. States are required to provide detailed information on a range of fiscal issues, from the share of revenue generated through the extractives sector to standards generated for revenue-sharing arrangements. Notably, the following is required.

- Financial or tax incentives provided.
- Steps taken to address illicit financial flows through amendments to national tax laws and policies, rules on related party transactions, company

---

11. The "Paradise Papers" is a global investigation into the offshore activities of some of the world's most powerful people and companies undertaken by the International Consortium of Investigative Journalists. For more information on the Paradise Papers, see www.icij.org/investigations/paradise-papers.

laws and policies, banking laws and policies and laws and policies governing the financial services sector.
• Measures put in place to renegotiate agreements that limit the state's
ability to collect adequate revenue from commercial activities within the
extractives sector.
• Legislative, administrative and judicial measures put in place to combat
corruption in the extractive industries sector.
• The extent to which the state is involved in joint ventures and the tax
implications of such ventures.

The list of categories of information required under the heading of fiscal
regulation is both unique and detailed. If it is enforced, it could provide the
basis for more specific concluding observations regarding corrective action.

There are positive obligations for non-state actors on fiscal and transparency issues. To fulfil these reporting requirements, the state should implement a system to obtain information from the non-state actors operating
within its territory. The guidelines requires that non-state actors should:

• disclose the identities of owners, shareholders and local partners;
• fully declare profits they make from their operations in the host country;
• disclose financial terms of agreements relating to licence fees, national and
local taxes, custom duties, royalties and shares due to the government in
terms of the contract and applicable laws of the country; and
• adopt measures to comply with requirements against illicit financial flows.

My examination of the 16 state reports[12] that were submitted and the six
concluding observations[13] that were issued after the adoption of the 2018
guidelines reveals that none of the state parties followed the fiscal reporting guidelines. Seven of the reporting countries are listed on the Financial
Secrecy Index (FSI).[14] Five of them are listed on the Corporate Tax Haven
Index (CTHI).[15] Of greater importance, the African Commission's concluding observations did not impress upon state parties the need to comply

---

12. The periodic state reports are for The Gambia 2018, Egypt 2018, Botswana 2018, Lesotho
2018, Zimbabwe 2019, Niger 2019, Cameroon 2020, Mauritius 2020, Malawi 2020, Benin
2020, Namibia 2021, Kenya 2021, eSwatini 2021, Seychelles 2021, Mauritania 2022 and
Côte d'Ivoire 2022.
13. The African Commission adopted concluding observations in respect of Botswana, The
Gambia, Lesotho, Zimbabwe, Malawi and eSwatini.
14. The FSI ranks jurisdictions according to their secrecy and the scale of their offshore financial activities.
15. The CTHI ranks them in terms of those most complicit in helping multinational corporations underpay corporate income tax.

with the fiscal reporting requirements.[16] Nevertheless, state parties' representatives are often asked to ensure compliance with reporting guidelines
during public sessions. Consequently, the potential embarrassment during
the presentation of the periodic report is insufficient to ensure that delegates
will comply next time.[17]

Why did the African Commission miss these opportunities?

On the rationale behind these missed opportunities, we may conclude, on
the surface, that it can be attributed to the limited capacity and understanding within the African Commission, and with each state party's delegation.
Further, the state party's team may have had limited capacity in addressing
fiscal issues from a human rights lens in its report. As with other specialized
focus areas, establishing the necessary reporting systems takes time. In addition to time, it requires civil society organizations, working with the African
Commission, to promote the new guidelines and support states to develop
such systems.

However, the African Commission's reaction to state reports is the first step.
It is perplexing that the Commission failed to mention the non-compliance of
the periodic report with the 2018 guidelines, at the very least, referencing the
required list of information in the concluding observations. Furthermore, the
press statement on the "Paradise Papers" had a sound technical foundation
and made clear recommendations, dispelling any notion of limited capacity
and understanding within the African Commission in terms of engaging with
the state representatives from both Mauritius and the Seychelles.

Clearly, there must be another reason for this choice. Potential reasons
range from the possible capture of key members of the African Commission
by neoliberal networks to the fear of losing foreign investment.

Perhaps the South African experience offers insights into the potential
dynamics at play. South Africans are learning every day that during the liberation struggle we all fought together *against* a common enemy but, importantly, we did not all fight *for* the same outcome. For many, the goal was
to change the colour of wealth owners, while dealing with the underlying
inequality was not as important. On the other hand, many of us were involved

---

16. At the time of writing this chapter, the African Commission had not published the latest
concluding observations for Mauritius and Niger. The statement is based on the concluding
observations for Botswana, The Gambia, Lesotho, Zimbabwe, Malawi and eSwatini.

17. It is embarrassing as a fellow African to highlight that the concluding observations under
Article 21 were almost the same, word for word, for two countries: Zimbabwe and The
Gambia. That the Commission, through the WGEI, could abdicate its responsibility on
such an important part of its mandate defies any form of serious analysis.

in the liberation struggle to build an egalitarian society rooted within a social democratic order. That tension persists to this day in South Africa.

Similarly, at the African Commission, in the African Union and even within civil society, not all are working towards the same economic model. On the one hand, there is growing acceptance of the importance of the social solidarity economy in advancing the African Union's Agenda 2063 plan (ILO 2022c). However, on the other hand, there is another school of thought that so-called "brown" tax havens ought to be tolerated, perhaps even supported, but certainly not heavily criticized. Instead, the attack ought to be directed against the tax havens of the Global North. This approach plays into the hands of the neoliberal networks, to maintain rather than disrupt the status quo.[18] As with South Africa, we are all fighting against an unjust international economic order, but we are not necessarily all working towards the same notion of a just international economic order.

How could a special mechanism on human rights and illicit financial flows at the African Commission turn the tide?

A special mechanism at the African Commission with a special focus on the human rights dimensions of IFFs could elevate states' duty to work in solidarity with each other to curtail illicit financial flows as an obligation under international human rights law.

If the special mechanism is structured like other working groups, and supported by external experts, it could enhance the quality and weight of the interpretative tools. It could question state representatives in a more robust and engaging manner and prepare clear concluding observations to state parties on targeted steps that need to be taken. It could, moreover, actively engage with member states on the steps taken to address IFFs. Afterwards, state parties would have additional pressure to act. If this special mechanism kept abreast of developments and was adequately supported, it could also feed into the international efforts to develop international human rights norms and standards to address human rights dimensions of taxation, trade and investment and illicit financial flows as they evolve, including putting out general comments on Article 29(6) and advisory opinions on complex international law questions when there are competing norms, such as within the African Continental Free Trade regime and the African Charter or between

---

18. For example, the Center for Freedom and Prosperity (CF&P) rallied the Congressional Black Caucus in the United States under the administration of George W. Bush to challenge the OECD project on harmful tax competition. The CF&P argued that the hard-won sovereignty of small Caribbean states was being threatened by what it described as a cartel of rich Western states (Ring 2008).

bilateral investment treaties and the African Charter. Importantly, it could also contribute to the growth and support of the social solidarity economy in Africa.

Significantly, in 2022 the Commission adopted General Comment 7 on state obligations under the African Charter, in the context of the private provision of social services (ACHPR 2022). This process was led by the Working Group on Social, Economic and Cultural Rights and supported by civil society organizations and a team of activists and experts. General Comment 7 is geared to reversing the trend towards the privatization of public services such as healthcare and education. In the past, human rights practitioners focused on the state's obligation to allocate adequate resources towards social services. However, General Comment 7 expands that lens to include the state obligation to mobilize resources, and includes fair and progressive taxation and the elimination of illicit financial flows, corruption, tax evasion and tax avoidance (ACHPR 2022). Although this is a great leap forward in norm elaboration, it is unfortunate that the reporting guidelines at the end of the general comment revert to the focus only on the allocation of resources and do not include the mobilization of resources. Nevertheless, the next step is to ensure that these norms are made known and enforced, at first by the African Commission itself, but also by civil society organizations in their advocacy and litigation.

Similarly, in addition to developing new norms, a special mechanism on illicit financial flows and human rights, or perhaps a special mechanism on a Rights-Based Economy, could take responsibility for ensuring that the African Commission uses, refers to and advocates for the use of its findings on the state's obligation to eliminate IFFs and the obligation to construct a Rights-Based Economy.

CONCLUSION

To correct the paradox of scarcity in the midst of abundance, African states can do very little alone, but together they can certainly achieve much. African values form the basis of the body of peoples' rights, bolstered by the duty to pay tax contained in the African Charter. They are not just platitudes but create obligations on state parties to work together to eliminate all forms of foreign economic exploitation and enable their peoples to fully benefit from the advantages derived from their national resources.

The African Commission has elaborated upon Article 21 and its sub-articles on the right of peoples to dispose of their natural resources for their own benefit, and has concluded that this article creates obligations for both state parties and non-state actors to curtail IFFs. It has also alluded to the obligations that arise from the duty to pay tax on states, individuals and corporations, under Article 29(6). However, the African Commission needs to deepen its efforts into developing a normative framework for a human-rights-based response to illicit financial flows.

States and corporations took concrete, deliberate and conscious action to develop the system that gave rise to and currently facilitates IFFs. It will similarly take concrete, deliberate and conscious action by states, corporations, African Union organs and, importantly, the African Commission to transform the system that keeps Africa in a paradoxical state of poverty in the midst of plenty. It will take even more coordinated effort to build a new economic system based on principles of equity, founded in egalitarian values and sustained within a framework of African unity and solidarity.

State parties to the African Charter need to go back to basics and remember the reason behind the establishment of the regional human rights system. As the continent moves towards regional integration, a common market and perhaps a common currency, the fundamental tenets of solidarity and unity that gave rise to the pan-African project need to be revived to ensure that Africa and its people do indeed benefit from its vast resources and abundant wealth.

CHAPTER 9

SOCIAL AND SOLIDARITY ECONOMY AS AN ALTERNATIVE ECONOMY FOR THE PROTECTION OF HUMAN RIGHTS

Ilcheong Yi

INTRODUCTION

States are obligated to fulfil, protect and respect basic economic and social human rights and ensure equal enjoyment of these rights for all. Laissez-faire free-market-centred or neoliberal economic theories, models and policies negatively affect or sometimes violate these human rights, particularly those of women, racial and ethnic minorities and other economically marginalized groups. The impact of the neoliberal economic theories, models and policies adopted by national governments often crosses national borders, affecting human rights in other countries. This is considered strong evidence of the extraterritorial implications of national economic policies, models and policies for human rights.

In this chapter, alternative economies are understood as economic relations and activities that challenge, address or replace these negative consequences of economic relations and the actions of laissez-faire free market economics or neoliberalism. Their concepts, theories and models often diverge from those of mainstream neoclassical economics, on which laissez-faire free-market-based or neoliberal economies, such as market equilibrium, rationality and methodological individualism, are founded.

The interest of policy-makers, activists and scholars in alternative economies is growing more than ever, because of the incapability of current economic systems to prevent and address crises such as climate change and the extraordinarily high levels of inequality. Search for viable alternative economies guaranteeing human rights is one of the most urgent tasks, since unexpected challenges such as Covid-19 and the Russo-Ukrainian war have exacerbated the degree of inequality and increased negative social and economic impacts, especially as politicians with a fascist leaning mobilize those who feel injustice in the current economic and social systems to attack democratic institutions and shape economic relations (Watkins & Seidelman 2019).

In this regard, it is key to address the following questions. What are alternative economies viable, egalitarian and ecologically sound enough to address the negative consequences of a laissez-faire free market? What concepts, theories and models underpin these alternative economies? Do these alternative economies have human rights concerns in their concepts, theories models and/or practices? If they do, in what sense are they human-rights-based economies?

Aiming to answer these questions, this chapter reviews diverse economic models and approaches considered alternatives to the current neoliberal laissez-faire market economy. The chapter explains alternative economies' conceptual and theoretical underpinnings, focusing on their differences from those with a foundation in the laissez-faire market economy. It elucidates potential implications for human rights. It focuses on the social and solidarity economy (SSE), since the SSE is one of the alternative economies officially recognized at local, national and global levels (ILO 2022b, 2022d; UNGA 2023b). The SSE encompasses various economic activities and relations, prioritizing social and often environmental objectives over profit motives. It organizes resource allocation and the exchange of goods and services around the principles of reciprocity and solidarity rather than those of price and competition. The SSE addresses the negative effects of markets. It has emerged as a countermovement of society to the tendency of capitalism to disembed the market from society and the environment. With an experimental methodology focusing on principles prioritized by diverse economies, this chapter explains alternative economies and elucidates their implications for human rights.

WHY AND HOW DOES NEOLIBERALISM NEGATIVELY AFFECT HUMAN RIGHTS?

A market economy is only one type of the various economies we come across daily. Different forms of organizations and institutions exist at diverse levels and sectors. They are not mutually exclusive but intermingled with each other to produce values. We can categorize these economies into four types of economies – at least, along the lines of the principles they prioritize. They are the principles of market, redistribution, reciprocity and ecology (Costanza *et al.* 1997; Laville 2010). The market principle consists of the supply and demand of goods and services, and a price system resulting from supply–demand dynamics should be the basis of exchange to meet our needs. Contracts based on rational individuals' agreement on mutual interests establish economic relations and facilitate economic activities.

Contemporary mainstream economies, their economic practices or their economics as conceptual and theoretical entirety are based on the principle of the market. Economies often categorized as neoliberal are also based on this principle of market underpinning specific relations between the state and the economy (Harvey 2005; Healy 2009). Neoliberalism, in particular its application to political economy, has several distinctive elements. From a human rights perspective, noteworthy elements are privatization, financialization, deregulation, marketization, anti-union sentiment and legislation, and negative externalities for the natural environment. These distinctive elements affect human rights in negative ways.

Privatization can be defined as various "modalities for for-profit organizations that provide (public) services or are involved in significant activities in service provision ... including multinational and national enterprises and public companies with a significant proportion of shares owned by private investors" (Special rapporteur on the human rights to safe drinking water and sanitation 2020: 2). The for-profit sector's provision of public goods and services has a high risk of violating human rights. The for-profit sector might attempt to extract the maximum net gains from the provision of services and goods by either reducing costs or raising revenues, or both, which are more likely to undermine service quality and expansion. When a for-profit company is a single operator in the provision of a service or goods in a sector, which is common in the privatized provision of public services, the regulatory bodies are more likely to be captured by that single operator too. As a result of the lack of technical expertise, accurate information and financial strength, public authorities are less likely to negotiate favourable user conditions or succeed in complex and prolonged litigation when conflict arises (Special rapporteur on the human rights to safe drinking water and sanitation 2020). In many cases, in particular in the water and sanitation sector, investment funds buy shares or have full ownership of companies providing services, which results in a high risk of financial interests' neglect of human rights to water and sanitation (Special rapporteur on the human rights to safe drinking water and sanitation 2020). For-profit organizations operating with the market principle treat public goods and services as economic goods based on supply and demand and price-setting principles, which tend to fail to provide equitable and affordable access for people, particularly vulnerable groups of people, to public services.

As a key element of neoliberalism, deregulation also has a high risk of violating human rights, such as the right to decent work and the right of access to various public services in sectors such as transportation, housing, telecommunication, energy and finance sectors. Deregulation has long been used as a norm to legitimize poor business practices on health, safety and the well-being of workers and, often, users of goods and services (Human Rights Watch 2019b; Nadj 2019). The abolition or weakening of regulations and regulatory bodies, as well as the relaxation or shift to a more flexible interpretation of standards, allow free hands for the for-profit sector to seek maximization of profits by reducing costs – sometimes the costs needed to ensure health and safety.

The anti-union sentiments, legislations and policies of neoliberalism have also been accompanied by the proliferation of low-paid and insecure employment in the context of the flexible labour market. Consistently, high levels of incidents of killings and other attacks against trade unionists are closely related to these anti-union sentiments, legislations and policies of neoliberalism (UN OHCHR 2022). Neoliberalism strengthens employers' power through its increased capacity to move jobs and investments globally. Within the neoliberal policy framework, for-profit companies often abandon their responsibility for fair wages and working conditions in expanded value chains or increase the pool of unemployed and underemployed workers in a flexible labour market (Luce 2014).

ALTERNATIVE ECONOMIES AND HUMAN RIGHTS

Alternative economies are those economies prioritizing principles other than market principles: principles of redistribution, reciprocity and ecology. They have different understandings and practices from those of an economy prioritizing market principles on various issues, relations and activities of political economy. Likewise, discrepancies rely upon what is produced, whom and what services and goods are produced for, how services and goods are produced and how services and goods are consumed. The principles of alternative economies mentioned above can be outlined as follows.

The principle of redistribution is about allocation by an authority, be it the state or monarch, of what is produced through various rules of collection and use of resources. Obligation and compliance with the authority's redistributive decisions are the key constituents of this principle. Although policies and systems based on the principle of redistribution vary, ranging from land reforms using confiscation to welfare states, they share an emphasis on the "social dimension of wealth creation and the need for strong collective action to protect individual citizens from the vicissitudes of the market" (Jackson 2008)

The principle of reciprocity prioritizes relations established between groups or persons through actions creating reciprocal social links or solidarity. The prioritized relations by this principle are emerging among people rather than given by authority. They are based on harmony rather than competition over recognition and power (Laville 2010). Various forms of economic organizations and activities, such as the SSE, solidarity economy and popular economy, are based on this principle.

The principle of ecology prioritizes resource allocation that adequately accounts for protecting the stock of natural capital. All economic activities should not exceed the sustainable carrying capacity of the Earth. A fair distribution of resources and opportunities between present and future generations, as well as among groups within the present generation, should be achieved by economic policies and institutions prioritizing the principle of ecology (Costanza *et al.* 1997). Such concepts and practices as degrowth, post-growth and the circular economy are the kinds affiliated with this principle.

These alternative economies share some features. First, all contend for *re-embedding economy into larger contexts*, such as institutions, society and physical, biological and ecological contexts (Polanyi 1944; Boulding 1966; Titmuss 2019; Laville 2010). For instance, the economy prioritizing the principle of redistribution (and its material forms of the welfare state and social policy) is also an attempt to re-embed market capitalism in collective norms determined by representative democracy (Laville 2023a).

Second, all these economies challenge key concepts of the measurement units of economic activities, such as gross domestic product (GDP) and other national income accounting measures. Economies prioritizing market principles tend to use GDP or measurement units focusing on monetary transactions as a basic unit. In contrast, economies prioritizing ecology and reciprocity criticize measurement units focusing on monetary transactions, since they overweight market transactions, understating resource depletion and the importance of well-being, omitting pollution damage and failing to consider social as well as economic values created by various relations and activities of human (Costanza *et al.* 1997). Recently, for instance, economists have expressed their concern about GDP as an imperfect measure of well-being and started to develop measurement units for non-market factors such as the value of leisure, health and home production – such as care – as well as the negative by-products of economic activities: pollution and inequality (Bannister & Mourmouras 2017; UN Statistics Division 2020).

In the business sector, the concern about these economic measurement units has accelerated the development of non-financial reporting or sustainability reporting over the last four decades, often labelled "ESG reporting", as it focuses on environment, social and governance-related performance. However, the ESG indicators also have a bias towards financial materiality – i.e. measuring ESG factors only if they affect the financial conditions of companies (conceptualized as single materiality) rather than measuring the impact of the company's activities on broader sustainability issues (conceptualized as double materiality) (Yi *et al.* 2023).

Finally, all these economies are associated with a much broader concept of human rights. As the issue areas of human rights and development discourse and practice based on market fundamentalism or neoliberalism expand and converge with each other, these economies also begin to shape and clarify specific understandings, interpretations and positions on human rights issues and concepts (O'Manique 1992). For instance, the economy prioritizing market principles considers individuals' right to "claim autonomy and freedom in the face of government authority" more important than other rights (Laqueur & Rubin 1990: 61; O'Manique 1992). Further, neoliberal economic thinking – with its exclusive stress on market autonomy and reducing the state's regulatory power – tends to confine the discourses on human rights to rights associated with autonomy and freedom in the dimensions of consumption and flexible labour (Martins 2010).

Economies prioritizing other principles contrast with this reductionist stance on human rights. Economies prioritizing the principle of redistribution, specifically the welfare state as its manifestation, grant citizens human rights, insuring them against social risks or providing a safety net for the most disadvantaged.[1] The supply of goods and services in welfare states is based on the principle of redistribution from rich to poor and from the active to the inactive, which is laid down by public authority subject to democratic control (Laville 2010). The economy prioritizing the principle of reciprocity also favours rights to social security as being equal as other rights. Notably, the economy prioritizing the principle of reciprocity is closely associated with collective rights or rights of collectivities or minorities, such as Indigenous people's rights. An example of this collective rights approach is the right of Indigenous people to the "improvement of their economic and social conditions" (UNGA 2007: 9, art. 7) and the encouragement to the state to take effective measures and, when appropriate, special measures to ensure continuing improvement of their economic and social conditions, and provide opportunities and spaces for the establishment and growth of economic organizations, institutions and activities for and by Indigenous people, based on principles of reciprocity and solidarity among Indigenous community members.

---

1. The right to social security is recognized in numerous human rights instruments, including the Universal Declaration of Human Rights (Article 22), the International Covenant on Economic, Social and Cultural Rights (Articles 9 and 10), Article 11 of the Convention on the Elimination of All forms of Discrimination against Women, Article 26 of the Convention on the Rights of the Child, Article 27 of the International Convention on the Protection of the Rights of All Migrant Workers and Members of Their Families and Article 28 of the Convention on the Rights of Persons with Disabilities. See UN Economic and Social Council (2008).

The economy prioritizing the principle of ecology expands the boundary of rights from human rights to nature rights. This expansion understands human rights as a subset of nature rights and places the relationship between human and non-human nature at centre stage in the rights discourse (Challe 2021).

The SSE is one of the good examples of economic organizations, relations and activities with a human rights stance of protecting the most disadvantaged and centring collective rights and the right to nature.

HOW CAN THE SSE CONTRIBUTE TO PROTECTING AND REALIZING HUMAN RIGHTS?

Although there are various definitions and approaches highlighting the SSE values and principles, the recent International Labour Conference (ILO 2022d) and the UN General Assembly resolution on the SSE (UNGA 2023b) provide a clear and comprehensive definition of the SSE based on a set of values and principles, as follows:

> The social and solidarity economy encompasses enterprises, organizations and other entities that are engaged in economic, social, and environmental activities to serve the collective and/or general interest, which are based on the principles of voluntary cooperation and mutual aid, democratic and/or participatory governance, autonomy and independence, and the primacy of people and social purpose over capital in the distribution and use of surpluses and/or profits as well as assets. Social and solidarity economy entities aspire to long-term viability and sustainability, and to the transition from the informal to the formal economy and operate in all sectors of the economy. They put into practice a set of values which are intrinsic to their functioning and consistent with care for people and planet, equality and fairness, interdependence, self-governance, transparency and accountability, and the attainment of decent work and livelihoods. According to national circumstances, the social and solidarity economy includes cooperatives, associations, mutual societies, foundations, social enterprises, self-help groups and other entities operating in accordance with the values and principles of the SSE.
>
> (ILO 2022d; UNGA 2023)

The SSE's voluntary cooperation and mutual aid principles are, in fact, a more detailed explanation of the principle of reciprocity. This alternative

125

economic primacy of people and social purpose over capital in the distribution and use of surpluses and/or profits, as well as assets, points to its
allegiance to the principle of redistribution at the organizational level. The
SSE aspiration for long-term viability and sustainability and values consistent
with care for the planet and people shows an affinity with the economy prioritizing the principle of ecology.

How, then, can the SSE contribute to protecting and realizing human
rights? I now review the contribution of the SSE to human rights, with a focus
on key issues and groups associated with the following core international
human rights instruments: the International Convention on the Elimination
of All Forms of Racial Discrimination (CERD); the International Covenant on
Civil and Political Rights (CCPR); the International Covenant on Economic,
Social and Cultural Rights (CESCR); the Convention on the Elimination of All
Forms of Discrimination against Women (CEDAW); the Convention on the
Rights of the Child (CRC); the International Convention on the Protection
of the Rights of All Migrant Workers and Members of Their Families (often
called the Migrant Workers Convention: MWC); and the Convention on the
Rights of Persons with Disabilities (CRPD).

The first generation of neoliberalism, such as that of Friedrich Hayek,
centres on the primacy of competition in market society and limiting democracy. Social purpose capitalism or social business initiatives – the latest
version of neoliberalism, albeit with different weights – are also based upon
various kinds of neoliberalism. This is the neoliberal version of the solidar-
istic argument that social business seeks to or can reduce or eliminate poverty somehow through shifting responsibility from the public sector to the
for-profit sector or the financialization of the public service. In this sense,
the neoliberal version of solidarity or reciprocity is about benevolence and
solicitude at best – which is also commendable, of course.

However, solidarity – one of the principles underpinning the SSE – relies
upon equality (the so-called political and social solidarity) instead of benevolence and solicitude (the so-called philanthropic solidarity). And equality
is the cross-cutting principle of human rights. Solidarity is drawn from the
political and cultural tradition of associationalism and its demand for democratization, which is predominant in the SSE community. Political and social
solidarity based on equal rights or democracy is against discrimination in
all forms.

Neoliberalism has dismantled or weakened institutions and policies regulating markets. They include those institutions and policies to: (a) prevent
the use of the assets of commercial banks for speculative activities, (b) regulate financial markets (and/or financial markets' innovations, such as hedge
funds, derivatives, financial futures, swaps, etc.) and (c) regulate interest rates
to prevent the emergence of excessively large financial institutions.

Governments adhering to neoliberal ideas have also established policies and institutions to facilitate financial markets. They include measures for bailing out financial institutions and replacing illiquid assets with liquid assets funded by government budget. Cyclical crises stemmed from these measures and policies, including the deliberate weakening of legislative changes or the removal of regulatory mechanisms for risky financial products. Likewise, the failure to extend government oversight of the private sector has created serious challenges for the realization of human rights (Heintz & Balakrishnan 2014).

The SSE is an economic approach with a strong focus on the political and social dimensions of economic activities and realities such as democracy and solidarity. It seeks systemic change, social transformation and political engagement at multiple levels of governance. The SSE promotes the replacement, or at least addresses the negative consequences, of neoliberalism (Hillenkamp & Wanderley 2015; Laville 2023a). Its economic activities are designed to respond to the needs of the community, its people and its land (territory). Rooted at the grassroots level and local economy, SSE organizations are more resilient than for-profit enterprises of similar size. This resilience ultimately contributes to reducing instability (or crisis), preventing financialization of the economy and protecting human rights from the vagaries of economic crises (Marcuello, Errasti & Bretos 2023). Solidarity finance, which is one of the SSE forms, such as micro-credit, concessionary lending, barter and complementary currencies, is still small in terms of its scale compared to the neoliberal finance mechanisms. However, it is continuously growing, and it contributes to financially empowering and protecting vulnerable groups (Jenkins *et al.* 2021).

Economic activities of the SSE are particularly concerned with marginalized and vulnerable groups of people, including women, children, ethnic minorities, Indigenous people and persons with disabilities. Despite the recommendations of various international human rights treaties that governments must create the "enabling conditions" for substantive equality in various dimensions including the economic dimension, women and those of other vulnerable groups are still affected disproportionately by the negative impacts or crises caused by neoliberalism (Donald *et al.* 2020). The SSE can significantly contribute to creating enabling conditions for substantive equality for those of vulnerable groups, particularly women at the grassroots level. In fact, some of the key players in the development of the SSE in its initial period were women, particularly Black women who ran small businesses or mutual aid organizations in Chile and the United States (Laville 2023a). These organizations were often combined with social movements protesting against exclusion from the political sphere (Gordon-Nembhard & Ajowa Nzinga 2023; Austin & Wright 2023). As the SSE movement grows in terms of size and power, women's role in the SSE becomes more crucial, which contributes to challenging and addressing the discrimination against women. In the Global North, ethnic minority women and Black women who have been and still are over-represented in low-paid job and stuck in a permanent situation of in-work poverty established and joined SSE organizations such as community-based economic and welfare organizations (Yi & Bruelisauer 2020).

In developing countries where the informal economy is more prevalent, women, particularly poor women, organize themselves in various types of SSE organizations, such as cooperatives and women's self-help groups. They reclaim their due share by enhancing their security, autonomy and self-confidence. Empowered women, improved women's and children's health and well-being and political mobilization contribute to rebalancing the power asymmetry between women and men in these countries (Christabell 2023).

The so-called post-welfare-state social model is another form of neo-liberalism. This model transfers the function of the public sector's service provision to the private sector through public sector contracts with the private sector (Baeten, Berg & Lund Hansen 2015). It is often accompanied by austerity. The SSE has an opportunity to transform this post-welfare-state social model into a much more transformative welfare state model.

Concerning marginalized and vulnerable groups, SSE organizations and enterprises (SSEOEs) can change the nature of the post-welfare-state model by filling the big gap left by the post-welfare-state model, particularly those workers in the informal economy who are excluded from social policy and labour market regulations (Utting 2023).

SSEOEs rooted in a local context can provide local social services that are tailored to the community's needs. They can create a new institutional arrangement that addresses government failures or bureaucratic problems in the conventional welfare state or social policy (Elsen 2023). SSE's prioritized principle of reciprocity implies that people in need are not just defined as social service users and receivers of social support, but active agents – if they are willing – with an opportunity to participate actively in a meaningful way as co-producers of solutions. Therefore, SSEOEs tend to facilitate empowerment, promote the participation of social service users and create opportunities for improving self-determination, which provides a fundamental basis for protecting human rights (Elsen 2023).

Not all SSEOEs claim to be an alternative to social policy, but they do argue for a socially productive culture of active and formative local social policy, requiring social acceptance and support (Elsen 2023). An exemplary case for this argument is SSE organizations involved in Rwanda's community-based mutual health insurance schemes. In this system, promoted and supported by the state at the national level, SSE organizations have played a significant role in moving towards universal health coverage (Yi 2023). However, SSEOEs also pose a risk in the context of the post-welfare-state model. As the dependence of SSEOEs on public funding and its neoliberal standards, criteria and principles, such as those of efficiency and competition, grows, SSEOEs run the risk of isomorphism and co-optation by neoliberal ideas and practices (Yi 2023). Legal protection of SSEOEs from the market and the state itself is central to avoiding isomorphism and co-optation. The co-construction of legislation that fully involves SSE stakeholders and movements is more likely to generate this legal protection (Jenkins *et al.* 2021).

SSEOEs and their members (particularly the informal workers), whether at the national or subnational level, can address such issues beyond the typical issue area of trade unions covering formal workers. When they make a partnership with unions, one of the main institutions to address inequality and create a more just economy, their contribution to the improvement of various aspects of human rights can be significant. They include but are not limited to freedom of association and the effective recognition of the right to collective bargaining; the elimination of all forms of forced or compulsory labour; the effective abolition of child labour; and the elimination of discrimination in respect of employment and occupation, such as discrimination against migrants (ILO 2022a).

The SSE can help to build a broader social movement that fights for the realization of human rights. It can contribute to extending a cross-national supply chain based on solidarity and global social movements, including women's organizations, consumer groups, Global North–South coalitions and unions, which can protect both unionized and non-unionized (in most cases vulnerable) workers (Luce 2014).

The SSE and the economies prioritizing the principle of ecology, which involves systemic thinking and concerns about the economy's impact on life on our planet, are complementary. Both propose an alternative way to manage natural resources sustainably in local contexts (Šimleša 2023). A strong critique of the growth paradigm by economies prioritizing the principle of ecology came from their emphasis on the rise in equality, human potentials and life satisfaction instead of the rise in material outputs and resource flow. These elements emphasized by the economies prioritizing the principle of ecology are closely related to the SSE's concerns with solidarity-based equality, empowerment of the vulnerable and marginalized groups and meeting the needs of people and community. Further, both the SSE and the economies prioritizing the principle of ecology have elective affinities in goals, their world perspective and operational norms and practices. Re-embedding the economy in a larger system (economy embedded in society in the case of the SSE and society embedded in nature in the case of the economies prioritizing the principle of ecology), the pursuit of wider and deep transformation and concern for the vulnerable and marginalized groups of society are common features of both economies that provide a strong framework for the protection of human rights within and beyond social and economic areas and the rights of nature.

CONCLUSION

Although the principles prioritized by alternative economies vary, such as principles of redistribution, ecology and/or reciprocity, all of these economies have a similar stance on human rights. They understand human rights in a much wider context and protect and promote them in multiple sectors. The SSE, one of the alternative economic approaches embodying these three principles, offers a viable economic approach that can address various human rights issues such as poverty, equality, social service, gender and labour.

However, making the SSE a mainstream economic approach faces many challenges, such as lack of finance and legal protection. One critical challenge it faces is that the SSE is still largely unknown to many. Being mostly locally rooted and small in size, the benefits and impacts of the SSE on various aspects of development, including human rights, are not well known beyond the communities in which it operates. This leads to a lack of support for and promotion of the SSE at the policy level in many countries. However, as of 2022 more than 20 counties have already established laws for the SSE (ILO 2022a). Likewise, the International Labour Conference passed a recommendation on the SSE as a key instrument to address issues related to decent work in 2022 (ILO 2022d). And in April 2023 the UN General Assembly adopted Resolution 77/281 on the SSE entitled "Promoting the social and solidarity economy for sustainable development" (UNGA 2023b). All of these actions contribute to raising awareness and improving the environment for the spread of the SSE.

According to the United Nations secretary-general's report on "Cooperatives in social development" (UNGA 2021b), the SSE contributes about 7 per cent to the world's GDP. The share of GDP cannot capture the impact of SSE as a whole because of its significant impacts, which mostly cannot be measured by conventional measurement tools developed for market economies. Nevertheless, using it as a proxy, we may be able to say, when the share reaches a level similar to that of the market economy, that we then have a better environment for the promotion, protection and fulfillment of human rights.

CHAPTER 10

JUDICIAL ENFORCEMENT OF SOCIO-ECONOMIC RIGHTS AS A WAY TO CHALLENGE NEOLIBERALISM: POST-2008 AUSTERITY IN EUROPE

Kári Hólmar Ragnarsson

INTRODUCTION

Courts are often viewed as operating in the field of the legal, as opposed to the political or the economic. Yet we know, of course, that such distinctions are ultimately difficult to maintain. Markets and economic power are products of, and shaped by, law. The question of the role of courts in political economy is an unavoidable one, since the issue at hand is not whether to exert public power through the law to impact the economy but, rather, how to do so (Klare 1989: 17–18). This chapter explores that question in the context of the possibility of challenging the dominant neoliberal model through socio-economic rights adjudication,[1] looking to build on experience following the 2008 financial crisis.

In the aftermath of the crisis, international financial institutions and other market actors often demanded that states implement austerity measures, and courts rarely struck such measures down as human rights violations. In many cases socio-economic rights were interpreted as conforming to neoliberal rationality, as courts accepted trade-offs to serve financial market considerations. This interpretation was linked to the traditional view that courts should defer to other branches of the state on social and economic issues. This chapter argues that this view should be revised in our political-economic context.

---

1. The term "socio-economic rights" is used here to indicate those rights protected in the International Covenant on Economic, Social and Cultural Rights (hereafter ICESCR). In this chapter examples of socio-economic rights adjudication also include cases in which socio-economic rights are adjudicated indirectly – i.e. through the application of other rights or principles, such as non-discrimination, solidarity or dignity.

As public finances have become marketized, deference to legislatures amounts to deference to markets. In the light of severe representation failures when legislatures become tools of market justice, we might, subject to various caveats, view a more active judicial role as a potential counterweight in favour of social justice. Drawing on post-2008 case law, the chapter sketches the mechanisms by which judicial enforcement of socio-economic rights could challenge neoliberalism, namely by immunizing certain social goods from market logic[2] or disrupting policy-making processes that are overly responsive to markets.

The chapter begins by clarifying the understanding of neoliberalism. Although the term has many applications, the focus here is on two key tenets. First, there is the *encasement of the economy*, meaning the distancing of economic policy-making from democratic control; and, second, there is *economization*, meaning the expansion of market logic to ever more aspects of social life. Following this, the chapter addresses the role of courts, explaining how adjudication often legitimizes neoliberal rationality, but argues that, in fact, courts have good reasons to scrutinize social and economic policy implemented through neoliberal processes. Whether the adjudication of socio-economic rights translates into a challenge to neoliberalism depends on the approach taken by courts. The subsequent section presents how we can think about adjudication challenging the encasement of the economy through *destabilization*, by disrupting policy-making processes that are captive to market logic and replacing them with other processes. Adjudication also has the potential to contest economization through *decommodification*, by immunizing certain social goods from market-based trade-offs. The next section places the abstract analysis in context through examples from post-2008 austerity cases. I conclude by noting that we should certainly not expect adjudication to be the primary tool of a shift towards a Rights-Based Economy. Nonetheless, adjudication may create openings in an otherwise unresponsive system to mobilize towards transformation.

TWO KEY TENETS OF NEOLIBERALISM

This section focuses on two aspects of neoliberalism – encasing the economy and economization – whatever else one might think about the term.

Encasing the economy is the neoliberal idea that the functioning of the economy, the operations of capital-friendly markets, the flow of capital and the accumulation of wealth, among others, should be protected (encased)

---

2. For an analysis of the harmful effects of economization in healthcare, see Chapter 11 in this volume.

from the reach of democratic institutions (Slobodian 2019). Attempts by democratic institutions to influence the economy are treated as market distortions. Capturing the point, Milton Friedman stated in a 1988 interview: "I believe a relatively free economy is a necessary condition for freedom. But there is evidence that a democratic society, once established, destroys a free economy" (cited in Slobodian 2019). In his essay "The containment of power and the dethronement of politics", Friedrich Hayek (1993 [1978]: 150–1) speaks of the need to "protect democracy against itself", as democratic politics carry the risk of economic redistribution. For the ordoliberals, such as Walter Eucken, democracy unleashes "the demonic powers of peoples", as the masses demand "interventionism", leading "to the reverse of what they had sought: weakening of the state and disorganization of the economy" (Eucken 2017 [1937]: 67). This line of thinking formed the basis for the ordoliberals' emphasis on a strong technocratic state.

After 2008 the encasement of the economy, in the context of socio-economic rights, was displayed most obviously by the influence of supranational institutions such as the European Union, the International Monetary Fund and the World Bank (Clifton, Diaz-Fuentes & Lara Gómez 2018), independent central banks (Braude *et al.* 2013), the requirements of constitutional balanced budget rules (Biebricher 2018) and expressly technocratic governments, such as Mario Monti's government in Italy (Mair 2013). Less obvious but just as important, there is a de facto shifting of the locus of decision-making to financial markets (Roos 2019).

Economization as used here refers to the application of market-based logic to more and more aspects of life, previously treated as "the social" or "the political" (Brown 2015: 30–5).[3] Wendy Brown builds on Michel Foucault's (2004 [1979]) early analysis of neoliberalism as a mode of normative reason that constructs people as *Homo oeconomicus*; all activities are conceived as market activities, even when money is not strictly speaking involved. Neoliberal relationality constructs each of us as an entrepreneur of the self, as bits of human capital. Others refer to the logic of neoliberalism as "market fundamentalism, that is the belief that all areas of politics, society, culture and knowledge, and not just economics, should succumb to and be ordered by market logic" (Nolan 2014: 1; see also Stiglitz 2009 and Crouch 2011). Similarly, David Harvey (2005: 3) writes that neoliberalism "holds that social good will be maximized by maximizing the reach and frequency of market transactions, and it seeks to bring all human action into the domain of the

---

3. Similarly, the term "economization" has been used in economic sociology to identify "processes that constitute the behaviours, organizations, institutions and, more generally, the objects in a particular society which are tentatively and often controversially qualified, by scholars and/or lay people, 'economic'" (Çalışkan & Callon 2009: 70).

market". However, for Harvey (2005: 9), existing neoliberalism is, above and beyond this utopian vision of welfare maximization, a class-based project to cement the power of economic elites. This means that, in specific contexts when marketization would not serve the interests of this economic elite, no marketization takes place.

In the context of the post-2008 rolling back of socio-economic guarantees, economization appeared in the emphasis on financial markets as sites of "veridiction", in Foucault's terms (Brown 2015: 67). The market is the truth. When actors on the sovereign debt market, or supranational institutions working to assist countries re-entering that market, have a policy preference – communicated through price signals in the purest form of the model, but also more crudely through lobbyism, rule-making (deficit caps, etc.) or other forms – that preference should be acted on and, within this logic, socio-economic rights are to be traded away for market gain.

THE ROLE OF COURTS

It is often claimed in human rights literature that "neoliberalism as a doctrine is hostile to socioeconomic rights at a foundational level" (Wills & Warwick 2016: 633). Even so, it is far less clear that courts will interpret and apply socio-economic rights to challenge neoliberalism (O'Connell 2011). Rather than claiming that human rights *are* in opposition to neoliberalism (MacNaughton, Frey & Porter 2018) or, alternatively, aligned with it (Whyte 2019), it is necessary to identify *how* rights adjudication interacts with neoliberal processes. It will become evident that the involvement of courts does not have a predetermined effect. The impact depends not only on the wider context but on the different approaches courts may take. This section highlights examples of courts' non-challenging, or neoliberal-conforming, approaches, mostly from the context of post-2008 austerity, and question the assumptions regarding the proper role of courts that underlie these decisions.

In this non-challenging mode, courts interpret rights as readily subject to trade-offs based on economic reasoning. Sometimes courts not only fail to challenge neoliberalism but also legitimize neoliberal processes. The European Court of Human Rights (ECtHR) has accepted "protecting the public purse" as a legitimate aim to restrict rights (see *Krajnc v Slovenia* [2017]). The Canadian Supreme Court has highlighted the importance of a good credit rating in the context of justifying discrimination (*Newfoundland (Treasury Board) v N.A.P.E.* [2004], para. 75). The Irish High Court has stated that, in the aftermath of 2008, "the welfare of the entire citizenry is hugely dependent on the capacity of the State to be able to raise money without hindrance on international markets" (*Collins v Minister for Finance & Ors* [2013], para. 124) and held that austerity measures were "in the urgent national interest" (*McKenzie v Minister for Defence & Ors* [2010], para. 5.3).

Although such express openness to financial market concerns as justifications for restrictions of rights is not necessarily the rule, a related central theme in the post-2008 austerity case law in Europe is clear: courts tended to adopt an initial stance of deference to other branches of government. This holds true for courts in Ireland (Nolan 2009; O'Connell 2012), Iceland, Germany and France, and even in Latvia and Portugal, where courts did in fact strike down certain austerity measures (Ragnarsson 2019). The same applies at the regional level, as the ECtHR has granted a wide margin of appreciation in cases concerning austerity measures,[4] and this deferential approach to social and economic policy issues has travelled back to national courts, including the United Kingdom's Supreme Court.[5]

Standard arguments in favour of judicial deference to other branches and concerns of judicial overreach focus on a perceived lack of legitimacy and institutional capacity on the part of courts as non-representative bodies (Neier 2015; Landau 2010; Waldron 2006; see also the summary in King 2012: 3–8). These concerns have been incorporated into socio-economic rights doctrine through an emphasis on judicial restraint. For example, the Optional Protocol to the ICESCR includes a "reasonableness" standard, whereby states "may adopt a range of possible policy measures" (UNGA 2009).

Neoliberalism should cause us to question these arguments. The legitimacy concerns in particular rest on assumptions about the quality and responsiveness of the democratic process in comparison to the judiciary (Waldron 2006). The emergence of marketized state finance in the neoliberal era has undermined these assumptions. Wolfgang Streeck's (2017 [2014]) stylized model of thinking about the neoliberal state may assist in identifying the issue. Streeck argues that the modern state serves two constituencies: the *Staatsvolk* (the people of the state: the citizenry, voters), exercising influence through politics and voting; and the *Marktvolk* (the people of the market: creditors, investors, international bondholders), exercising influence through financing (or not) the state through debt instruments (Streeck 2017 [2014]: 84). The *Staatsvolk* of course also finance the state, through taxes, but Streeck emphasizes that in the neoliberal era the best

---

4. See *Koufaki & ADEDY v Greece* [2013], *Mateus & Januário v Portugal* [2013], *Da Silva Carvalho Rico v Portugal* [2015], *Mihăieş & Senteş v Romania* [2011], *Sulcs v Latvia* [2011] and *Mockienė v Lithuania* [2017].

5. *R (on the application of DA and others) v Secretary of State for Work and Pensions* [2019].

off have successfully resisted steep progressive taxation while the importance of debt has multiplied, describing this as a historic shift from the "tax state" to the "debt state". The state must maintain the loyalty of its voters/taxpayers while not losing "investor confidence". Neoliberal processes entail that the balance shifts in favour of the *Marktvolk*. By encasing the economy, decisions are made at the level of international financial markets. And, as fiscal policy has become marketized through public debt, then decisions on, for example, taxing and spending on social welfare programmes are economized – that is, designed on the basis of how they might be received by financial market actors and the impact they may have on yields in public debt markets.

An illustrative example of the dynamics between the state and investors is the 2022 tax reform in Colombia. The reform raises various taxes to fund an increase in social spending (Fitch Ratings 2022). It was designed to maintain investor confidence by avoiding deficits and maintaining full debt service. In a stylized version, the tax reform managed internal *Staatsvolk* tensions without involving the *Marktvolk*; the state's options were limited by what the *Marktvolk* would accept. Politicians respond to the market not (necessarily) out of self-interest or ideology but, rather, in response to these neoliberal processes and real or perceived economic necessity, revealing a structural representation failure.

Meanwhile, courts' independence provides (comparative) freedom from responding to market forces. Unlike the legislative and executive branches, courts are not directly exposed to the market and its "people" when executing their tasks. Likewise, the courts' non-representative nature becomes an asset rather than a weakness. Because of the courts' detachment from the second constituency compared to legislators' over-responsiveness to markets, we look to courts for disruption of the status quo.

The marketization of public finance calls for an Ely-esque argument for judicial scrutiny. Just as John Hart Ely's (1980) theory emphasizes minorities' lack of access to the democratic process, the reality of marketized public debt supports robust judicial review. We can identify three distinct, but partly overlapping, underrepresented groups: first, the voting citizenry, whose influence over the state's institutions has been diluted; second, the beneficiaries of public services, impacted by the consolidation of state budgets arising from debt burdens or the demands of market confidence; and, third, future generations of citizens, who have to deal with the state's efforts of "buying time" when the next crisis hits.

Accordingly, courts have good reasons to scrutinize the actions of other branches of government, even with respect to social and economic policy. In this case, the next question is whether such adjudication can, in fact, challenge neoliberalism.

SOCIO-ECONOMIC RIGHTS ADJUDICATION AS A CHALLENGE TO NEOLIBERALISM

Above, I have noted how adjudication might legitimize neoliberalism by accepting economization as a frame for rights-based analysis, or, less starkly, by deferring to other branches that over-respond to financial market concerns. I now turn to the question of whether a different mode of adjudication is possible: which types of judicial enforcement of socio-economic rights, if any, challenge which aspects of neoliberalism?

As the chapter explains below, if neoliberalism encases the economy, a challenge must entail a disruption of this isolation, injecting democratic influence in non-responsive processes and institutions: *destabilization*. If neoliberalism means economization, whereby value judgements are made in market-based terms, a challenge disengages this process and actively removes certain goods, resources or spheres from the reach of market logic: *decommodification*.

A rights-based challenge to the encasement of the economy requires disrupting unresponsive institutional processes. If the equilibrium between the market and the social is unacceptably tilted in favour of the market, this equilibrium must be displaced, leading to a recalibration of the balance of power between the actors. The term I use for this theme, borrowed from Roberto Mangabeira Unger (2001 [1987]: 530–5), is "destabilization rights", which involve not the "unilateral imposition of a duty" to enforce a defined legal claim but opening areas of social practice to ordinary conflict.

The idea of socio-economic rights as destabilization rights has been explored by several authors (Young 2012; Liebenberg & Young 2015; Rodríguez-Garavito & Rodríguez-Franco 2015, Liebenberg 2019; Gerstenberg 2014), building on earlier work analysing public law litigation as enforcing destabilization rights (Sabel & Simon 2004). In this context, the role of courts is to "force new action and linkages to remove the institutional intransigence, incompetence, or inattentiveness that have led to the economic and social rights infringements" (Young 2012: 268). Katharine Young (2012: 167–91) characterizes the South African Constitutional Court as a "catalytic court", producing interaction between legislatures, governmental agencies, rights-holders, social movements, landlords, hospitals, and so on, rather than exercising judicial supremacy as traditionally understood. César Rodríguez-Garavito and Diana Rodríguez-Franco (2015: 21–3) characterize the decision of the Colombian Constitutional Court on internally displaced persons (IDPs) as an application of socio-economic rights as destabilization rights. The court took an expressly structural approach, declaring an "unconstitutional state of affairs" and ordering, among other things, the government to draft a policy to protect IDPs' rights and set deadlines for progress. More broadly, the authors argue that socio-economic rights litigation has proved most impactful when courts engage in "dialogic activism", meaning, among other things, that court-issued remedies set the broad goals for policy and include processes, deadlines and ongoing monitoring, but leave substance and details up to government agencies (Rodríguez-Garavito & Rodríguez-Franco 2015: 16). This mode of adjudication is closely aligned with the idea of destabilization rights (see Rodríguez-Garavito 2019).

In the context of a challenge to neoliberalism, and encasement of the economy in particular, courts' enforcement of socio-economic rights as destabilization rights would not entail a substantive solution – for example, prohibiting cuts to specific social programmes or ordering the provision of specified goods or services – but to "put in motion processes of contestation" (Young 2012: 269), forcing a shift in institutional procedures and thus interrupting the current state–market–people equilibrium of power. On this basis, destabilization might take the form of ordering new policy design, following improved, more inclusive, procedures, substantively guided by constitutional socio-economic rights, and ongoing monitoring, or revisiting by the court, of the implementation.

Decommodification focuses on substance rather than processes. As a challenge to neoliberalism, decommodification rights replace economization with non-market rationality, insisting that "certain things (goods and services) are so fundamental to human flourishing that they should be exempted from market rationality" (O'Connell 2018: 87). In Mangabeira Unger's (2001 [1987]: 524) terminology, such rights would be "immunity rights" protecting elements of "essential security", including "freedom from violence, coercion, subjugation and poverty", in order to provide people with the safety to be able to "participate actively and independently in collective decision making" (Mangabeira Unger 2001 [1987]: 525). Similarly, in Gøsta Esping-Andersen's (1990: 21–2) classic work on welfare states, the core of providing a service within the welfare state as a "right" ensures that "a person can maintain a livelihood without reliance on the market". An earlier classic, T. H. Marshall's 1949 articulation of social rights (Marshall 1992 [1950]: 42), refers to "a basic conflict between social rights and market value" as social rights grant a claim to "real income which is not proportionate to the market value of the claimant" (Marshall 1992 [1950]: 28), and "imply an invasion of contract by status, the subordination of market price to social justice, the replacement of free bargain by the declaration of rights" (40).

An understanding of socio-economic rights as decommodification rights challenges the economization associated with neoliberalism. A strong version of this position is expressed by Paul O'Connell (2018: 987), viewing this role of socio-economic rights as a potential "fundamental challenge" to capitalism on the basis that commodification and marketization are the core of the system.

In this mode, socio-economic rights act as a decoupling of market logic. In a simple version, decommodification requires that at least some level of essential goods – primary education, basic nutrition and healthcare, to name the obvious examples – are provided as a right, regardless of ability to pay and regardless of other economic considerations. The economization of (previously) public goods and services has been a key neoliberal development in the context of marketized fiscal policy and the associated state–people–market dynamic. Even when goods and services relevant to the enjoyment of socio-economic rights are not expressly marketized, such as through privatization, the broader field of fiscal policy is marketized by the reliance on sovereign debt markets. A logic of decommodification is, therefore, about making socio-economic rights immune to market logic and trade-offs by reference to market-based arguments.

POST-2008 AUSTERITY CASES AS FIRST STEPS

The previous section has described in abstract terms the potential function of socio-economic rights adjudication as enforcing destabilization rights or decommodification rights, challenging different aspects of neoliberalism. The next questions relate to how court practice fits with the abstract construct and which tools currently employed by courts might be developed further to approximate these functions. For this purpose, I look again at case law on post-2008 austerity in Europe.[6] Various challenges were mounted to austerity measures, and, as noted above, the overall picture is that courts rarely struck down such measures. Nonetheless, in the post-2008 case law, different approaches to the interpretation of rights and the role of courts can be identified as potential first steps towards adjudication as a challenge to neoliberalism.

As a first example, the Latvian Constitutional Court, in a 2009 decision, struck down reductions of pensions: a 10 per cent cut for old age pensions for unemployed pensioners and 70 per cent for those employed. The government argued, among other things, that because of bad credit ratings the state could not access financial market funding and needed to rely on financing from the European Union and the IMF, which, according to the government, required the disputed pension cuts. In deciding the case, using a proportionality framework, the court emphasized the lack

---

6. There is a rich practice of socio-economic rights adjudication in other parts of the world, not least in the Global South. It is more than likely that this practice offers clearer examples of adjudication challenging neoliberal practices than the European sample discussed here.

of quality of the decision-making process. Notwithstanding the legislature's discretion during times of economic hardship, the court found that insufficient care, consultation with social partners, assessment and review of alternatives had been carried out when the austerity measures were designed. The court also required the legislature to approve conditionalities attached to international loans, as opposed to simple negotiations between lenders and the executive (Latvijas Republikas Satversmes Tiesa [2009]: 48–51, paras. 13).

This emphasis on the process resonates with the idea of destabilizing decision-making structures that are unresponsive to democratic challenge. When processes are overly responsive to the demands of market actors and policy is made based on broad assertions of economic necessity, without input from civil society or other interested actors or groups, courts may interject to replace the equilibrium of power with different processes to ensure that excluded voices are heard. If trade-offs are to be made, courts applying a process-based approach may indicate that such trade-offs must be substantiated under a logic of rights, rather than purely the logic of the market. Importantly, courts do not, under this approach, impose a substantive outcome of what rights require in each case.

The second example from the post-2008 case law involves courts protecting "strong rights" (Tushnet 2009), in the sense that courts dismiss the government's economic justifications as irrelevant. A 2010 decision by the Romanian Constitutional Court's struck down a 15 per cent cut to pensions, holding that the right to pension in Article 47(2) of the constitution[7] gives rise to an "acquired right" based on the pensioners' social security contributions. This acquired right means that a person's pension should reflect the income level enjoyed while the person was economically active and making contributions. The Romanian constitution prevents the legislature from reducing pension payments, even temporarily, and the general limitations (proportionality) clause of Article 53 does not allow restrictions on active pensions (Curtea Constituțională a României [2010]).

From the broader catalogue of socio-economic rights adjudication, the best-known example of such strong protections is the Brazilian courts' healthcare adjudication. Courts issued individual remedies for the provision of medical treatments and medicine, rejecting any defences based on the state's resource constraints: "Between the protection of the inviolable rights

---

7. Constitution of Romania of 1991 (as subsequently amended) in its Article 47(2): "Citizens have the right to pensions, paid maternity leave, medical care in public health centres, unemployment benefits, and other forms of public or private social securities, as stipulated by the law. Citizens have the right to social assistance, according to the law." See www.cdep.ro/pls/dic/site.page?den=act1_2.

to life and health ... and the upholding ... of a financial and secondary interest of the State ... ethical-juridical reasons compel the judge to only one possible solution: that which furthers the respect of life and human health" (Supremo Tribunal Federal, Recurso Extraordinario no. 271.286-8 [2000], quoted in Ferraz 2011: 1658).

A key characteristic of this approach is to aim at socio-economic rights enforcement as decommodification rights, but not as destabilization rights. Courts dismiss any balancing of rights against economic arguments, immunizing the relevant social service or resource from market-based consideration.

Falling between these two categories of emphasizing process (Latvia) and protecting strong rights (Romania) are cases in which courts engage substantively with the economic justifications offered by governments as a *rationale* for restricting or not fulfilling socio-economic rights. Concrete examples from the post-2008 case law are not easy to pinpoint. However, the practices of the Portuguese Constitutional Court[8] and the European Committee of Social Rights (ECSR) are worth noting.

In 2013 the Portuguese court struck down cuts to the salaries and pensions of public employees, emphasizing that, despite the existence of a financial crisis, the economic objectives of the state do not automatically prevail over constitutional rights (Ruling no. 187/13 [2013]). In particular, the court held that the government's austerity measures placed a disproportionate burden on certain groups, specifically public employees, and that the government should have adopted an alternative route, namely by adjusting the tax system. The court thus engaged directly with the appropriateness of the fiscal policies choices of the government.

The ECSR also took, in some cases, a substantive position on the merits of fiscal policy choices. In a case concerning Greece decided in 2017, the ECSR firmly stated that the disputed austerity measures had failed to achieve their purpose. The ECSR found that the relevant economic indicators (unemployment, GDP, public debt levels) had worsened. Likewise, the various violations of socio-economic rights represented more than problems for individuals, as they "pose a challenge to the interests of the wider community and to the shared fundamental standards of all the Council of Europe's member states, namely those of human rights, democracy and the rule of law" (*General Confederation of Greek Workers (GSEE) v Greece* [2017], para. 250).

The examples from Portugal and the ECSR interject rights into the economic reasoning by the government – which is often grounded in the demands of international financial institutions (encasement of the economy) or price signals from financial markets and economic analysis (economization). As the

---

8. See Canotilho, Violante and Lanceiro (2015), De Almeida Ribeiro (2013) and Guerra Martins (2015).

emphasis is on the substance of policy, the aim is not set for destabilization but, rather, for a soft version of decommodification, as in principle, economic justifications are accepted as legitimate reasons for restrictions of rights. In fact, although the mentioned Portuguese and ECSR decisions revealed violations of rights, there are more examples from post-2008 case law when courts adopted a *prima facie* similar approach – that is, a proportionality or balancing assessment of limitations of rights – and held that the relevant austerity measures were justified (Kilpatrick 2017).

The three categories of examples from the post-2008 case law demonstrate that different judicial approaches to socio-economic rights adjudication may produce different variations of challenges to neoliberalism. A court can emphasize either destabilization or decommodification. The examples are, at best, small steps in any direction, but they demonstrate a potential that requires further exploration.

CONCLUSION

Analysing socio-economic rights adjudication and its relationship with neoliberalism provides a means of examining the larger theme of the role of courts in a shift towards a Rights-Based Economy. As a result of neoliberal processes encasing the economy and economizing social goods, traditional arguments to the effect that courts lack legitimacy when scrutinizing social and economic policy are unpersuasive. Adjudication may function to destabilize and reinvent decision-making processes or to decommodify basic necessities, immunizing them from market-based logic. The examples from post-2008 austerity case law in Europe can be interpreted as steps towards these adjudication functions. The cases indicate that courts may need to prioritize destabilization or decommodification by focusing either on process or on substance.

All judicial interventions, as well as non-interventions, carry institutional costs for courts, including in the sense of backlash from political elites, market actors, international institutions or the public. The relative merits of different approaches warrant further study concerning their effectiveness, legitimacy and robustness. However, it is clear that the role of socio-economic rights adjudication vis-à-vis neoliberalism is shaped by the details of courts' interaction with neoliberal processes. In this regard, many paths are open for innovation.

What is the value of such judicial innovations? Even if, as suggested here, some types of adjudication challenge neoliberalism, courts will hardly lead a paradigm economic shift. The partial examples of judicial challenges to neoliberalism discussed in this chapter have yet to yield obvious structural changes. However, through the mechanisms identified here, adjudication may create opportunities for mobilization towards new institutional arrangements or new moral or legal distinctions between market justice and social justice. In some contexts, adjudication may thus delegitimize neoliberalism and, by disrupting neoliberal processes, create openings for steps towards a Rights-Based Economy.

CHAPTER 11

HEALTH AND HUMAN RIGHTS: WHAT ARE THE LESSONS FROM THE COVID-19 PANDEMIC?

Jasmine Gideon and Kate Bayliss

INTRODUCTION

In 2018 the Astana Declaration was endorsed by all World Health Organization (WHO) member states, 40 years after the Alma Ata Declaration, which committed governments to provide "health for all". Although this was ostensibly a celebration of four decades of work promoting primary healthcare (PHC) and universal health provision, critics used it as a moment to reflect on how far the global health agenda has moved away from the commitment to social justice and the right to health that is at the core of the Alma Ata Declaration.

The debate around a universal provision in health is highly contested and open to diverse interpretations of universalism and the best way to implement and finance the universal health coverage (UHC) agenda (Yi, Koechlein & de Negri Filho 2017). Nevertheless, critics argue that UHC typically encourages systems with state-purchased services, provided either entirely by the private sector or by a mix of private and public providers. Such configurations encourage the participation of private, for-profit insurance corporations. Benefits packages purchased in these configurations generally utilize tiers for the poor and non-poor (Smithers & Waitzkin 2022: 1). For the People's Health Movement (PHM), a global movement of health activists, academics and civil society organizations, the Astana Declaration clearly articulated this shift. It became the "de facto international strategy for financing health services" (PHM 2022: 86).

Within this vision, governments are relegated to a regulatory and governing role.[1] Thus, if states are no longer tasked with financing healthcare

---

1. Although the Astana Declaration does not explicitly state that the financing for health services will be provided by the private sector, it is important to acknowledge the push for private finance to achieve the Sustainable Development Goals, including the rolling out of UHC programmes.

services, what does this mean for the right to health? As of 2022 171 state parties have signed up to the International Covenant on Economic, Social and Cultural Rights (ICESCR), which recognizes the right to health (UNGA 1966: art. 12). The right to the highest attainable standard of health is codified in numerous legally binding international and regional human rights treaties, and over 100 constitutions worldwide (Khosla, Allotey & Gruskin 2022). Furthermore, there is also a consensus on the importance of a holistic view of this right. Paul Hunt (2006: 604), former special rapporteur on the right to health, contends:

> The right to health … goes beyond health care to encompass the underlying determinants of health, such as safe drinking water, adequate sanitation and access to health-related information. The right includes freedoms, such as the right to be free from discrimination and involuntary medical treatment. It also includes entitlements, such as the right to essential primary health care.

Yet, despite the states' commitments to deliver on the right to health, significant gaps in provision and health inequalities persist, especially in many low-income countries. In 2019, in an assessment of progress towards UHC, the WHO estimated that only between 39 and 63 per cent of the global population will be covered by essential healthcare services by 2030 (PHM 2022: 87).

Healthcare systems are integral to the social determinants of health. Khosla, Allotey and Gruskin (2022) point out that allocating health services is an inherently political process. We argue that the embedding of neoliberal ideology in recent decades is more profound. Because of the expansion of the private sector and the increased individualism in understanding health outcomes, austerity has affected the right to health.

Furthermore, the current UN special rapporteur on health, Tlaleng Mofokeng, expresses concern that healthcare privatization will probably increase racialized disparities in accessing high-quality healthcare services (UNGA 2022b). Considerable research has already highlighted the gendered impacts of privatization in health (Gideon 2016). This is a serious concern because of the significant presence of the private sector in financing and delivering healthcare services.

The "real-world" implications of these deeply embedded inequalities in health systems were made highly visible by the Covid-19 pandemic. The gendered and racialized impacts of Covid-19 have been stark (Escalante & Maisonnave 2022; Wenham, Smith & Morgan 2020). Many public health services were ill resourced and unprepared to manage and control the pandemic. The growth of private provision has left systems fragmented. Peru proves that this was the case in much of Latin America (Gianella, Gideon &

Romero 2021). In sum, the long-term effects of the privatization of healthcare systems have eroded the first line of emergency public health response (PHM 2022).

As we argue in the chapter, despite the inequalities generated by private healthcare provision, international finance institutions (IFIs) and the WHO have reaffirmed their support for the private sector to finance and deliver healthcare services. Nevertheless, a counter-narrative has emerged. It pushes for more public finance and challenges the dominant narrative of neoliberalism, predominantly based on private finance. The agenda of the 2022 UN Inter-Agency Task Force on Financing for Development attests to it, setting out greater reliance on public finance (UN Inter-Agency Task Force on Financing for Development 2022). However, this counter-narrative has yet to gain sufficient traction to make a significant impact in challenging the role of private finance.

The first section of this chapter reflects on the reframing of UHC in the past few decades from an understanding of universal healthcare to one in which care has been replaced with coverage. We consider the growing role of private financing in implementing UHC policies, particularly promoted by the World Bank, and enquire into its implication for the right to health. Building on this, the second section focuses on the impact of Covid-19 on depleted health systems. The chapter questions whether the continued push for more private finance by the World Bank and other IFIs will allow states to effectively deliver "health for all" and address the devastating impact of the Covid-19 pandemic. We contend that, instead, considering the evidence for the private sector's inability to address health inequalities, increased public investment is necessary to ensure high-quality public health services for all.

FROM UNIVERSAL HEALTHCARE TO UNIVERSAL HEALTH COVERAGE: THE LINK TO NEOLIBERAL POLICY-MAKING?

Current understandings of UHC deviate significantly from the notion of "universal healthcare" that was a central tenet of advocates in the 1970s. In Latin America, for example, there was relatively widespread support for ideas around social justice and health. This was evident in the advancement of primary healthcare access in countries such as Cuba and Costa Rica (Vasquez, Perez-Brumer & Parker 2019). The 1978 Alma Ata Declaration provided international recognition of this push for social justice (Birn & Krementsov 2018). It asserted health as a universal human right, promoting a more active role for governments and international actors and organizations to address all health inequities. The Alma Ata Declaration promoted a broad approach to healthcare, with universal primary healthcare at the centre of a wider social justice agenda (Jensen, Kelly & Avendano 2022).

By the early 1980s "health for all" had become too vague and unattainable. It was soon replaced with more targeted approaches to PHC so that outcomes could be more easily evaluated (Jensen, Kelly & Avendano 2022). The WHO moved away from explicitly pursuing a political agenda pushing for health and health equity as part of a broader social justice agenda (Cueto 2004; Jensen, Kelly & Avendano 2022).

The 1980s and 1990s saw the widespread diffusion of neoliberalism, which celebrates the power of the market and reduces the state's role to regulator rather than one of direct responsibility for healthcare financing and provision. At the same time, based on neoclassical economics, neoliberalism considers the public sector inefficient and advocates for a more significant role for the private sector in delivering healthcare services. Asa Laurell (2016: 2) contends that "the neoliberal reform basically challenges the idea of health as a human and social right and moves toward its commercialization".

This period witnessed the rise of the World Bank as the most prominent actor in the field of international health policy (Ruger 2005). The Bank published two key documents that clearly laid out its neoliberal health agenda. In 1986 it published "Financing health services in developing countries: an agenda for reform" (World Bank 1986), underlining the need for improved healthcare financing and advocating the importance of user fees – arguably the most controversial aspect of neoliberal healthcare (James *et al.* 2006). The idea underpinning user fees was that individuals should contribute to healthcare since public spending was unsustainable and inefficient. In essence, the shift from an expansionary, publicly funded health system to a contractionary model based on user fees was a reversal of the policy on access to healthcare on the basis of need. Ideologically, by levying the sick to access services, the policy was a burden on the heavy users of care and a direct contradiction to the egalitarian tenets of solidarity and cross-subsidization (Mhazo & Maponga 2022: 5). The 1986 report also called for healthcare services to be financed by insurance schemes rather than general taxation to avoid the system subsidizing the wealthy.

With the publication seven years later of the *World Development Report* (WDR) subtitled *Investing in Health* (World Bank 1993), the Bank gained greater legitimacy in the health sector and explicitly promoted a greater role of the private sector in health. The 1993 WDR has been seen as "crystalizing the neoliberal 'turn' in health" (López Cabello 2021: 1336).

Although Chile had first initiated neoliberal health reforms in the early 1980s, following the publication of the 1993 WDR Latin America became a testing ground for neoliberal health reforms. In the subsequent two decades most countries in the region implemented health sector reforms guided by the World Bank's neoliberal model (Laurell 2016). Even so, in Chile, most of the population remains within the public sector (76.5 per cent). In contrast, only a small percentage of the population is covered by private health insurance, the ISAPRES (15.4 per cent) (Cabieses *et al.* 2022). Nevertheless, Chile has one of the highest levels of out-of-pocket (OOP) payments for health among the Organisation for Economic Co-operation and Development countries and increasingly unequal access to healthcare (OECD 2018a).

The failure of Latin American health reforms to address health and wider socio-economic inequalities has been widely documented (Birn, Nervi & Siqueira 2016). The reforms' primary beneficiaries were private health insurance companies and high-income healthcare users, who enjoyed a decrease in their out-of-pocket expenditure (Homedes & Ugalde 2005).

The World Bank's health reforms aimed to diminish states' control over health issues and increase the role of the private sector (López Cabello 2021). The wider reform packages, known as structural adjustment policies, sparked a wave of "ruthless policies" (Birn & Nervi 2019: 5). Policies include the expansion of private insurance programmes; state health systems becoming privatized "from within", with public funds used to contract private hospitals and providers; management and human resources outsourcing; and subcontracting to private entities of profitable services (laboratories, pharmacies, food services, cleaning and patient transportation). User fees were also introduced into health systems across the region (Birn & Nervi 2019).

Kentikelenis (2017) identifies three main pathways through which structural adjustment affects health: policies directly targeting health systems, such as cuts to the health budget and the introduction of user fees; policies that indirectly impact health systems, such as public sector pay cuts and deregulation; and policies that affect the social determinants of health, such as with a rise in economic inequality, insecurity and poverty. These austerity measures can significantly impact the right to health. Austerity measures include wage cuts or layoffs for medical personnel, increases in co-payment and OOP expenses, rationing of treatment, altering eligibility, cuts to services and, ultimately, adverse impacts on the social determinants of health (CESR 2018; Kentikelenis 2017).

UHC sees health as a commodity with a minimal role for the state, with funding based on the pooling of private and public funds, and encourages private health insurance (Birn & Nevri 2019). UHC focuses on individual care and creates segmented access and fragmented services, increasing overall costs and marginalizing the social determinants of health. UHC encourages private participation in health financing. The expansion of UHC has been influenced by economic interests facing market saturation in the United States and Europe and seeking new markets in middle-income countries (MICs). UHC proposes *financial* coverage consisting of everyone who should be incorporated into an insurance programme to avoid potentially catastrophic out-of-pocket payments. UHC promotes the privatization of health insurance and health services on the understanding that the public sector is unable to meet the population's health needs (Giovanella *et al.* 2018).

These features differ significantly from the universal healthcare model, known as the "universal health system" (UHS) model. UHS conceives health as a human right provided by the state and financed by progressive taxation. Access is guaranteed for the whole population by comprehensive primary healthcare networks, with attention to intersectionality and the societal determinants of health. UHS provides "greater solidarity, redistribution and equity" (Giovanella *et al.* 2018: 1766).

Moreover, the term "coverage" rather than "care" either suggests a limited scope of care or is being used to suggest enrolment in an insurance scheme (Sanders *et al.* 2019). For many low-/middle-income countries (LMICs), this has meant operationalizing UHC through government-funded health insurance schemes but with the involvement of the private for-profit sector. Public sector funds are transferred into the private health sector, thereby reinforcing existing health inequities. Insurance-based models of UHC risk being promoted at the expense of funding PHC and other public health programmes (Sanders *et al.* 2019).

Although UHC is seen as a solution to the problems of health access, the long-term perspective demonstrates that it reproduces

> the features of neoliberalism that have plagued healthcare systems and overall societal wellbeing over recent decades: proliferating user fees, privatization and outsourcing, public subsidies to the for-profit sector, subcontracting of public roles and jobs to private interests, greater precarity and loss of union protection for health workers, increased market entry for profiteering corporate interests ...   (Birn & Nervi 2019: 8)

At the same time, debt crises resulting from costly bailouts of the financial sector have amplified the claims asserting the unaffordability of existing welfare systems (Sell 2019: 2).

Financial market volatility and reduced tax revenue have curbed efforts to expand UHC further. Capital mobility has facilitated tax evasion and tax havens. Financial stability and adequate tax revenue are necessary (if not sufficient) conditions for achieving UHC (Sell 2019: 2). The US-based Disease Control Priorities Network (DCPN)[2] estimates that low- and lower

---

2. In collaboration with the University of Washington, the Center for Global Health Research and the Public Health Foundation of India, the DCPN aims to improve the efficacy of health

middle-income countries would, on average, need to raise their respective annual per capita health expenditures by $53 and $61 per person to achieve coverage with the essential UHC package of 218 core interventions, a sizable burden in relation to average expenditure increases in recent years (Bloom, Khoury & Subarraman 2018: 1).

COVID-19, PUBLIC HEALTH AND THE FATAL EFFECTS OF AUSTERITY

The onset of the Covid-19 pandemic in March 2020 placed immense strain on global health systems. Breaking from the neoliberal trajectory, the pandemic led to extensive state intervention and an immediate hike in health budgets. High-income countries increased their year-on-year health spending by an unprecedented 7.5 per cent of gross domestic product once the pandemic had started. For MICs, government spending increased by 3.2 per cent of GDP (Kentikelenis & Stubbs 2022).

For many countries, health services have been weakened by decades of neoliberal policy. Austerity has led to reductions in healthcare expenditure and chronic underinvestment, with devastating effects on health services. In Spain, public healthcare spending dropped by 12.7 per cent from 2009 to 2013. In Greece, public expenditure on health fell by 42.8 per cent between 2009 and 2017 following the 2010 economic crisis. Austerity introduced co-payments for health treatments and cuts in health workers' remuneration, resulting in a decline in access to and the quality of healthcare (Amnesty International 2018, 2020). In Lombardy, Italy, private health has expanded while public services have weakened, being forced to compete with the private sector for funds (Tansy 2021). In Nigeria, health spending fell from 7.3 per cent of GDP in 2006 to 4.4 per cent in 2018 (Global Initiative for Economic, Social and Cultural Rights [GI-ESCR] 2021). In many LMICs, poor-quality healthcare has been a major driver of excess mortality, and many are pushed into poverty due to out-of-pocket payments (Ahmed *et al.* 2022). In Nigeria, enrolment in the national insurance system covers only around 5 per cent of the population, mostly informal workers, while OOP spending accounts for 76 per cent of all health expenditure (GI-ESCR 2022).

Moreover, the role of the private sector has expanded, representing 20 per cent of all hospital beds in Europe (European Union of Private Hospitals [UEHP] 2021). In some cases, the private sector is also the dominant form of healthcare, such as in the United States and India (Williams 2020). In Nigeria, the share of health expenditure through the private sector rose

---

resource spending in various contexts around the globe. The DCPN is funded by the Bill & Melinda Gates Foundation.

from 64 per cent in 2000 to 78 per cent in 2018 (GI-ESCR 2022). The WHO (2022) estimates that, in Africa, private for-profit sectors deliver 35 per cent of outpatient care and informal providers an additional 17 per cent. Research shows that, in a sample of 70 LMICs, the private sector is the dominant source of treatment for children with a fever or cough (Clarke *et al.* 2020). They also contend that the private sector provides nearly 40 per cent of healthcare across most WHO regions, rising to 62 per cent in the eastern Mediterranean region, including some of the world's poorest countries, such as Yemen, Somalia and Afghanistan. The nature of the private sector varies widely, accounting for large hospital chains through to traditional and religious healers. Often in LMICs these are poorly regulated and not well integrated into national health systems (Williams 2021; GI-ESCR 2021; Initiative for Social and Economic Rights [ISER] 2021).

This backdrop created major challenges in addressing the pandemic. Privatization and austerity were associated with the worse outcomes from Covid-19. Assa and Calderon (2020) analysed data from 147 countries, evaluating 93 per cent of the world's population across continents and income levels. They find that, even when controlling for income, urbanization, globalization and democracy, a 10 per cent increase in private health expenditure resulted in a 5.84 per cent increase in Covid-19 cases and a 6.91 per cent increase in Covid-19 deaths. Data from OECD countries indicates that a higher share of GDP allocated to public health, higher doctors per population and higher bed availability are associated with lower fatality rates from Covid-19 (Sherpa 2020). This demonstrates austerity's fatal impacts.

Although some governments moved to sequestrate private sector capacity and equipment to manage the pandemic – such as Egypt, Ireland, South Africa, Pakistan and India – the sector was not well suited to managing the pandemic. In India, the private sector lacked coordination across provider types and had difficulties accessing data from private hospitals, leading to pandemic control issues (Williams, Chun Yung & Grépin 2021). Companies with market power were able to negotiate generous terms with governments. In South Africa, three firms dominate the private hospital market, Netcare, Mediclinic and Life, with more than 80 per cent of the hospital beds and 90 per cent of all the admissions, despite serving just 27 per cent of the South African population (Williams, Chun Yung & Grépin 2021).

Moreover, access to testing and treatment deepens inequalities when subject to payment ability. In the United States, 12 per cent of the population is uninsured. Although the state provided Covid-19 testing and acute care, many experienced financial barriers to medical treatment and rising debts because of out-of-pocket spending (Unruh *et al.* 2022). Inequalities were deepened by opportunistic behaviour by the private sector, in a demonstration of "disaster capitalism". Some private providers charged exorbitant fees for Covid-19 testing and hospital treatment, with high costs for add-ons such as oxygen. Often large deposits were required, and dead bodies were withheld until the high fees had been paid (see Williams, Chun Yung & Grépin 2021, Marathe *et al.* 2022 and ISER 2021).

Profiteering was also in evidence in the United Kingdom, with some companies reporting a surge in profits because of Covid-19 contracts (*Guardian* 2022a), especially those with political connections (*Guardian* 2022b). The starkest manifestation of private sector exploitation was the production and distribution of the Covid-19 vaccine, through a system that created billions for shareholders of pharmaceutical companies while denying access to many in poor countries (Ahmed *et al.* 2022; ACT Alliance 2021).

Although some have profited from it, the pandemic significantly strained private health providers. Many faced a liquidity crisis soon after the pandemic started for several reasons: elective care and outpatient treatments stopped because of Covid-19 restrictions; a weakened ability to pay, either out of pocket or through insurance as a result of the economic impacts; costs escalating as a result of infection control and personal protective equipment (PPE) requirements; and medical tourism drying up (Hellowell *et al.* 2020; Williams 2020).

Clarke *et al.* (2020) argue that many countries relied on private health services during the Covid-19 pandemic and sought to prop up the private sector by drawing on its resources and capacity. They contend that this "all hands on deck" approach was considered critical, especially in LMICs. Governments introduced emergency legislation and funding to "bail out" private providers. Williams, Chun Yung and Grépin (2021) evidence this in LMICs, such as in the Philippines, Jordan and Morocco. Regarding Africa, the WHO (2022) notes that Covid-19 bolstered the engagement with the private health sector and "exposed the limitations of not having a strategy or the corresponding resources, the 'skill and will' necessary to effectively work with the private sector in health" (WHO 2022: 15).

In England, the pandemic boosted the ailing private health industry, with the government paying for private sector beds to be on standby to support a potential overrun of the public system; most of this capacity was not used. The private sector tends to cherry-pick the least complex cases and has little intensive care capacity, contributing little to public health during a pandemic (Bayliss 2022; Tansy 2021).

In the case of Africa, the WHO calls for policy to "shift mindsets to the private sector as co-investor and thought partner in health systems". The WHO also calls for "consumers" to be at the centre of "health value chains" (WHO 2022: 16). Although Covid-19 brought the need for investment in public health systems and the risks of engaging with private providers to global attention, it appears that no lessons were learned, and the policy direction remains unchanged. Global institutions continue to advocate for profit-making in health services, rather than promoting the respect and fulfilment of human rights. Moreover, private health is set to be boosted by widespread spending cuts, as an expanding private sector in health is often a corollary of austerity.

Analysis of the International Monetary Fund expenditure projections indicates that governments have begun to cut back public spending at a time when it is most needed to promote social protection. Based on IMF projections, it has been estimated that austerity would affect 6.7 billion people in 2023 – 85 per cent of humanity – (Ortiz & Cummins 2022). In health policy, austerity brings in reforms such as increased charges for health services, reductions in medical personnel, cost-saving measures in public healthcare centres, discontinuation of allowances, the phase-out of treatments and services and increased co-payments for pharmaceuticals (Ortiz & Cummins 2022). Post-Covid-19 fiscal contraction is expected to affect many LMICs (Kentikelenis & Stubbs 2022). The Covid-19 recovery plan for west Africa has been described as "austerity on steroids" (Oxfam International 2021).

Covid-19 has also shifted global attention in health spending. International donors such as the World Bank and major donors such as the Bill & Melinda Gates Foundation are prioritizing investments in "global health security". There is a heightened focus on "pandemic preparedness", so that outbreaks of infectious diseases can be contained. Hence, health spending is framed in terms of vulnerability to risks of emergent infectious diseases, which is based on the policy agendas of the Global North. The countries of the Global South would do better to prioritize equitable and effective health systems to cater for a wide range of health conditions (Kentikelenis & Stubbs 2022).

CONCLUSION

A Rights-Based Economy is grounded in a holistic understanding of human well-being and supported by the widely agreed framework of human rights' values and obligations. It demands action to redistribute resources, remedy inequalities, and rebalance power in our economies (see Chapter 1). As we have demonstrated in this chapter, assigning a greater role to the private sector in health is unlikely to address health or wider socio-economic inequalities and raises significant concerns over government's human rights obligations. As Balakrishnan & Elson (2011b: 17) note, "There are a variety of ways to achieve economic growth, and states have the duty to pursue growth strategies that are compliant with their human rights obligations."

Sustained levels of public spending are vital for health systems (Kentikelenis & Stubbs 2022). Public spending requires a boosting of government finances.

Fiscal space can increase with debt write-offs, curbing illicit financial flows and increased tax revenue. Notably, private sector involvement does not increase fiscal space but is likely to reduce it.

Covid-19 demonstrated that massive public spending could be mobilized and that policy orthodoxy could be overruled. Governments mobilized over $16 trillion in response to the pandemic, with some of the largest support programmes since the Second World War, showing "their ability to provide fiscal firepower when it is needed" (Ahmed *et al.* 2022). Some have suggested this might be a "window of opportunity to rethink the role of the private health sector in national health systems and to promote much-needed reform and strengthening of regulatory systems" (Williams, Chun Yung & Grépin 2021: 1327).

Despite the failings of neoliberalism, austerity and privatization, policy and practice are not responsive to evidence. In terms of addressing these entrenched positions, we outline three distinct examples of initiatives that are seeking to bring change.

(a) The work within the WHO Council on the Economics of Health for All (2020). The focus here has been on shifting global narratives on health and economics and placing a commitment to health and well-being at the centre of policy-making. In its manifesto, the WHO Council proposes a "fundamental rethink of how value in health and wellbeing is measured, produced and distributed across the economy" (WHO 2020: 3). Health is seen as central to a thriving society rather than "a peripheral concern of economic policies" (WHO 2021: 3).

(b) The role of social movements continues to be critical. As the People's Health Movement reflects in its most recent triennial *Global Health Watch* publication: "[T]he idea of changing the global and political economic system, and the underlying power structures can seem like an impossible task" (PHM 2022). Yet the PHM's work is testimony to the strength of social movements and health activists working at the local, regional and national levels pushing for more inclusive change and constituting a "global people's health movement". Similarly, hundreds of different types of civil society organizations have worked on the 2022 Santiago Declaration for Public Services; "The Future Is Public"[3] is, again, testimony to the work that is being done to push for greater accountability to citizens in all public services and to ensure that governments deliver on their obligations to provide comprehensive and accessible services for all.

---

3. See https://futureispublic.org.

(c) Legal action is another significant arena for advocacy groups aiming for change. Amnesty International has taken steps to hold the Greek authorities accountable at the Council of Europe for violating people's rights to health and non-discrimination, as well as failing to protect the population against austerity measures (Amnesty International 2022).

Overall, there is a remarkable disconnect between the wide support for equitable and sustainable access to health services for all, as set out in Sustainable Development Goal 3, and the fact that the policy reality continues to be anchored in austerity and private provisioning, which are known to weaken health services. More research is needed to unpack the reasons behind this scenario.

CHAPTER 12

FROM RECOVERY TO TRANSFORMATION? ASSESSING ARGENTINA'S COVID-19 ECONOMIC RESPONSE THROUGH A FEMINIST LENS

Magalí Brosio and Edurne Cárdenas

INTRODUCTION

The Argentinian feminist movement has a long and rich tradition, which is crystallized in – among other things – 35 editions of Encuentros Plurinacionales de Mujeres, Lesbianas, Trans, Travestis, Bisexuales, Intersexuales, y No Binaries (Plurinational Meetings of Women, Lesbians, Trans, Travestis, Bisexuals, Intersex, and Non-Binary People), which started in 1986 and were interrupted only during the Covid-19 pandemic. The Encuentros are a unique phenomenon in the world: yearly open meetings in which tens of thousands of women and people with diverse sexual orientations and gender identities (SOGI) from all geographic regions, social stratifications and political orientations get together to think and discuss the movement's agenda collectively.

In 2015 the first demonstration under the slogan "Ni Una Menos" ("No One [Woman] Less") further enhanced the vitality and massification of the feminist movement in the country. This protest constituted a historic event, which gave political, social and cultural volume to the condemnation of gender violence (Centro de Estudios Legales e Sociales [CELS] 2019). It contributed to the prioritization of gender issues within the public agenda, which included demands related to the rights to legal, safe and free abortions and the unfair sexual division of labour.

In this context, it is unsurprising that feminists have progressively gained space, albeit not without effort, in the political arena. Cross-party alliances between legislators, for example, played a key role in bringing the demands of feminists from the streets to the National Congress and, ultimately, in achieving, after several attempts, the enactment of the Voluntary Interruption of Pregnancy Law (Congreso Nacional de la Nación Argentina 2020).

Likewise, gender units have been gradually institutionalized within the government (Lopreite & Rodríguez Gustá 2021), and have slowly gained hierarchy and autonomy, although these changes have not always resulted in an increase in budget allocation. The path towards the institutionalization of gender machinery within the national government has not been linear; nevertheless, the change of government administration in 2019 was a turning point. Since the election to the presidency of Alberto Fernández late that year there has been a shift at the national level in terms of the political discourse and priorities, moving away from the previous government's very orthodox neoliberal positions and proposing a recovery of the role of the state as a guarantor of the well-being of society. The emphasis placed on gender equality – at least discursively – had been unprecedented.

Evidence of this was the creation of the first Ministerio de las Mujeres, Géneros y Diversidades (MMGyD; Ministry of Women, Gender and Diversity) by decree (Presidente de la Nación Argentina 2019a, 2019b) on the same day as the presidential inauguration, and the establishment of the Dirección Nacional de Economía, Igualdad y Género (National Directorate of Economy, Equality and Gender) within the Ministry of Economy just a few weeks later (Ministerio de Economía [Mecon] 2020a). The new government's plans were soon interrupted by the outbreak of the Covid-19 pandemic.

In a context of widespread uncertainty, what was certain was that the economic crisis linked to the pandemic was disproportionately affecting women and people with diverse SOGI, particularly trans* and non-binary people, further exacerbating pre-existing inequalities and erasing the modest progress made over decades. Around the world, women and people with diverse SOGI have been disproportionately impacted by increased economic insecurity, higher unpaid care workloads and rising levels of gender-based violence (Human Rights Campaign Foundation n.d.; ILO 2020; UN Women 2020a; CELS 2021).

Thus, in Argentina, the recently established gender units and their agendas had to be quickly reconverted to provide a response to this crisis that incorporated a gender perspective in both design and implementation.[1] Logically, not only Argentina but all governments faced this challenge, regardless of the level of importance assigned to it. In this scenario, UN Women and the United Nations Development Programme (UNDP) developed a tracker to monitor the extent to which the policies adopted to alleviate the effects of the crisis in the different governments contained a gender perspective in their design.

---

1. According to the Technical Coordination Group of the National Cabinet for the Mainstreaming of Gender Policies (GNTPG), to December 2022 there were 16 gender units in all ministries and decentralized agencies of the federal administration, included the GNTPG. Fifteen of these units were created as of December 2019, showing the influence of MMGyD.

At its launch, in September 2020, the tracker (which analysed a total of 2,500 measures in 206 countries) found important gaps in the global response to Covid-19.[2] The initial data showed that 42 countries (equivalent to 20 per cent of the countries reviewed) were not implementing any gender-sensitive measures.[3] The countries deploying gender-sensitive policies were, in most cases, circumscribed to the area of violence against women and girls. In contrast, only 10 per cent of all the measures surveyed focused on women's economic security, and fewer than one-third of the countries adopted measures linked to the care system (UN Women 2020b). These statistics are more concerning if we consider the trackers' failure to measure resource allocation and policy impact.

Even though implementing this type of gender-sensitive emergency policies constituted essential support for protecting women and people with diverse SOGI in a highly critical context, feminists have pointed out on multiple occasions that returning to the pre-pandemic world was not a desirable objective for these population groups. In this sense, without denying the urgency of providing answers amid an unprecedented global crisis, we understand that this tracker is an important tool. Even so, it is of limited usefulness, since it does not evaluate the potential of the surveyed measures in contributing to a true transformation of the economy that allows women and those with diverse SOGI to fully enjoy their human rights.

This chapter proposes to revisit the approach to the economic crisis associated with the Covid-19 pandemic and to analyse its transformative potential.[4] With this goal in mind, in the two following sections we present the UN Women and UNDP tracker in greater detail and contextualize the measures implemented in Argentina. In the third section we complement the findings of the tracker with the qualitative analysis of a specific case: that of the Inter-Ministerial Committee on Care Policies (Mesa Interministerial de Políticas de Cuidado; hereafter la Mesa), coordinated by the MMGyD. We find a transformative seed with the ability to respond to a crisis context in this policy.

---

2. See https://data.undp.org/gendertracker.
3. For this tracker, UNDP and UN Women define gender-sensitive measures as "those that seek to directly address the risks and challenges that women and girls face during the Covid-19 crisis, notably violence against women and girls, unpaid care work, and economic insecurity" (UNDP & UN Women 2022: 1)
4. The UNDP and UN Working Group on Business and Human Rights (2019: 63) define transformative measures as being "able to respond to differentiated, intersectional and disproportionate adverse impacts on women's human rights as well as to discriminatory norms and patriarchal power structures. The consequent measures and remedies should be transformative in that they should be capable of bringing change to patriarchal norms and unequal power relations that underpin discrimination, gender-based violence and gender stereotyping."

It also lays the foundations for a long-term systemic change in how care is understood and organized.

We find that the institutionalization of the gender perspective and the incorporation of feminists in positions of power played a key role in designing and implementing policies with these characteristics. We also recognize that this is necessary but not sufficient: political will is needed to give content, resources and direction to these initiatives. These reflections are elaborated on in the fourth section of the chapter. In the last section we synthesize the key findings to identify crucial elements for designing and implementing feminist economic policies beyond the Covid-19 context.

BETWEEN CHALLENGES AND OPPORTUNITIES: CAN THE RESPONSE TO THE PANDEMIC HAVE TRANSFORMATIVE POWER?

The measures implemented to contain the pandemic further exacerbated inequalities for women and people with diverse SOGI. The Office of the United Nations High Commissioner for Human Rights has emphasized that confinement measures (even when necessary) led to an increase in gender-based violence in the intra-family sphere (UN OHCHR 2020).[5]

The International Labour Organization has highlighted that the economic security of women – in all their diversity – was disproportionately harmed through four main ways: (a) as a group over-represented in the sectors and economic activities hardest hit by the pandemic and the related isolation measures; (b) in their role as domestic workers – an occupation with high rates of feminization and that in many countries concentrates a large part of female employment – as their usually precarious working conditions made them more vulnerable to employment suspension or termination without receiving any kind of compensation; (c) as the majority of the health sector workforce, an essential job and with particularly exhausting conditions throughout the pandemic; and (b) through the increase in unpaid care work performed within the household,[6] particularly in closures of educational establishments (ILO 2020).

---

5. See the thematic report of the UN independent expert on protection against violence and discrimination based on sexual orientation and gender identity on the impact of the Covid-19 pandemic on the human rights of LGBT people (UNGA 2020).

6. The reliance on women's unpaid work to make up for gaps in the state provision of care services is not a new trend nor unique to the Covid-19 pandemic. According to feminist economists' research, economic policies are frequently underpinned by gender stereotypes that presume that women will step up to fill any emerging gaps when states shrink and their role in providing care services diminishes (Donald & Lusiani 2017). The Covid-19 pandemic further exacerbated this trend, in so far as both public and private services were either collapsed or unavailable, shifting the burdens almost completely to households and ultimately to women.

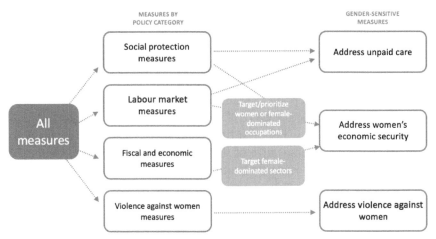

Figure 12.1 Selection criteria for determining gender-sensitive measures in UN Women and UNDP's policy tracker

Source: UNDP & UN Women (2022).

It is within this framework that UN Women and the UNDP developed a tracker to monitor to what extent the policies adopted to alleviate the effects of the crisis in the different governments contained a gender perspective in their design (hereafter, the tracker).

This tool surveyed social protection measures; labour market measures; economic and fiscal measures; and measures to address violence against women (see Figure 12.1). The last group measures were considered gender-sensitive by default. For the rest of the categories, a more in-depth analysis of their content was necessary for determination.[7] Social protection and labour market measures were considered "gender-sensitive" if they targeted women's economic security, unpaid care work or occupations in which women are over-represented (textile manufacturing, domestic work, education and healthcare). Regarding economic and fiscal measures, the criteria revolved around whether they supported sectors with high female participation rates, under the assumption that this protects women's employment and, ultimately, their economic situation (UNDP & UN Women 2022).

The tracker recognized Argentina as one of the countries that most rapidly and systematically integrated the gender perspective in its response to the

---

7. The tracker's methodological note defines the integration of a VAWG perspective in Covid-19 response plans, awareness-raising, a strengthening of services and the collection of data as gender-sensitive by default, saying that "measures under this policy category recognize this risk and are aimed at prevention and response as well as the generation of evidence on incidence, needs and readiness to respond" (UNDP & UN Women 2022: 4).

Covid-19 pandemic. A regional report on the implementation of measures during the first months of the pandemic finds that, of the 44 measures implemented by the country, 26 had a gender perspective (that is, 59 per cent). Thus, Argentina was highlighted as an example within Latin America and the Caribbean. This performance is attributed in part to the influence of feminists in key positions in public administration and the weight of the women's movement on the public agenda (UN Women & UNDP 2020). Prior to detailing these measures, it is important to highlight that the tracker claims to evaluate the gender perspective of the implemented measures. Even so, it considers only policies associated with women, offering a limited conceptualization of gender and replicating a binary logic.[8] Hence, since we use the tracker as a starting point for discussion, the subsequent analysis is focused almost exclusively on the impact of the different measures on women. We recognize the limitations of this approach, and criticize it. Further, it is crucial to underline that, in Argentina, people with diverse SOGI were explicitly included in the design of policies linked to the Covid-19 pandemic. Any assessment of whether these measures effectively addressed the situation and needs of this collective remains an urgent and pending account that, unfortunately, exceeds the objectives of this chapter.

In line with the recorded global trends by UN Women and UNDP, most of the gender-sensitive measures in Argentina focused on the area of violence against women (see Table 12.1). These measures were aimed at providing comprehensive protection to victims, carrying out awareness-raising campaigns, expanding the available communication channels and reinforcing the services offered in cases of complaints. These policies are in line with promising practices identified globally by the OHCHR. Standout examples are the declaration of services associated with gender violence as essential; expanding the availability of alternative accommodation to avoid confinement together with abusers; the implementation of accessible, diverse and proactive alert systems; and the provision of information to victims about available services (UN OHCHR 2020).

It is difficult to judge the impact of these measures. Yet, after an increase in complaints registered at the beginning of the pandemic, in the first year of widespread containment measures (between 20 March 2020 and 19 March 2021, including lockdown, isolation, quarantine and *cordon sanitaire* measures, albeit with different levels of stringency) a total of 288 femicides were registered, compared with 334 in the previous year. In this sense, despite

---

8. Despite some recent promising developments (such as the appointment of the first independent expert on sexual orientation and gender identity in 2016), the United Nations has failed to make substantial improvements in the recognition and protection of people with diverse SOGI, reflecting the stiff resistance of some member states.

Table 12.1 Gender-sensitive measures adopted by Argentina to respond to the Covid-19 crisis

Focus area	Number of measures	Key measures
Unpaid care work	5	The establishment of the Mesa Interministerial de Políticas de Cuidado, a network coordinating care-related actions since the beginning of the pandemic (MMGyD n.d.).
Women's economic security	8	The implementation of an emergency family income (Ingreso Familiar de Emergencia: IFE), a series of cash transfers targeting the most vulnerable populations, including women domestic workers and informal workers.
Violence against women	13	Recognition of shelters as essential services and expansion of the network in collaboration between MMGyD with unions, the private sector and local governments. Expansion of the violence hotline through new channels (WhatsApp and email).

Source: Own elaboration based on UN Women and UNDP (2020).

gender violence continuing to be a central problem for women in Argentina, the pandemic measures may have contributed to containing the issue.

Regarding women's economic security, one of the central measures, frequently highlighted as a promising practice, was the establishment of the Emergency Family Income (Ingreso familiar de emergencia: IFE), which included a series of non-contributory cash transfers to the most vulnerable groups in the population.[9] Beyond its magnitude, this tool stands out for incorporating a gender approach. First, one of the explicit objectives was to reach the segment of informal workers who, in many cases, are excluded from state policies and their benefits. Within this group, women are over-represented. Second, one of its few eligibility requirements was not being registered as an employee, with domestic work as the only exception – a sector comprised almost exclusively of women and characterized by precarious conditions. This programme was aligned with the recommendations of the Committee on the Convention of the Elimination of All Forms of Discrimination against Women (CEDAW). The UN mechanism emphasized the significance of implementing Covid-19 measures that address

9. The payment was done in three instalments of $AR 10,000. For reference, when the programme was launched, Argentina's minimum wage was $AR 16,875 (President of Argentina's Resolution 6/2019; see www.argentina.gob.ar/normativa/nacional/resolución-6-2019-327580/texto).

gender inequalities in employment, facilitate women's transition from informal to formal work and improve relevant social protection systems (UN OHCHR 2020).

IFE was originally expected to cover between 3.6 and 4 million households. Ultimately, it reached a total of 9 million beneficiaries (almost a fifth of Argentina's total population), with most recipients female (55 per cent). This indicator suggests positive progress for the tool in terms of gender. Moreover, the discrepancy between the initial estimates and the actual number of beneficiaries sheds light on a segment of the vulnerable population that was not considered in the design of pre-pandemic social protection policies. In this sense, the innovation of the IFE opens a door for groups usually ignored, such as informal workers or full-time unpaid care workers, to be considered when designing social and economic policies in the future (D'Alessandro 2022).

The coverage achieved by the IFE is even more impressive when contrasted with global and regional averages. For instance, a Global South cross-country study coordinated by the Financial Transparency Coalition (FTC) finds that, on average, only 4.22 per cent of all Covid-19 recovery spending went towards the informal sector. Notably, Argentina (together with Colombia and Jordan) was recognized as a champion in allocations to the informal sector, reaching 13.84 per cent (FTC 2022). All in all, the IFE case demonstrates that, even in difficult contexts, if there is political will it is possible to design and implement policies reaching those further towards the margins. This has huge implications for women, in so far as social protection systems that are built around male-biased stereotypes (i.e. assuming continued career trajectories in formal employment as the normal, and anything else as deviance) tend to systematically exclude women from receiving coverage.

Beyond the mitigation success of these policies, it is worth asking whether these policies can exercise a transformative function and contribute to real change in how gender relations are structured. As previously mentioned, for women and people with diverse SOGI, returning to the pre-pandemic "business as usual" situation was not a satisfactory objective. Active efforts were needed to reverse the course we were on before 2020. In particular, the pandemic highlighted the unresolved or poorly solved tensions between the productive and reproductive realms, demonstrating the incompatibilities that arise if responses are to be devised exclusively and individually from each household and its internal organization.

In this sense, the creation of the Mesa Interministerial de Políticas de Cuidado crystallizes in an emergency context a long-standing demand of the feminist movement. Despite its early stages, we detect in it a transformative potential, as it lays the foundations for rethinking care and its organization not just in but also beyond the Covid-19 pandemic.

THE MESA INTERMINISTERIAL DE POLÍTICAS DE CUIDADO: SHIFTING THE PARADIGM?

The care policies at the federal level in Argentina were recognized as key measures to address unpaid care work in the first version of the tracker. In this area, we find particularly valuable the creation of la Mesa, a network to facilitate the coordination across different national governmental units, aiming at the construction of a formal and transversal space under the feminist leadership of the MMGyD.

For the MMGyD, the establishment of la Mesa is an outstanding and innovative measure, as it is an articulating space for "periodic exchange, essential for discussing and building consensus to generate public policies that recognize care as a necessity, a job, and a right; and that allow for the equal redistribution of care between men, women and other identities" (Mecon 2020b). In addition to the MMGyD, la Mesa is constituted of 14 additional organizations that have an impact on the social organization of care.

The initiative was first introduced in February 2020 and formalized in October of that year, through an administrative decision of the Executive Office of the Cabinet of Ministers. This administrative decision explicitly links the establishment of la Mesa with the obligations assumed by the Argentine state through the ratification of multiple international treaties, including the CEDAW, the Convention on the Rights of the Child (CRC), the Convention on the Rights of Persons with Disabilities (CRPD) and the Inter-American Convention on the Protection of Human Rights of Older Persons.

The issue of care was already on the agenda of many different public organizations that were implementing policies without a comprehensive view, with isolated actions and with major shortcomings. In this vein, in their final observations on their last periodic country review, both the CEDAW Committee and the ESCR Committee recommended to the Argentine state the equitable distribution of domestic and family tasks between men and women, providing sufficient and adequate childcare services and increasing incentives for men to exercise their right to parental leave (UN CEDAW 2016: 12, para. 31). Furthermore, the UN Economic and Social Council (2018: 6, para. 29) recommends emphatically "strengthening and expanding a comprehensive public care system that eliminates social and territorial gaps through the effective implementation of the Equal Opportunities Plan, and more actively promote reconciliation policies between work and family life for men and women".

The objectives defined in the regulatory instruments for the establishment of la Mesa undoubtedly aimed to account for these gaps referred to in the recommendations made by the aforementioned committees. Hence, the conceptualization of care and care work that underpins the vision of la Mesa is firmly grounded on feminist analysis of the economy and the economic system. Therefore, the aims constitute good tenets for a gender-transformative Rights-Based Economy.

At the time of writing this chapter, la Mesa is still functioning in a sustained manner. Among the measures adopted in the context of the Covid-19 pandemic are the preparation and dissemination of a document with basic notions towards a comprehensive care policy with a gender perspective; the deployment of the national campaign "Cuidar en igualdad: necesidad, derecho, trabajo" ("Caring for Equality: Need, Right, Work"); and the programme "Registradas", which focuses on domestic workers' formalization[10] (Mesa Interministerial de Políticas de Cuidado 2021, 2022).

La Mesa also promoted other actions oriented towards structural change in the longer term. One example is the Mapa Federal del Cuidados (Federal Map of Care), a virtual tool with a national scope that enables the identification and geopositioning of available care services for the different population groups that require it, as well as the provision of training services focused on care. Another good example is the Cuidar en Igualdad (Care in Equality) Bill. La Mesa was deeply involved in developing this bill, which was done in a participatory process coordinated by the MMGyD. It included a drafting committee made up of experts in the field, activists and academics. Within its mandate, several consultations were performed with other stakeholders, including organizations for people with disabilities, the elderly, children, chambers of commerce, feminist and diversity organizations and popular economy organizations.

FROM MAINSTREAMING TO INSTITUTIONALIZATION: A NECESSARY BUT NOT SUFFICIENT CONDITION FOR TRANSFORMATION

Reflecting on the conditions that made possible the emergence of a policy with transformative characteristics such as la Mesa, we find that the shift from mainstreaming towards the institutionalization of a gender perspective within the government played a central role.

At the time of the fourth and final World Conference on Women (1995), the focus was on the concept of *gender mainstreaming*. As María Rigat-Pflaum (2008: 41) points out:

> Gender mainstreaming, translated into Spanish as "*transversalidad*", can be understood in various ways: as a strategy that involves all social actors in the search for gender equality, or as the name of

---

10. Created by National Decree 660/2021 by the president of Argentina.

certain tools for gender analysis. In reality, it is a transformative approach, endowed with its own theoretical body, which aims to analyse the differentiated impacts of the gender system on men and women, which makes it possible to take into account the specificities of people as integral beings and which, at the same time helps with the implementation.

Almost 30 years later, it has become increasingly clear that gender mainstreaming does not guarantee by itself the achievement of gender equality.[11] A complementary concept has emerged: *the institutionality of gender*. This refers to changes in the organizational structure for managing public policies on women's rights and gender equality at all levels of government and across all its branches. The concrete institutional designs or modalities are heterogeneous and vary from country to country. Even so, they consist of various mechanisms for the advancement of women, including the gender equality units in sectoral ministries, the legislature, the judiciary, decentralized organizations and intersectoral and interinstitutional coordinating bodies (UN ECLAC 2016).

The government administration, headed by Alberto Fernández and Cristina Fernández de Kirchner, placed the centrality of the feminist agenda as a campaign issue and a government promise. In this sense, the creation of the MMGyD was presented as the response to the social demands of the feminist movement. For the first time, a gender mechanism was granted at the highest institutional status (a national ministry), accompanied by an expansion of the matters within its purview.

The establishment of the MMGyD was not the only measure adopted in this regard: gender and diversity offices and units were created or granted a higher rank across different ministries. Evidence of this is that, in 2021, Argentina had its first ever gender-responsive national budget. Hence, although the illusion of a Cabinet with equal representation of men and women was far away, renowned feminists (from politics, academia and activism) occupied key decision-making positions in the second and third lines.

Formal mainstreaming spaces were also created. Some initiatives in the federal administration aimed at mainstreaming the gender perspective and coordinating actions and policies across units. In addition to the case of la Mesa, it is worth mentioning the Programa Interministerial de Presupuesto con Perspectiva de Género y Diversidad (hereafter el Programa) and the Gabinete Nacional para la Transversalización de las Políticas de Género (hereafter el Gabinete).

---

11. Some critics indicate the "emptying" of meaning and depoliticization of some terms, such as "gender mainstreaming"; see Cornwall and Eade (2010).

El Programa is a transversal measure implemented by the Executive Office of the Cabinet of Ministers and the National Ministry of Economy to promote the development of budgets with a gender and diversity perspective at all government levels. In turn, the creation of el Gabinete, chaired by the head of the Cabinet of Ministers and integrated by the highest authorities of each of the ministries forming the National Cabinet and other key agencies (the Administración Nacional de la Seguridad Social [ANSES], Instituto Nacional de Estadística y Censos [INDEC] and Programa de Atención Médica Integral [PAMI]), has the objective of ensuring the inclusion of a gender perspective in the design, implementation and evaluation of all national public policies, based on the regular work coordinated by the MMGyD.

These initiatives were complemented by informal coordination mechanisms, such as an instant messaging group that seeks to bring together all the "women in government", with more than 250 officials working in different ministries and decentralized agencies, to strengthen personal ties and streamline coordination within different areas of public administration (Cafferata 2020).

Finally, although the creation of institutions constitutes a key point to establishing a specific gender agenda with concrete responsibilities, past experiences have shown that formal institutions are not enough on their own and that political will is necessary to provide content, finance and direction to these initiatives.

In this vein, the presence of feminists with decision-making power seems to be the engine to keep these institutional spaces alive. This is not enough: gender institutionality and mainstreaming should be transformed into state policies.

Thus, creating institutionality through ministries, offices and programmes is key to establishing a specific agenda with concrete responsibilities. However, as noted before, institutionality without the political will that gives content, resources and direction to these initiatives is emptied of meaning.

CONCLUSION

First, we would like to assert the importance of evaluating measures and policies from a gender perspective. With all its flaws and limitations, the tracker developed by UNDP and UN Women is a step in the right direction. It gave visibility to the importance of incorporating a gender perspective into the response to the Covid-19 crisis. It also granted some degree of recognition to those who were applying the gender-sensitive measures (and perhaps even some shame to those who were not).

Nonetheless, it is also worth reflecting critically on this tool and recognizing that simply counting measures is an extremely limited approach. Some of the problems that we have identified through our analysis are the binary nature of the tracker and the lack of any information on the actual impact of these policies. In addition, there is a lack of information on the resources actually allocated to the measures captured by the tracker, as well as the failure to include an intersectional approach to identify how these policies and programmes impact different groups of women.

Although the tracker equalizes all gender-sensitive measures, we wish to set them apart and recognize that, even though they all might be necessary (especially during an economic crisis and a global pandemic), only very few of them have the transformative potential of subverting existing gender relations through tackling structural inequalities.

In the case of Argentina, we have identified some policies that are worth noting thanks to their gender perspective, which enabled them to capture segments of the population traditionally excluded from social protection. The case of the IFE is an excellent example of how a feminist perspective can shed light on blind spots in policy design if there actually is the political will to identify and fill any existing gaps. Equally important is to recognize that, although this policy provides a much-needed relief to those further towards the margins, it does not substantially alter the gender inequalities and power relations that underpin the economic system.

In the establishment of the Mesa Interministerial de Políticas de Cuidados we find a policy firmly grounded on a feminist analysis of the economy. We consider that the initiative offers a conceptualization of care and its place within the economic system, which constitutes a stepping stone towards a gender-transformative Rights-Based Economy.

We find multiple and overlapping enabling conditions, including political will, state structure, high levels of gender institutionalization and legal systems with strong linkages with human rights law. The differential factor seems to be the presence of feminists in decision-making positions, with real power and resources to operationalize (at least to some extent) their vision.

The case of Argentina demonstrates that, even when resources are scarce, governments can find or create fiscal space to fund social protection and other necessary policies when it is needed. One question that remains unanswered is whether this would have been possible in a context in which economic policies were mandated by external actors. Although the IMF allowed for some leeway in terms of government spending during Covid-19 (Razavi *et al.* 2021; FTC 2022), it has now fully returned to its usual prescription for achieving financial and macroeconomic stability: a set of austerity measures (Ortiz & Cummins 2022). Furthermore, through its recently adopted gender strategy, the IMF has made explicit its intention to include gender conditionalities in its agreements with member countries in the future (IMF 2022b).

Argentina has spent 41 of the last 65 years under IMF programmes (Brenta 2021) and is currently the recipient of the largest loan in the history of the IMF (Rúa 2021). There is a real danger not only that this institution will impose austerity measures that further undermine the livelihoods of women and people with diverse SOGI but that it will force its own perspective on gender equality; this, essentially, means an instrumentalist approach to women's economic empowerment that is focused mostly on women's access to the labour market – over the more transformative approach promoted by Argentinian feminists in key decision-making positions.

As a next step, we need to continue searching for policies that move away from recovery to transformation and bring us closer to a Rights-Based Economy with care at its centre.

CHAPTER 13

A FEMINIST AND DECOLONIAL GLOBAL GREEN NEW DEAL: PRINCIPLES, PARADIGMS AND SYSTEMIC TRANSFORMATIONS

Bhumika Muchhala

INTRODUCTION

The current paradigm of the global economy is characterized by three broad features. First, neoliberalism, and its enduring agenda of liberalization, privatization and deregulation (Craig & Porter 2006). Since the 1970s neoliberalism has led to the deployment of the state to serve the interests of corporations and private investors rather than to fulfil people's rights. Second, the economic financialization, or the systemic deregulation of finance capital, whereby financial markets, motives, institutions and elites dominate the global economy, affecting everything, from production, consumption and regulation to health. And, third, intellectual monopoly capitalism, in which owners of intellectual property act as a monopoly force by reducing competitive supply, excluding others from using patented knowledge and increasing prices. At the centre of these paradigms is the overarching emphasis on export-oriented development models for the Global South through fossil-fuel-dependent global value chains and private investment governed by developed countries.

The historical extraction of ecological colonialism has expanded in scale and sophistication by exporting primary commodities and natural resources, such as timber, coffee, cotton and sugar (Malm 2016). The manifold harms of air pollution, soil erosion, desertification, deforestation and monocrops replace a diversity of local production, exploit many workers and often violate their human rights and exacerbate climate change. Unsurprisingly, the climate catastrophes we witness today are being felt the hardest in countries where colonization decimated natural resources, altered infrastructures and compromised traditional ways of living that respect the environment (Perry 2020). Powerful corporations and markets controlled by colonizers become the foundation of a "global economy" underpinned by several centuries of strategies of wealth drain, slavery or indentured servitude, deindustrialization and the creation of commodity and extractive enclaves.

A feminist and decolonial Global Green New Deal (GGND) is a collective project within the ecological and climate justice social movements to radically reimagine these reigning paradigms towards redistribution, equity and praxis of reparations, linking it to structural change and ideological transformation. A feminist and decolonial GGND resists the socially constructed hierarchies of racial, gender, class, caste sexuality and ability-based inequalities, which underpin colonial, neoliberal and capitalist structures, ideas and societies. It recognizes that the current ecological collapse directly results from an unequal social contract in which these hierarchies shape our social and economic relations. A feminist and decolonial GGND creates a plurality of new paradigms that forge active links between climate change, racialized and gendered labour exploitation, trade rules and the economic structures that reproduce inequalities both within and among nations. It is critical for a feminist and decolonial GGND to be global, as no country or region exists in isolation in a world that is inextricably interdependent through trade, human, capital and climate flows.

SYSTEMIC INEQUALITIES IN THE WORLD ECONOMIC ORDER

Starting with ecological extraction in the colonial era, further amplified by fossil capitalism during the Industrial Revolution, trade expansion, and the formation of a global market through colonial conquest and Indigenous land dispossession, this system thrived on the wealth generated by slave labour (Williams 2021). The Industrial Revolution in Britain started the process that led to the emission of vastly larger scales of carbon emissions, resulting in today's anthropogenic global warming (McGregor *et al.* 2016). Entire political and economic institutions and designs were assembled to expand and strengthen fossil fuels as a central fulcrum of capitalist extraction and accumulation, which required an unequal balance of power rooted in colonial structures and relations (Táíwò & Bigger 2022). This fundamental inequality has been embedded into international organizations and multilateralism, which manages and determines global economic and political affairs today. International "development" continues to be organized through modernist notions that flattened difference and disregarded economic structuralism (Chang 2002). The field of development studies reinforces notions and concepts such as "stages of development" and "comparative advantage", denigrating the Global South to monetized resources, land and harvest waiting to be commodified or exploited for production and consumption elsewhere.

Reforming global economic governance is at the heart of a feminist and decolonial GGND, which is still shaped by colonial-era inequities in power and voice within the Group of 20, the Organisation of Economic Co-operation and Development, the Institute of International Finance, the International Monetary Fund and the World Bank. In many ways the archetypal unapologetic neoliberal institution, the IMF has the power to shape and manage the social provisioning of its borrower governments. Governance power in the Fund's executive board is disproportionately skewed towards rich countries, holding more than a half of the voting power; developing countries, which constitute 85 per cent of the world's population, have a minority share. For every vote that the average person in the Global North has, the average person in the Global South has only one-eighth of a vote (Hickel 2019).

PRINCIPLES, POLICY PARADIGMS AND DECOLONIAL FUTURES

Coherent foundations underpin the design and implementation of a just and equitable GGND. These foundations involve three dimensions: principles, policy change and decolonial praxis. The principles involve a Rights-Based Economy, structural feminism and common but differentiated responsibilities. Structural policy transformations involve centring public expenditure and dismantling the austerity bias. They also include achieving debt justice through restructuring and cancellation, as well as tax justice through international cooperation within a UN tax convention, averting green financialization and carbon colonialism. Decolonial theory offers a praxis of countering the singularity of neoclassical economics and expanding into a plurality of economic methods. In an exchange with each other, a heterogeneous spectrum of economic approaches, including feminist, heterodox, ecological and political theory, generates a powerful toolbox to construct a legitimate GGND.

A RIGHTS-BASED ECONOMY AS A FOUNDATION FOR A GGND

An RBE is based on a holistic understanding of human well-being, supported by the values and obligations of human rights (CESR 2020). It involves policy change and political action to redistribute resources, remedy inequalities and rebalance unequal power dynamics and social relations in our economies and societies. An RBE is a foundation for a GGND, providing a coherent set of values and mechanisms for economic justice and social equality. Three dynamic human rights frameworks are particularly relevant to a Rights-Based Economy: the International Covenant on Economic, Social, and Cultural Rights (ICESCR), extraterritorial obligations (ETOs) and the Declaration on the Right to Development (DRTD).

The ICESCR clarifies the requirement of states, as duty-bearers, to employ the maximum available resources to realize economic and social rights by all appropriate means, including the adoption of legislative measures (UNGA 1966). The ICESCR highlights progressive realization to mobilize the maximum available resources: the avoidance of retrogression, such as by refraining from cutting expenditures on public services; non-discrimination and equality, such as by ensuring that distributive impacts of services and funds are equitable across social and class groups; and minimum core obligations, for example, to ensure the basic needs of the whole population (UNGA 1966; UN Economic and Social Council 1990).

Extraterritorial obligations have emerged as critical human rights tools to address the dynamics and impacts of finance and macro policy in a globalized economy. ETOs are defined as the obligations relating to the acts and omissions of a state, within or beyond its territory, that affect the enjoyment of human rights. The Maastricht Principles on Extraterritorial Obligations of States in the area of Economic, Social and Cultural Rights assembles these obligations. Grounded in human rights instruments and principles, especially ICESCR, it calls for international cooperation and assistance (ETO Consortium 2013; UNGA 1966: 2, art 2).

The DRTD reiterates the inalienable nature of the right to development and the prerogative of providing an equal opportunity for the enjoyment of the right (UNGA 1986). Although the rights of individuals and peoples, and equality of opportunity for nations, comprise the central focus of the declaration, its articles spell out states' responsibilities of the state, such as the "right and the duty to formulate appropriate national development policies that aim at the constant improvement of the well-being of the entire population and of all individuals" (UNGA 1986: art. 2.3); the primary responsibility of the state "for the creation of national and international conditions favourable to the realization of the right to development" (UNGA 1986: art. 3.1); and the duty of states to "co-operate with each other in ensuring development and eliminating obstacles to development" (UNGA 1986: art. 3.3).

The DRTD is unique for its application to the state as a collective body and for addressing the macro policy constraints to the state's pursuit of economic and social development. Meanwhile, international financial institutions routinely argue that their mandate does not include the fulfilment of human rights. The GGND approach addresses such claims by holding international institutions accountable regardless of their mandate. Their bodies are comprised of member states as shareholders, which are human rights duty-bearers.

Inclusive economic rights are central to remaking an extractive and unequal world economy into a rights-based one. It requires a shift from values of self-interest, boundless accumulation and exploitation to a moral economy underpinned by economic inclusion, human dignity, social equity, sustainability and participatory accountability.

STRUCTURAL FEMINISM

Feminist theory confronts gender as a system structuring unequal power relations. This frame is foundational to feminist climate justice, as a system of patriarchal fossil capitalism exploits and abuses both nature and gender in intertwined ways. Patriarchy, as both ideology and praxis, constructs hierarchical gender differences through a global sexual division of labour. Consequently, the social reproductive economy becomes indispensable to capital accumulation through unremunerated, or free, labour, including the creation of labour supply. As Lenore Palladino and Rhiana Gunn-Wright (2021) point out, care-based employment supported by an RBE delivering family-sustaining wages, social protection and public services contributes to the creation of green jobs and the well-being of both current and future generations by regenerating natural resources and ecosystems. The global climate crisis amplifies the need for care in response to increasing health impacts and disaster response needs, making care infrastructure indispensable in redressing climate crises (Muchhala 2021). No other community leads the protection of the world's biodiversity as the Indigenous communities do, as the small amounts of Indigenous land cultivate almost 85 per cent of the world's biodiversity (Raygorodetsky 2018).

A feminist foundation for a Global Green New Deal generates accountability for women's human rights. The Convention on the Elimination of All Forms of Discrimination against Women (CEDAW) and the Beijing Platform for Action uphold women's rights norms (UNGA 1995). Article 2 of CEDAW commits to a policy of eliminating discrimination against women by all appropriate means and upholds the key human rights principles of equality and non-discrimination (UNGA 1979). The Beijing Platform commits states to analyse the structural links between gender relations, environment and development, emphasizing on sectors such as agriculture, industry, fisheries, forestry, environmental health, biological diversity, climate, water resources, and sanitation (UNGA 1995: para. 258).

COMMON BUT DIFFERENTIATED RESPONSIBILITIES

Within GGND narratives, two paradigms are at play: the existential threat of carbon emissions and climate crisis; and the systemic inequalities. A decolonial paradigm collapses this binary and argues that a GGND must simultaneously strive for ecological sustainability and the human right to equitable development through historical responsibilities (Muchhala 2021). The 1992 Rio principle of common but differentiated responsibilities (CBDR) upholds an interdependent approach rooted in the unequal history of climate harm. The UN Earth Summit held in Rio de Janeiro in 1992 recognized that states have different historical responsibilities and national capacities in addressing the climate crisis (UNGA 1992). A decolonial basis for a Global Green New Deal is grounded in the CBDR principle (Muchhala 2021).

Implementing CBDR requires political will to transform tilted consumption and production patterns. At the core of transforming consumption patterns is the recognition that the global disparity in carbon footprint must be reduced (World Economic Forum 2019). The disparity can be exemplified by the average carbon footprint per person in the United States of 15.74 metric tons of carbon emissions, relative to 7.72 metric tons in China, 2.28 in Brazil, 1.90 in India and 0.65 in Ghana.[1] Globally, the average carbon footprint is close to 4.69 metric tons of carbon emissions, which reflects an enduring global reality of crude oil dependence in sourcing primary energy supplies. CBDR also implies the Global North taking the lead in reducing pollution and the use of toxic materials and cutting down the use and waste of natural resources.

CENTRING ON PUBLIC SYSTEMS AND SERVICES

A growing global consensus recognizes that public services and systems are the first line of defence in climate disasters (Intergovernmental Panel on Climate Change [IPCC] 2018).[2] For marginalized communities, including women and children, the lack of access to high-quality public services has long-term negative impacts on the human rights to health, education and work (Elson & Seth 2019; Rao & Akram-Lodhi 2021). For women across the Global South, the public sector is a crucial source of employment. For example, in Ecuador, 60 per cent of workers in the health sector are women, and 85 per cent of those in the nursing profession are women (Muchhala & Guillem 2022). When policy-makers retrench or fail to deliver public financing for public services, typically in response to pressure from international financial markets and

---

1. See Our World in Data: https://ourworldindata.org/grapher/co-emissions-per-capita.
2. See also the "Global manifesto for public services": https://futureispublic.org/global-manifesto.

their institutional agents, social provisioning is shifted onto women and marginalized communities (Razavi & Staab 2012). Generating the political will for public investments in a GGND entails redressing the defunding of the public purse through interest-laden debt payments to international creditors, tax evasion by transnational corporations and fiscal austerity directed by the IMF, credit rating agencies and private investors. A rights-based public services regime is undergirded by the values of dignity, equity, accountability and justice. As CESR (2020: 7) states, "More than just meeting people's needs, rights-based public services have promoted greater equality of opportunity and outcome as an explicit goal".

AUSTERITY VIOLATES ECONOMIC AND SOCIAL RIGHTS

History has repeatedly demonstrated the cost of maintaining debt sustainability through fiscal austerity, primarily, but not always, imposed through IMF loan conditions. Austerity exacerbates inequalities as well as exclusion and discrimination, across the registers of income, gender, race, caste, disability and sexuality (Muchhala 2021). Research shows a correlation between increases in inequality and IMF loan programmes recommending fiscal austerity, documented by both relative and absolute losses of income by the poor (Lang 2021) and, over time, by increases in income shares to the top 10 per cent of the population at the expense of the bottom 80 per cent (Stubbs *et al.* 2021). Empirical data confirm how budget cuts harm health and education outcomes; erode hard-earned pensions and social protection programmes; increase unpaid care work; impose consumption taxes; reduce or freeze public wages; and generate layoffs affecting public sector employees who are essential to public system resilience (Ortiz & Cummins 2019; IEO 2014). Since the onset of the Covid-19 pandemic the role of the IMF has heightened to an unprecedented level, with 221 loans being arranged with 88 developing countries as of August 2021 (Kentikelenis & Stubbs 2022). Through both loans and country surveillance reports, the IMF advised 154 developing countries in 2021 and 159 in 2022 to commence fiscal tightening measures, following a brief duration of fiscal spending in 2020 to respond to the immediate health and economic damage inflicted by the pandemic (Ortiz & Cummins 2019; Tamale 2021). The austerity measures, more premature and severe than in the aftermath of the global financial crisis of 2007–08, were projected to affect approximately 85 per cent of the world population in 2022. The pandemic led to a threefold increase in austerity measures, touching an estimated 2 billion people, or around 25 per cent of the world's population, in 2019. Some 80 per cent of the affected individuals are in developing countries across the Middle East and north Africa, sub-Saharan Africa, south and east Asia, the Pacific, Latin America and the Caribbean.

The effects of austerity measures on women occur through three dominant channels: diminished access to essential services; loss of livelihoods; and increased unpaid work and time poverty (Muchhala & Guillem 2022). Social protection programmes, which are a critical source of financial resources for low-income women, in large part because of the enduring gender pay gap and other factors that concentrate women more heavily in lower-income deciles, are often the first services to be reduced, even in countries that suffer extreme poverty (Razavi 2016).

FROM DEBT COLONIALISM TO DEBT JUSTICE

Sovereign debt crises overshadow much of the Global South today (World Bank 2022b). Debt payments will have increased by 150 per cent since 2011, as the world's poorest countries face their greatest debt servicing bills in 25 years (UNCTAD 2023). Repayments on public debt owed to foreign creditors in 91 low- or lower middle-income countries amounted to 16 per cent of government revenues in 2023 (Debt Justice 2023). Over 60 per cent of low-income countries are in debt distress or at high risk of debt distress, and 11 countries have defaulted since 2020, with several more sovereign defaults being predicted (IMF 2022a), Debt servicing amounts to approximately 25 per cent of total government spending across all developing countries. Debt servicing is twice education spending across all countries, 9.5 times that of health spending and 13.5 times social protection; for a smaller group of countries reporting climate spending in their United Nations Framework Convention on Climate Change nationally determined contributions, debt service is 32 times as high as climate spending (Martin & Waddock 2022). The poorest countries now spend more on servicing their debt as a proportion of gross national income than at any point in the past three decades, according to the 2022 *World Development Report* (World Bank 2022c). The proportion of debt servicing relative to public expenditure is a striking illustration of the violation to economic rights induced by the inability to restructure and relieve debt burdens.

The debt crisis today is playing out in a transformed landscape of borrowing and lending, in which the creditor composition of sovereign debt has made a sharp turn over the last several decades from official bilateral creditors, nearly all of whom were Paris Club members, to commercial creditors. As a result, 47 per cent of sovereign debt across the Global South is owed to private lenders, 27 per cent to multilateral institutions, 12 per cent to China and 14 per cent to other governments (UNCTAD 2022). Private debt is characterized by high and variable interest rates, foreign currency denomination and a lack of enforceability over private lenders to ensure comparability of treatment in debt restructuring exercises – all of which generates systemic risk for the many nations that rely on foreign debt to access international capital.

The G20's Common Framework, established in 2020, opens the door to major bilateral creditors excluded by the Paris Club, namely China and Saudi Arabia. However, almost two years later its myriad flaws led many to call it a "slow-motion debt tragedy" (Gill 2022). The key dilemma is the inability or unwillingness to enforce or regulate private creditor participation in the Common Framework. Middle-income countries, where the vast majority of the world's poor reside and where serious debt defaults are taking place, are – problematically – excluded from the Common Framework, further confirming its operational failure. The political economy of global debt creates continual challenges for those countries, especially developing countries, that repudiate or default on their external debt. The risks include, for example, being cut off from access to external financing, credit rating downgrades, a worsening of borrowing terms and/or capital outflows.

This intractable context makes urgent the need for a binding and transparent debt workout mechanism within a multilateral framework for debt crisis resolution. Calls for such an enduring pillar of economic justice have been made by developing countries within the UN General Assembly, global movements for social and economic justice, the international human rights community and various other developing countries (UNGA 2014). Global justice movements call for such a mechanism to address the unsustainable and illegitimate debt and provide systematic, timely and fair restructuring of sovereign debt, including debt cancellation, in a process convening all – bilateral, multilateral and private – creditors (Civil Society Financing for Development (FfD) Mechanism 2020). An ambitious, immediate and unconditional debt cancellation must also be central to a debt architecture reform. Past cases show how reducing debt stock and debt payments allows for countries to increase their social investments and climate financing.

CRAs effectively weaponize climate vulnerabilities as a risk factor that increases liabilities or costs (Crotti & Fresnillo 2021). This leads to higher borrowing costs, with higher interest payments or shorter maturities, to access money from international lenders, resulting in more debt. Sovereign debt interest rates for the most climate-vulnerable countries are higher than they would be if only macroeconomic indicators were considered. This leads to a vicious circle. As climate vulnerability increases borrowing costs, developing countries' debt burdens increase, in turn undermining investments and capacities to address loss and damage (UNCTAD 2023). When Global South nations are unable to invest and finance climate adaptation adequately, their climate vulnerabilities increase even more. The cyclical effects here are inherent to the amorality of a world financial design in which debt repayments to wealthy state, institutional and private creditors supersede the economic and social rights of people as well as the national policy space for developing countries, and especially climate-vulnerable countries such as small islands, to address climate change. In a Rights-Based Economy, global economic governance, including such measures as a debt workout mechanism, would aim to realize economic and social rights, the right to development and the Universal Declaration of Human Rights so as to move towards a world economy in which rights are realized for all (CESR 2020). The incorporation of CBDR into a Rights-Based Economy is reflected in the long-standing demand of debt justice movements that ecological debt owed to the Global South by the countries of the Global North must be incorporated in sovereign debt (Asian People's Movement on Debt and Democracy 2020).

TAX JUSTICE IS DECOLONIAL RECLAMATION

Illicit financial flows (IFFs) entail a systematic drain of financial resources from the Global South to the Global North. In the decade between 2004 and 2013 approximately $7.8 trillion was rerouted out of the developing world into tax havens. Illicit financial outflows accumulate into tax havens belonging to the richest businesses in the world (Kar & Spanjers 2015).

A decolonial and feminist GGND redresses tax-related financial drain through international cooperation on tax matters that advance rights-centred international tax policy. The mechanism long advocated for by developing countries in the UNGA, global justice advocates and movements and a growing number of international institutions, academics and policy-makers is precisely a universal and intergovernmental UN tax convention through which South states have a voice and shape their fate (Global Alliance for Tax Justice 2020). A feminist lens highlights how forgone public resources from systematic tax evasion and avoidance violate women's economic and social rights, as public services and the social-reproductive economy are chronically underfinanced and eroded.

DECOLONIZING ECONOMICS: HOW WE THINK IS AT THE ROOT OF OUR CRISES

The project to decolonize economics is gaining traction across academia, civil society and cross-border social movements for justice. One starting point is the recognition that neoclassical economics is a colonial construction.

The characteristics of a universal theory of supply and demand, quantitative methodologies and an origin in the European context supply neoclassical economics with the linear, techno-modernist and singular language of modernism (Mignolo 2009). What, then, are the strategies through which the discipline of neoclassical economic can be not only contested but also reshaped? A conscious engagement with a pluralism of economic knowledge, methods and praxis is one place to start. At least nine major schools of economics and various other smaller schools can be considered in delinking, including feminist, ecological, Marxist, Keynesian, developmentalist and structuralist (Chang 2018). Whereas neoclassical economic theory says that societies are made up of rational and selfish individuals, risk is calculable, choices, exchange and consumption are most important and the free market will automatically correct inefficiencies, structural, feminist and development economists say that societies are composed of gender-unequal class structures, the world is complex and uncertain, the most important domain of economies is production and human welfare, including the care and informal economies, and the state must use active fiscal policy to redistribute income to poor people, diversify economies, create jobs and protect local and small businesses.

A significant body of research on decolonizing research methodology asserts that Eurocentric ways of teaching and research are inadequate in explaining Southern experiences, while a plural landscape of knowledge exists not only as critique but in its own legitimacy (Tuhiwai Smith 2012). Methodological sophistication in economics, based on quantitative-heavy econometric modelling, limits the research questions that can be asked in the first place, and particularly their relevance outside industrialized economies. At the same time, the rigid scripture of econometric methodology is a prerequisite for publication in top-tier academic journals (Kvangraven & Kesar 2021). Similarly, most institutions of higher education in the South operate within Eurocentric canons and methodologies that lack social science and liberal arts interdisciplinarity, particularly with histories of economic thought in the era of political decolonization. This would elevate the thinking of Southern thinkers associated with the new international economic order, such as C. L. R. James and Kwame Nkrumah, who proposed centralized federal states, critiqued international hierarchy and sought to secure national self-determination towards political and economic equity on a global scale (Getachew 2019). Given that a central unit of analysis in macroeconomics is the nation state, the way such thinkers questioned the legitimacy of the state as a post-colonial construction marked by divisive and arbitrary features of colonial rule and proposed ways to disperse and delegate sovereignty beyond the state fuels a decolonial turn in economic thinking.

A key channel through which conventional economics can be decolonized is that of embodied knowledge, which accesses experiences and intuition within the life experiences of individuals and communities. The bodily experience of austerity is visible through the prisms of gender and race and detailed in a vast body of empirical research and feminist economics analysis (Elson & Çagatay 2000; Sen & Grown 1987). In moving from the abstraction of finance to the experiential imprint on women's bodies and livelihoods, embodiment as a form of knowledge expands political economy by illuminating the role of social-reproductive economies. Embodied knowledge, as opposed to textual knowledge, has the potential to shift three aspects. First, it unites the human condition to its natural condition, making economics material. Second, embodiment joins theory to praxis, making the politics of economic policy historically sensitive and accountable. Third, embodiment unites the experience and knowledge of women and racialized people through the material conditions of their daily life (Muchhala & Guillem 2022: 288).

DECOLONIAL FUTURES

The twentieth century may have dismantled colonialism's juridical-political institutions, but its colonial logic and systemic organization of governance and unequal power relations not only prevail but reproduce and expand in more insidious and sophisticated forms (Kataneksza, Ling & Shroff 2018). The coloniality of power thus institutionalizes, socializes and embeds structures of domination through the conceptual and operational registers of epistemic violence, unequal hierarchies of humanity and ruptured relations (Maldonado-Torres 2007; Mignolo 2009). The erasure of non-Western knowledge systems under the colonial narrative of civilizing the Other positioned modernity, science and rationality as superior to the knowledge of Indigenous and non-Western people, and to unwritten or uncoded forms of knowledge and ways of life (Maldonado-Torres 2007; Mignolo 2007). Historical narratives, lived experiences, cosmologies and thought systems originating from Indigenous cultures were (and still are) appropriated and/or suppressed and denied existence. Aníbal Quijano (2000: 540) writes, "Europe's hegemony over the new model of global power concentrated all forms of the control of subjectivity, culture, and especially knowledge and the production of knowledge under its hegemony." The notion of an individual separate from and superior to nature necessitates an undoing and remaking as part of a decolonial agenda for a green new deal (Muchhala 2021). Two historical falsehoods were promulgated: nature is proclaimed "dead" and land is proclaimed "empty" (Merchant 2019). If land is "empty", then Indigenous and rural communities can be displaced or eliminated; if nature is "dead", it can be exploited for unlimited resources. A decolonial ethos involves delinking from the knowledge systems that are still rooted in the Cartesian paradigm that assumes thinking comes before being. It involves reimagining humanity with the epistemologies of all who live on the margins, in particular the Indigenous (Muchhala 2021). Ultimately, we need a transformative decolonial turn towards asserting a humanity in which hierarchies of supremacy collapse and interactive and interdependent ways of being in unity with nature, with others and within ourselves arise to form a new reality.

CONCLUSION

A decolonial and feminist GGND is, at its very centre, about redressing systemic inequalities in the world economic order through principles, policy change and decolonial praxis. The three principles outlined above are that of an RBE, structural feminism and common but differentiated responsibilities. An RBE prioritizes the duty of states to progressively realize economic and social rights by employing the maximum available resources, extraterritorial obligations in cross-border human rights impacts and the collective right to development of communities and nations. Structural feminism advances a feminist economics framework of a care economy supported by the long-term public financing of social protection and public services. The principle of common but differentiated responsibilities renders relevance to historical and current contexts of inequality that define separate responsibilities and liabilities, particularly with regard to consumption and production patterns.

Policy changes for a decolonial and feminist GGND encompass a broad yet holistic range of economic structuralisms, from economic diversification and the technology transfers required for articulating local production structures to centring public expenditure and dismantling the austerity bias, and to achieving debt justice through restructuring and cancellation and tax justice through international cooperation within a UN tax convention. In doing so, a pluriverse of perspectives and praxis will make it possible to dismantle unequal hierarchies of humanity through constructed divides of race and gender, and, eventually, repair human relations as well as human–nature relations.

Ultimately, a feminist and decolonial GGND requires a radical reimagining of economic, social, ecological and political relations and realities. And both the legitimacy and sustenance of such a project are possible only through grassroots and community-level ownership. History shows us, across regions, cultures and political regimes, that meaningful changes are rooted in people's movements and organized struggles. Social movements comprehend and act in intersectional and interdisciplinary ways as a function of pragmatism as well as existentialism. For how can natural disasters wrought by climate change be separated from social and economic inequalities as livelihoods, basic needs and income security are increasingly challenged? Through a decolonial and feminist lens, the GGND becomes a political standpoint that articulates exactly why structural policy and theory change, for equitable and redistributive policy action requires a concomitant process of ideological transformation. In this sense, a plurality of paradigms that forge economic, social and ecological justice stitch together a new social contract, one that invokes rigorous regulation of finance, market and foot-loose capital in order to ensure not merely the survival but the flourishment of communities and economies. By invoking the long-standing demands, priorities and aspirations of political and social movements across geographies, time and even the phases of capitalism, a feminist and decolonial GGND clarifies the depth and content of intersectional and systemic change towards equity. It may seem like a tall order. However, nothing less will ensure the survival of our one planet, and of *all* people, not merely the privileged few, from current and future climate change in a world economy that is designed in deeply unequal structures.

CHAPTER 14

CONCLUSION: "RIGHTING THE ECONOMY" AND BUILDING ON PLURAL AND DECOLONIAL MODELS TO CURTAIL THE EFFECTS OF NEGATIVE CORPORATE PRACTICE

Matti Kohonen and Marianna Leite

EMERGENCE OF A RIGHTS-BASED ECONOMY

In order to transform the economy and society, we first need to recognize that contemporary markets are largely a product of a concentrated effort of economization, defined as a set of practices that leads to the establishment and maintenance of economic markets (Çalışkan & Callon 2009). Economization since the Second World War – namely with the foundation of the Bretton Woods institutions in 1944 – has expanded the reach of Global North market actors and investors into countries in the Global South. The end of the gold standard in 1971 set in motion the shift towards flexible exchange rates and the end of capital controls, with the simultaneous rise of offshore tax havens (Bullough 2023; Shaxson 2005). The late 1970s and early 1980s saw the "Big Bang" of deregulation such as the control of capital, currency exchange, separation of investment from retail banking and other banking regulation. This caused risks to the wider economy and society in the form of successive financial crises, which led to large-scale bailouts of economic sectors, in most cases by states. Governments ended up enacting austerity measures and prioritizing in "saving the economy" rather than prioritizing human rights, as we have seen in particular both during and after the Covid-19 pandemic (Oxfam International 2023; Ortiz & Cummins 2022; FTC 2022).

Parallel to the rise of the dominant discourse of marketization, this volume has analysed the rise of the human rights language as the universally accepted "lexicon" that has been developed over the same period – since the Second World War (Balakrishnan, Heintz & Elson 2016; Dommen 2022; Bachelet 2021). Human rights have grown in importance as a counter-narrative to growing trends of economization and marketization. For instance, some governments are now looking to prioritize the human rights of their population by expanding fiscal resources through greater taxation of extractive industries, high incomes and wealth (Gobierno de Chile 2023). This trend is particularly evident with the growth in both recognition and articulation of the existence of economic, social and cultural rights (ESCRs), which originate from the Universal Declaration of Human Rights (UDHR). ESCRs also became institutionalized as a key part of international law through the establishment of the International Covenant on Economic, Social and Cultural Rights (ICESCR), the Convention on the Elimination of All Forms of Racial Discrimination (CERD), the Convention on the Elimination of all forms of Discrimination against Women (CEDAW) and the UN Declaration on the Right to Development (UNDRD). Wider collective rights such as the right to development are recognized by instruments such as the African Charter on Human and Peoples' Rights and the Arab Charter on Human Rights.

The dichotomy between the ever-expanding forces of markets and the mobilization of social forces and institutions, both with different interests and demands, around an alternative discourse of rights is part of what Karl Polanyi in *The Great Transformation* (Polanyi 1944) discusses as constituting a "double movement". Polanyi establishes two important notions. First, economic institutions are permanently *embedded* in social institutions, which provide the norms, legitimization and acceptance for market institutions to operate (Granovetter 1985). Second, markets tend to "disembed" from their social foundations, but, in doing so, provoke a backlash against them. In some cases, market actors may resist pricing certain goods and services as a result of there being *embedded* social and cultural frames (DiMaggio 1994), such as the use of child labour, environmentally harmful products or profiteering from health emergencies. As a result, new social institutions are created to advocate for alternatives – both progressive and illiberal ones – as he observed in the 1920s and 1930s in the simultaneous rise of the New Deal, centred on the welfare state in the Global North countries, as well as fascism and communism as authoritarian alternatives.

Polanyi (1944) also observes that society has four modes of exchange. (a) *The domestic sphere*, producing and engaging in reproductive work for the purpose of a basic unit of society, often defined as a household or extended family. (b) *Reciprocity*, made up by people who interact through gift exchange relationships that are established between different social units, which may specialize in the production of specific goods and services but in which such relationships are indistinguishable from broader social relationships. (c) *Redistribution*, whereby an institutional authority – in most cases a state, but potentially also a feudal authority, chief or traditional ruler, or a charismatic authority – has a role to provide or distribute certain goods and services on the basis of a political agreement, often in order to gain legitimacy and also

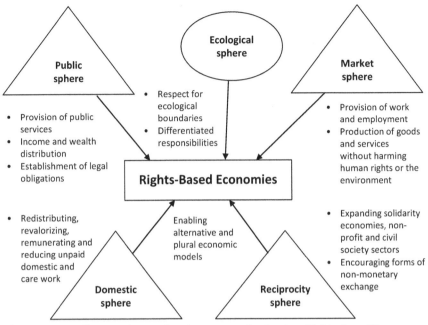

Figure 14.1 Different spheres of exchange contributing to a Rights-Based Economy

expand its reach. (d) *Market exchange*, as a site of production of goods and services where demand and supply meet for the purpose of exchange, and where exchange does not tend to create long-term social bonds, as money or money-like commodities are used as a form of intermediation (Mauss 1978 [1925]). To this, we today would also add (e) *the ecological sphere* (Brechin & Fenner 2017), to recognize the socio-ecological exchange, and the ecological dislocation that systems that centre on market exchange produce.

We can summarize how all the modes of exchange can contribute towards a Rights-Based Economy or economies in Figure 14.1.

REASSEMBLING ALTERNATIVE ECONOMIES

There are demands for alternative economic models, ones that often draw their inspiration from pre-colonial forms of exchange and resistance movements to neoclassical and neoliberal economics. In doing so, they create the seeds for change that allow for a reassembling of the economic sphere (Latour 2005: 7) and reconstructing it (Klare 1989) in such a way that we prioritize the attainment of all human rights.

As Ilcheong Yi notes in Chapter 9, "[A]lternative economies are understood as economic relations and activities that challenge, address or replace these negative consequences of economic relations and the actions of laissez-faire free market economics or neoliberalism" (119).

In terms of proposing to reassemble and to reconstruct economies, we need to focus on more than just the level of firms and individuals, which are generally considered as the key economic agents from the neoclassical perspective. Closer examination shows that neoclassical economies (Callon 1998) are heavily designed by economic experts, much as engineers design bridges and physical infrastructure. This realization opens up an avenue for economic alternatives – that is, if the design of the economic sphere was left to human rights activists and experts, or, at least, if they participated in the design of economic policies and economic spheres, then economies would indeed look fundamentally different from the current types of neoliberal and neoclassical economic assemblages.

That being said, and in reference to Yi's chapter in this volume, one should not assume that all "alternative economies are viable, egalitarian and ecologically sound enough to address the negative consequences of a laissez-faire free market" (Yi 2023: 95). Indeed, periods when policies were introduced to reduce inequalities were often followed by times that saw authoritarian regimes and narratives flourish (Phillips 2020). We see this in how disparities of wealth and power are often not tackled even in times of crises (Hamilton & Darity 2017).

Through the work of this book, we have found that the following set of non-exhaustive theories, shaping some plural alternative economic models, fit better with RBE principles and parameters and are therefore more likely to address the negative consequences of neoliberal policies.

Feminist economics and care economies

As noted in Chapter 13, by Bhumika Muchhala, a feminist economics centres the care economy as part of *a feminist and decolonial Global Green New Deal*. Feminist economics also strongly criticizes the idea of a utility-maximizing individual, considering the largely unpaid care and domestic work that women perform in disproportionate quantities in relation to men. Chapter 12, by Magalí Brosio and Edurne Cárdenas, also provides a vision of a care economy that addresses the unequal sexual division of labour at the heart of feminist economics. Women subsidize the economic system that most neoclassical economists still talk about in terms of formal wage labour and formal economic relationships, which could not occur without women's care and domestic work. The work around feminist economics also includes emotional labour and relational labour as spheres of feminized labour in maintaining social relationships. This aligns with existing human rights instruments, such as the Beijing Plan of Action and Platform for Action (UNGA 1995).

Degrowth, post-growth and post-extractivism

Chapter 2, by Olivier De Schutter, rightly notes that growth is often said to be the remedy for all the economic ills. Others in the ecological economics sphere have looked at ways in which the quest for endless growth is defined by planetary boundaries, as first noted by the Club of Rome's report on the limits of economic growth (Meadows *et al.* 1972). Later, this work developed into literature about degrowth (see Kallis, Demaria & D'Alisa 2015 and Hickel 2020). This body of work considers that the planetary overconsumption of resources in the Global North is a reason for poverty and inequality in the Global South, as resource scarcity makes it harder for those who do not have enough to build societies that meet human needs (Magalhães Teixeira 2021).

Although growth models have today been amended to become a green growth model, or climate-adjusted growth model (Brock & Taylor 2010; Bentley & Meckling 2021), to take into account the impacts of climate change and the depletion of non-renewable natural resources, these also come with socially detrimental aspects, such as lower taxes, derisking private capital flows and less protection on labour rights, which have been advocated to "attract" capital – a process labelled by Daniela Gabor (2021) as the "Wall Street Consensus".

The popular image of degrowth economics is the Doughnut Economy (Raworth 2012, 2017). However, the idea of endless green and circular economy-based growth has been debunked, notably by Jason Hickel and Giorgos Kallis (2019: 120), who state that "there is no empirical evidence that absolute decoupling from resource use can be achieved on a global scale against a background of continued economic growth, and [that] absolute decoupling from carbon emissions is highly unlikely to be achieved at a rate rapid enough to prevent global warming over 1.5°C or 2°C, even under optimistic policy conditions".

What Hickel and Kallis (2019) suggest is that the decoupling that sits at the heart of the green and circular economy models just is not possible. As Pedro Rossi indicates in Chapter 6, in the case of societies that experience severe material scarcity (or at least the perception of scarcity), degrowth is not possible, and at times even inadequate. Scholars such as Celso Furtado (1961, 1971) have developed a complementary vision aiming to define the kind of growth we seek, whose growth we are focusing on and at the benefit of whom.

A post-extractivist transition (Acosta 2021) of the economic model towards an RBE or new socio-economic missions that resignify growth is called for as an alternative, which also requires a deeper process of democratization of economic and social decision-making in achieving a structural transformation. Considering some of these discussions, Chapter 4, by Surya Deva and Harpreet Kaur, challenges the tenets of a free market economy, problematizing the theoretical underpinnings of existing business and human rights norms to propose having rights and rights-holders as the centre of these norms.

Social and Solidarity Economies

Social and solidarity economies (SSEs) are a worldwide range of economic practices that encompass enterprises, organizations and other entities that are engaged in economic, social and environmental activities to serve the collective and/or general interest, and are based on the principles of voluntary cooperation and mutual aid, democratic and/or participatory governance, autonomy and independence, and the primacy of people and social purpose over capital in the distribution and use of surpluses and/or profits as well as assets (Johanisova & Vinkjelhoferová 2019; ILO 2022c; Yi 2023). The term includes the eighteenth- and nineteenth-century movement of co-operatives and mutual societies, as well as more recent solidarity-based economic organizations (Borzaga & Defourny 2001).

In Latin America, the term "solidarity economy" (Singer 2001) draws on the decommodification of goods and services for the service of wider society, or terms such as "*sociedad abigarrada*" (Tapia Maella 2010; Zavaleta 1986), which one could loosely translate as a "hybrid society". *Sociedad abigarrada* states what could be a way of describing a system of production and life that mixes different types of production and exchange based on reciprocity and markets. Furthermore, the "popular economy" (Razeto 2001) considers that what is often seen as the "informal economy" (Hart 1973) is in fact a sphere of exchange that has many solidarity-based practices. Theories that describe social and solidarity economies (Laville 2023b [2010], 2003) often draw on both the concept of gift exchange (Mauss 2000 [1950]) and Polanyi's spheres of exchange in terms of hybridizing different forms of exchange.

By definition, social and solidarity economies are embedded into much wider social interaction, which is characterized not by "utility" or "gains" in the neoclassical sense but, rather, by the achievement of multiple aims, including income and livelihoods but also building ties with others based on principles of equality and reciprocity. In spite of not necessarily mentioning human rights as a cornerstone, SSEs align with human rights principles.

Decommodification of the commons

The commons can be defined as (a) a common pool of resources, collectively governed by (b) a community that (c) engages in sustainably shared life and resources (De Angelis 2019). The thinking around the commons has been further developed by Elinor Ostrom with Vincent Ostrom (Ostrom & Ostrom 1977). Models of the commons vary. In general, communities avoid conflicts on commons management via cases of collective ownership – cultural norms around shared duties to safeguard the commons more instead of using free markets and property rights. We believe that valuing the commons, as opposed to individualist interest, and decommodifying the commons, at least to a certain extent, are core components of the RBE.

As mentioned in Chapter 10, by Kári Hólmar Ragnarsson, it is important to decommodify certain social goods by immunizing certain social goods from market-based trade-offs. Chapter 11, by Jasmine Gideon and Kate Bayliss, and Chapter 3, by the Center for Economic and Social Rights, also touch upon the negative effects of commodifying social goods and removing them from the sphere of market exchange. We would take a step further by saying that immunizing a part of the commons from neoliberal policies and narratives is important.

Buen vivir *and ecological democracy*

Buen vivir (Gudynas 2011) draws upon an Andean philosophy of sustaining life. *Sumak kawsay*, a Quechua term that translates in Spanish as *buen vivir*, which now has constitutional recognition in both Ecuador and Bolivia, "expresses a deeper change in knowledge, affectivity, and spirituality, an ontological opening to other forms of understanding the relation between humans and non-humans which do not imply the modern separation between society and nature" (Chuji, Rengifo & Gudynas 2019). The Ecuadorian constitution states that "[t]he development regime is the organized, sustainable, and dynamic set of economic, political, socio-cultural, and environmental systems that guarantee the realization of good living, of sumak kawsay" (Asamblea Nacional de la República del Ecuador 2008: 117, art. 275). However, thus far, this has not stopped exploration for oil in key ecosystems in the Ecuadorian Amazon, namely the Tipnis national park.

Similarly, ecological democracy, or "Swaraj" (Kothari 2018), draws on south Asian concepts of living in communities that are in harmony with the ecological surroundings, and also not depending on industrial agriculture or agro-industry. Chapter 3, by the CESR, draws on the concepts of *buen vivir* and a pluriverse of alternative ways of living to construct an RBE. Although it does not necessarily depart from the concept of *buen vivir*, Chapter 13, by Bhumika Muchhala, proposes principles and paradigms for a systemic transformation that is aligned with it and the RBE.

THE ROLE OF THE STATE AS ENABLER OF HUMAN-RIGHTS-CENTRED TRANSFORMATIONS

We recognize the potential power of human rights regimes while acknowledging that these same regimes are in constant flux – "continually being interpreted, disputed, and transformed" (Sandwell *et al.* 2019: 6). Human rights can also be seen to be primarily achieved by autonomous movements that organize themselves apart from the state, while the state plays an enabling role in fostering, enabling and supporting such movements. In taking this position, it is important to recognize that human rights were conceptualized and still revolve around the central role of the state (Sandwell *et al.* 2019), and such a conceptualization of human rights is an evolution of this position.

De Schutter and Dedeurwaerdere (2022) mention three competing hypotheses that touch upon the need to re-envisage the role of the state when it comes to the realization of human rights. The first hypothesis focuses on the need to recapture and redemocratize the state (Freeman 2017). The second hypothesis looks at the power of critical consumers to affect and transform market forces (Mooney 2012). The third hypothesis argues for the need for an enabling state that gives freedom to local communities to experiment and push for transformative changes (De Schutter & Dedeurwaerdere 2022). We believe that, for an RBE to flourish as an enabling umbrella for plural and transformative economic models, it is crucial for the state to also act as a catalyst. The state, in this vision, is more than a redistributive state: it would catalyse human rights via its enabling capacities of financing, legislation and regulation to create the conditions for the diverse visions of alternative economies to flourish. This, in turn, would also reduce the power and disparities created by the over-reliance on growth and profit-orientated markets in organizing economic exchange.

In many ways, under neoliberalism, the state has been an enabler of market forces (Fraser 2022). Through the liberalization and loosening of rules pertaining to the role and the working of markets, many states – if not all, to some extent – have promoted a web of initiatives, policies and frameworks that put profit before human rights (Balakrishnan & Elson 2011a). Under the RBE, the enabling state would have an opposite role. As put by De Schutter and Dedeurwaerdere (2022: 1), in this case the enabling state would recognize that "[s]ocietal transformation, at the speed and scope required, also should be based on the reconstitution of social capital, and on new forms of democracy emerging from collective action at the local level". This "enabling state" would simultaneously reinforce the responsibilities of the welfare state, which remains essential to regulate market relationships, to tax corporations and wealthy individuals and to compensate for the inequalities that have their source in market relationships. In this sense, for all the transformations referred to in the above-mentioned section to thrive, it would be fundamental to have a state that enables creative thinking, collective power and re-assemblage. In short, for the appropriate rights and economic models to be front and centre, an enabling environment is needed. This is fundamental for the flourishing of a policy and praxis that are human-rights-centred.

CONCLUSION: WAY FORWARD AND RECOMMENDATION FOR POTENTIAL FUTURE WORK

The RBE attempts to frame the principles and parameters for human-rights-enabling economic policies while also considering the role of states in terms of enabling and lifting up plural economic alternatives that align with these same principles and parameters. This means that the rights-based economy can be used and understood as an umbrella term that encompasses the normative and aspirational aspects of different and plural alternative economic models, and the enabling environment for them to flourish.

Regardless of whether this book has presented a non-exhaustive set of examples, we believe that these are fundamental in further understanding what it means to transform or completely replace neoliberal policies. The main thread of this compendium also touches upon the importance of alternative initiatives for resistance to and the disruption and destabilization of the neoliberal status quo. In terms of theoretical underpinnings, we draw on the scholarship concerning different spheres of exchange to demonstrate that market-based exchange is by no means the dominant or only way to engage in economic exchange. This is especially true if we consider care economies, ecological concepts of the commons or, indeed, social and solidarity economies, which are often set up in direct response to the failures or emerging organically from the multiple crises of neoclassical or neoliberal economic policies.

The reality is that replacing neoliberalism will not be easy or straightforward, and to do so requires a closer understanding of how markets were constructed in the first place, by enabling states that maintain and reinforce them with their current set of economic policies. We should also not discount the past and present violence and force of colonialism and post-colonial policies in this context. Resistance, disruption and reassemblage will be key in keeping these ideas and principles alive and ensuring that collective work is strengthened, even when taking one step forwards and two backwards. However, as Polanyi (1944) also reminds us, a "double movement" of social forces keen to embed the economy back into society can indeed follow from a period of disembeddedness, which is a socially and ecologically harmful period, and is also characterized by polarization of the political sphere and calls for authoritarianism. Human rights offers, in such a process, a framework to re-embed, and reassemble, while resisting regressive and authoritarian alternatives.

To reach this reality, much work still needs to be done. We believe, for instance, that human rights indicators could be put in place through legislative measures to ensure that economic policies and reforms abide by human rights principles and normative values. Human rights principles should be used to design economic policies, including intergovernmental economic relationships. In addition, more research is needed to understand unexplored issues. For example, this book has been unable to cover gap areas, such as: the role of the private sector and of philanthropic institutions; the role of public enterprises or those of mixed capital; the role of the state in enhancing accountability and enabling plural alternatives; the role of localized examples based on Indigenous praxis such as *buen vivir*; or a more localized approach to the RBE, such as food sovereignty. We hope that future initiatives will still run in parallel while finding the points of synergy and collective wisdom. As we have seen during turning points in history, such as the French Revolution or decolonization movements, only the power of the collective is able to stand against oppressive structures that exploit people and the planet.

REFERENCES

Abdelal, R. & J. Ruggie 2009. "The principles of embedded liberalism: social legitimacy and global capitalism". In *New Perspectives on Regulation*, D. Moss & J. Cisternino (eds), 151–61. Cambridge, MA: Tobin Project.

Acosta, A. 2021. "Ocio y trabajo, en clave de Buen Vivir: reflexiones para construir otro futuro". In *Posdesarrollo: Contexto, contradicciones, futuros*, A. Acosta, M. Pascula & M. Ronaldo (eds), 411– 40. Quito: Editorial Abya-Yala.

ACHPR 2017a. "Statement on illicit financial flight and other concerns arising out of the Paradise Papers". 12 December.

ACHPR 2017b "Resolution on the Niamey Declaration on ensuring the upholding of the African Charter in the extractive industries sector", ACHPR/Res. 367 (LX). 22 May.

ACHPR 2017c. "Concluding observations and recommendations on 6th to 8th Combined Report of the Republic of Mauritius on the implementation of the African Charter on Human and Peoples' Rights. Banjul: African Union.

ACHPR 2018. "State reporting guidelines and principles on Articles 21 and 24 of the African Charter relating to extractive industries, human rights and the environment". Banjul: African Union.

ACHPR 2022. "General Comment 7: state obligations under the African Charter on Human and Peoples' Rights in the context of private provision of social services". Banjul: African Union.

ACT Alliance 2021. "Putting people first: equal access to COVID-19 vaccines". Geneva: ACT Alliance.

Adams v Cape Industries plc [1990]. Ch. 433 (27 July 1989).

African Tax Administration Forum 2021. "A new era of international taxation rules – what does this mean for Africa?". 8 October.

Ahmad, N. & A. Wyckoff 2003. "Carbon dioxide emissions embodied in international trade of goods", Science, Technology and Industry Working Paper 2003/15. Paris: OECD Publishing.

Ahmed, N. *et al.* 2022. "Inequality kills: the unparalleled action needed to combat unprecedented inequality in the wake of COVID-19", briefing paper. Oxford: Oxfam International.

Aizawa, M., D. dos Santos & S. Seck 2018. "Financing human rights due diligence in mining projects". In *Mining and Sustainable Development: Current Issues*, S. Lodhia (ed.), 99–122. Abingdon: Routledge.

Allam, L. 2021. "Failures at every level: changes needed to stop destruction of Aboriginal heritage after Juukan Gorge". *The Guardian*, 19 October.

Alliance Sud *et al.* 2016. "Swiss responsibility for the extraterritorial impacts of tax abuse on women's rights". Bern: Alliance Sud.

Amnesty International 2018. "Wrong prescription: the impact of austerity measures on the right to health in Spain". London: Amnesty International.

Amnesty International 2020. "Resuscitation required: the Greek health system after a decade of austerity". London: Amnesty International.

Amnesty International 2022. "Greece: authorities must be held to account after austerity measures violate right to health". 2 November.

Ampofo-Anti, O. & K. Donald 2022. "The Rights-Based Economy and the social contract: natural allies?". Christian Aid, 14 November.

Ampofo-Anti, O. & A. Saba 2022. "How a rights-based economy can help us overcome the social, economic and environmental challenges of our time". UNRISD, 29 September.

Antar 2022. "The destruction of Juukan Gorge". 23 November. https://antar.org.au/issues/cultural-heritage/the-destruction-of-juukan-gorge.

Asamblea Nacional de la República del Ecuador 2008. *Constitution of the Republic of Ecuador*. Quito: Asamblea Nacional de la República del Ecuador.

Asara, V. 2021. "Democracy, degrowth, and the politics of limits". *Green European Journal*, 9 September.

Asian Peoples' Movement on Debt and Democracy 2023. "Asia-wide mobilisations slam more loans for the South, demand finance for reparations, justice and equity". *Asia Debt Monitor* 2023 (2): 1–4.

Assa, J. & C. Calderon 2020. "Privatization and pandemic: a cross-country analysis of COVID-19 rates and health-care financing structures". UNDP, 30 May.

Aust, H. 2011. *Complicity and the Law of State Responsibility*. Cambridge: Cambridge University Press.

Austin, S. & D. Wright 2023. "The Black social economy". In *Encyclopedia of the Social and Solidarity Economy*, I. Yi *et al.* (eds), 92–6. Cheltenham: Edward Elgar.

Avi-Yonah, R. & G. Mazzoni 2019. "Taxation and human rights: a delicate balance". In *Tax, Inequality, and Human Rights*, P. Alston & N. Reisch (eds), 259–78. New York: Oxford University Press.

Azemi v Serbia [2013]. ECtHR, 11209/09 (5 November).

Bachelet, M. 2021. "Human rights update by the High Commissioner". 21 June. www.ohchr.org/en/2021/06/47th-session-human-rights-councilitem-2-human-rights-update-high-commissioner?LangID=E&NewsID=27178.

Baeten, G., L. Berg & A. Lund Hansen 2015. "Introduction: neoliberalism and post-welfare Nordic states in transition". *Geografiska Annaler: Series B, Human Geography* 97 (3): 209–12.

Bakan, J. 2004. *The Corporation: The Pathological Pursuit of Profit and Power*. New York: Free Press.

Balakrishnan, R. & D. Elson (eds) 2011a. *Economic Policy and Human Rights: Holding Governments to Account.* London: Zed Books.

Balakrishnan, R. & D. Elson 2011b. "Economic policies and human rights obligations: an introduction". In *Economic Policy and Human Rights: Holding Governments to Account*, R. Balakrishnan & D. Elson (eds), 1–26. London: Zed Books.

Balakrishnan, R., D. Elson & R. Patel 2010. "Rethinking macroeconomic strategies from a human rights perspective". *Society for International Development* 53 (1): 27–36.

Balakrishnan, R., J. Heintz & D. Elson 2016. *Rethinking Economic Policy for Social Justice: The Radical Potential of Human Rights.* Abingdon: Routledge.

Banković and Others v Belgium and 16 Other States [2001]. ECtHR 52207/99 (12 December).

Bannister, G. & A. Mourmouras 2017. "Welfare vs. income convergence and environmental externalities", Working Paper 17/271. Washington, DC: IMF.

Bantekas, I. & C. Lumina (eds) 2018. *Sovereign Debt and Human Rights.* Oxford: Oxford University Press.

Barclay, L. 2018. *Disability with Dignity: Justice, Rights and Equal Status.* New York: Routledge.

Bayliss, K. 2022. "Can England's national health system reforms overcome the neoliberal legacy?". *International Journal of Health Services* 52 (4): 480–91.

BBC News 2021. "Vale dam disaster: $7bn compensation for disaster victims". 4 February.

Bentley, A. & J. Meckling 2021. "Creative learning and policy ideas: the global rise of green growth". *Perspectives on Politics* 21 (2): 1–19.

Berik, G. & E. Kongar 2021. "The social provisioning approach in feminist economics: the unfolding research". In *The Routledge Handbook of Feminist Economics*, G. Berik & E. Kongar (eds), 3–19. Abingdon: Routledge.

Berik, G. & Y. van der Meulen Rodgers 2009. "Engendering development strategies and macroeconomic policies: what's sound and sensible?". In *Social Justice and Gender Equality: Rethinking Development Strategies and Macroeconomic Policies*, G. Berik & E. Kongar (eds), 1–43. New York: Routledge.

Berkhout, E. *et al.* 2021. "The inequality virus: bringing together a world torn apart by coronavirus through a fair, just and sustainable society", briefing paper. Oxford: Oxfam International.

Bernaz, N. 2014. "Establishing liability for financial complicity in international crimes". In *Making Sovereign Financing and Human Rights Work*, J. Bohoslavsky & J. Černič (eds), 61–76. Oxford: Hart Publishing.

Beveridge, W. 1942. *Social Insurance and Allied Services* [Beveridge Report]. London: HMSO.

BHRRC n.d. "Companies & investors in support of mHREDD". www.businesshumanrights.org/en/big-issues/mandatory-due-diligence/companies-investors-in-support-of-mhrdd.

Biebricher, T. 2018. "The rise of juridical neoliberalism". In *The Politics of Legality in a Neoliberal Age*, B. Golder & D. McLoughlin (eds), 97–115. Abingdon: Routledge.

Bielschowsky, R. 2014. "Estratégia de desenvolvimento e as três frentes de expansão no Brasil: um desenho conceitual". In *Presente e futuro do desenvolvimento brasileiro*, A. Calixtre, A. Biancarelli & M. Cintra (eds), 195–225. Brasília: IPEA.

Bilchitz, D. 2010. "The Ruggie framework: an adequate rubric for corporate human rights obligations?". *Sur: International Journal of Human Rights* 7 (12): 199–229.

Bilchitz, D. 2021. *Fundamental Rights and the Legal Obligations of Business.* Cambridge: Cambridge University Press.

Birchall, D. 2019. "Any act, any harm, to anyone: the transformative potential of 'human rights impacts' under the UN Guiding Principles on Business and Human Rights". In *University of Oxford Human Rights Hub Journal*, C. Meghan, F. Judy & F. Sandra (eds), 120–47. Oxford: Oxford University Press.

Birchall, D. 2021. "Corporate power over human rights: an analytical framework". *Business and Human Rights Journal* 6 (1): 42–66.

Birn, A.-E. & N. Krementsov 2018. "Socialising' primary care? The Soviet Union, WHO and the 1978 Alma-Ata Conference". *BMJ Glob Health* 3 (Supp. 3): 1–15.

Birn, A.-E. & L. Nervi 2019. "What matters in health (care) universes: delusions, dilutions, and ways towards universal health justice". *Globalization and Health* 15 (Supp. 1). DOI: 10.1186/s12992-019-0521-7.

Birn, A.-E., L. Nervi & E. Siqueira 2016. "Neoliberalism redux: the global health policy agenda and the politics of cooptation in Latin America and beyond". *Development and Change FORUM 2016* 47 (4): 734–59.

Bloom, D., A. Khoury & R. Subbaraman 2018. "The promise and peril of universal health care". *Science* 361. DOI: 10.1126/science.aat9644.

Blyth, M. 2013. *Austerity: The History of a Dangerous Idea.* New York: Oxford University Press.

Boesten, J. 2007. "Free choice or poverty alleviation? Population politics in Peru under Alberto Fujimori". *Revista europea de Estudios Latinoamericanos y del Caribe/ European Review of Latin American and Caribbean Studies* 82: 3–20.

Bohoslavsky, J. 2012. "Tracking down the missing financial link in transitional justice". *International Human Rights Law Review* 1: 54–92.

Bohoslavsky, J. & J. Černič (eds) 2014. *Making Sovereign Financing and Human Rights Work.* Oxford: Hart Publishing.

Bohoslavsky, J. & A. Esribá-Folch 2014. "Rational choice and financial complicity with human rights abuses: policy and legal implications". In *Making Sovereign Financing and Human Rights Work*, J. Bohoslavsky & J. Černič (eds), 15–32. Oxford: Hart Publishing.

Bohoslavsky, J. & M. Rulli 2010. "Corporate complicity and finance as a 'killing agent': the relevance of the Chilean case". *Journal of International Criminal Justice* 8: 829–50.

Borzaga, C. & J. Defourny (eds) 2001. *The Emergence of Social Enterprise.* London: Routledge.

Boston, D. 2021. "Caring communities for radical change". Transnational Institute, 5 November.

Boulding, K. 1966. "The economics of the coming spaceship Earth". In *Environmental Quality in a Growing Economy: Essays from the Sixth RFF Forum*, H. Jarrett (ed.), 3–14. Baltimore: Johns Hopkins University Press.

Bradlow, D. & D. Hunter (eds) 2010. "International law and the operations of the international financial institutions". In *International Financial Institutions International Law*. Amsterdam: Wolters Kluwer.

Branco, M. 2009. "Economics against human rights: the conflicting languages of economics and human rights". *Capitalism Nature Socialism* 20 (1): 88–102.

Braude, J. *et al.* (eds) 2013. *The Great Recession: Lessons for Central Bankers*. Cambridge, MA: MIT Press.

Brechin, S. & W. Fenner IV 2017. "Karl Polanyi's environmental sociology: a primer". *Environmental Sociology* 3 (4): 404–13.

Brenta, N. 2021. "Los acuerdos entre la Argentina y el FMI, 1956–2021". *Voces en el Fénix* 83: 26–33.

Brighouse, H. & A. Swift 2006. "Equality, priority and positional goods". *Ethics* 116 (3): 471–97.

Brinks, D. *et al.* 2021. "Private regulatory initiatives, human rights, and supply chain capitalism". In *Power, Participation, and Private Regulatory Initiatives: Human Rights under Supply Chain Capitalism*, D. Brinks *et al.* (eds), 3–34. Pittsburgh: University of Pennsylvania Press.

Brock, W. & M. Taylor 2010. "The Green Solow model". *Journal of Economic Growth* 15 (2): 127–53.

Brown, W. 2015. *Undoing the Demos: Neoliberalism's Stealth Revolution*. New York: Zone Books.

Bullard, R. *et al.* 2017. *Toxic Wastes and Race at Twenty: 1987–2007*. Cleveland: United Church of Christ Justice and Witness Ministry.

Bullough, O. 2023. *Butler to the World: How Britain Became the Servant of Tycoons, Tax Dodgers, Kleptocrats and Criminals*. London: Profile.

Bulmer, M. & A. Rees 2016. *Citizenship Today: The Contemporary Relevance of T. H. Marshall*. Abingdon: Routledge.

Cabieses, B. *et al.* 2022. "Health in Chile's recent constitutional process: a qualitative thematic analysis of civil proposals". *International Journal of Environmental Research and Public Health* 19 (24). DOI: 10.3390/ijerph192416903.

Cachalia, F. 2018. "Democratic constitutionalism in the time of the postcolony: beyond triumph and betrayal". *South African Journal on Human Rights* 35: 375–97.

Cafferata, M. 2020. "Mujeres Gobernando: más de cien funcionarias con altos cargos se organizaron en un grupo de WhatsApp". Página 12, 27 January.

Çalışkan, K. & M. Callon 2009. "Economization, part 1: shifting attention from the economy towards processes of economization". *Economy and Society* 38 (3): 369–98.

Callon, M. 1998. *The Laws of the Markets*. Oxford: Blackwell.

Canotilho, M., T. Violante & R. Lanceiro 2015. "Austerity measures under judicial scrutiny: the Portuguese constitutional case-law". *European Constitutional Law Review* 11 (1): 155–83.

Capraro, C. & F. Rhodes 2017. "Advancing feminist alternatives in the context of neoliberalism: reflections from advocating on unpaid care and domestic work". London: Gender and Development Network.

Case of the Río Negro Massacres v Guatemala [2012]. IACtHR Series C no. 250 (4 September).

CELS 2019. "Movimientos: las luchas por los derechos en democracia". In *Derechos humanos en la Argentina: Informe 2019*, 189–213. Buenos Aires: Siglo XXI Editores.

CELS 2021. *Post: Cómo luchamos (y a veces perdimos) por nuestros derechos en pandemia*. Buenos Aires: Siglo XXI Editores.

Černič, J. 2014. "Sovereign financing and corporate responsibility for economic and social rights". In *Making Sovereign Financing and Human Rights Work*, J. Bohoslavsky & J. Černič (eds), 139–60. Oxford: Hart Publishing.

CESR 2018. *Assessing Austerity: Monitoring the Human Rights Impacts of Fiscal Consolidation*. New York: CESR.

CESR 2020. *A Climate for Change: Trends Analysis Conducted for CESR's Strategy Planning Process*. New York: CESR.

CESR 2022. "Help us draw the blueprint for a rights-based economy". 11 July.

CESR & Christian Aid 2014. "A post-2015 fiscal revolution", human rights policy brief. New York: CESR.

CESR *et al.* 2022. "Submission to the independent expert on foreign debt, other related international financial obligations and human rights ahead of the 77th session of the General Assembly". www.cesr.org/sites/default/files/2022/Joint_Submission_to_the_Independent_Expert_of_Foreign_Debt_and_Human_Rights.pdf.

Chalk, N. & R. Hemming 2000. "Assessing fiscal sustainability in theory and practice", Working Paper 00/81. Washington, DC: IMF.

Challe, T. 2021. "The rights of nature: can an ecosystem bear legal rights?". State of the Planet, 22 April.

Chang, H.-J. 2002. "Kicking away the ladder: an unofficial history of capitalism, especially in Britain and the United States". *Challenge* 45 (5): 63–97.

Chang, H.-J. 2018. *Economics: The User's Guide*. London: Pelican Press.

Chaparro, S. 2014. "Presupuesto, derechos humanos y control judicial: una oportunidad para la convergencia entre constitucionalismo y hacienda pública", master's thesis. Universidad Nacional de Colombia, Bogotá.

CHRB 2019. "CHRB response to Brumadinho dam disaster: Vale suspension from Human Rights Benchmark". 28 January.

Christabell, P. 2023. "Women's self-help groups". In *Encyclopedia of the Social and Solidarity Economy*, I. Yi *et al.* (eds), 172–9. Cheltenham: Edward Elgar.

Chuji, M., G. Rengifo & E. Gudynas 2019. "Buen vivir". In *Pluriverse: A Post-Development Dictionary*, A. Kothari *et al.* (eds), 111–13. New Delhi: Tulika Books.

Cirefice, V. & L. Sullivan 2019. "Women on the frontlines of resistance to extractivism". *Policy & Practice: A Development Education Review* 29: 78–99.

Civil Society Financing for Development (FfD) Mechanism 2020. "Global economic solutions now!". 25 September. https://csoforffd.org/economic-reconstruction-and-systemic-reforms-summit-at-the-un.

Clarke, D. *et al.* 2020. "All hands on deck: mobilising the private sector for the COVID-19 response". UHC2030, 7 April.

Clifton, J., D. Diaz-Fuentes & A. Lara Gómez 2018. "The crisis as opportunity? On the role of the Troika in constructing the European consolidation state". *Cambridge Journal of Regions, Economy and Society* 11 (3): 587–608.

Collins v Minister for Finance & Ors [2013]. IEHC 530 (26 November).

Conectas 2019. "Urgent appeal: collapse of mining tailings dam owned and operated by Vale leaves several killed and hundreds missing in Brazil". 5 February. www.conectas.org/wp-content/uploads/2019/02/Urgent-Appeal-Brumadinho-05.02.2019.pdf.

Congreso de la Nacion Argentina 2020. "Law no. 27.610: Acceso a la Interrupción Voluntaria del Embarazo", adopted 30 December. Buenos Aires: Congreso de la Nacion Argentina.

Cornwall A. & D. Eade 2010. *Deconstructing Development Discourse: Buzzwords and Fuzzwords.* London: Practical Action Publishing.

Costanza, R. *et al.* 1997. *An Introduction to Ecological Economics.* Boca Raton, FL: CRC Press.

Cotula, L. & C. Tan 2018. "Public–private partnerships and aid's 'private turn': addressing the investment law dimensions". International Institute for Environment and Development, 30 January.

Craig, D. & D. Porter 2006. *Development beyond Neoliberalism? Governance, Poverty Reduction and Political Economy.* Abingdon: Routledge.

Crotti, I. & I. Fresnillo 2021. "The climate emergency: what's debt got to do with it?". Brussels: European Network on Debt and Development.

Crouch, C. 2011. *The Strange Non-Death of Neoliberalism.* Cambridge: Polity Press.

Csikszentmihalyi, M. 1997. *Flow: The Psychology of Happiness.* New York: Basic Books.

Csikszentmihalyi, M., R. Graef & S. McManama Gianinno 2014. "Energy consumption in leisure and perceived happiness". In *Flow and the Foundations of Positive Psychology*, M. Csikszentmihalyi (ed.), 127–33. Dordrecht: Springer.

Cueto, M. 2004. "The origins of primary health care and selective primary health care". *American Journal of Public Health* 94 (11): 1864–74.

Curtea Constituțională a României [2010]. Case no. 872/2010 (25 June).

Da Silva Carvalho Rico v Portugal [2015]. ECtHR, App. no. 13341/14 (1 September).

D'Alessandro, M. 2022. "Ingreso Familiar de Emergencia (IFE): notas sobre una política pública a contrarreloj". Fundar, 11 August.

Dann, P. 2013. *The Law of Development Cooperation: A Comparative Analysis of the World Bank, the EU and Germany.* Cambridge: Cambridge University Press.

Dann, P. & M. Riegner 2011. "Foreign aid agreements". In *Max Planck Encyclopedia of Public International Law*, vol. 4, 175–7. Oxford: Oxford University Press.

De Almeida Ribeiro, G. 2013. "Judicial activism against austerity in Portugal". *International Journal of Constitutional Law* blog, 3 December.

De Angelis, M. 2019. "Commons". In *Pluriverse: A Post-Development Dictionary*, A. Kothari *et al.* (eds), 124–6. New Delhi: Tulika Books.

De Schutter, O. 2019. "Taxing for the realization of economic, social and cultural rights". In *Tax, Inequality, and Human Rights*, P. Alston & N. Reisch (eds), 59–80. New York: Oxford University Press.

De Schutter, O. & T. Dedeurwaerdere 2022. *Social Innovation in the Service of the Social and Ecological Transformation: The Rise of the Enabling State.* New York: Routledge.

De Schutter, O., J. Swinnen & J. Wouters (eds) 2012. *Foreign Direct Investment and Human Development: The Law and Economics of International Investment Agreements.* Abingdon: Routledge.

De Witte, B. 2009. "Balancing of economic law and human rights by the European Court of Justice". In *Human Rights in International Investment Law and Arbitration*, P.-M. Dupuy, F. Francioni & E. Petersmann (eds), 197–207. Oxford: Oxford University Press.

Dean, J. 2002. "Does trade liberalization harm the environment? A new test". *Canadian Journal of Economics/Revue canadienne d'économique* 35 (4): 819–42.

Dean, S. & A. Waris 2021. "Ten truths about tax havens: inclusion and the 'Liberia problem'". *Emory Law Journal* 70 (7): 1659–84.

Debt Justice 2023. "Lower income country debt payments to hit highest level in 25 years". 11 April.

Del Valle, F. & K. Sikkink 2017. "(Re)discovering duties: individual responsibility in the age of rights". *Minnesota Journal of International Law* 26 (1): 189–245.

Demaria, F. 2018. "The rise – and future – of the degrowth movement". The Ecologist, 27 March.

Deva, S. 2021. "Covid-19, business, and human rights: a wake-up call to revisit the 'protect, respect and remedy' framework?". *International Community Law Review* 23 (5): 433–49.

Deva, S. 2023. "Mandatory human rights due diligence laws in Europe: a mirage for rightsholders?". *Leiden Journal of International Law* 36 (2): 389–414.

Deva, S. forthcoming. "Reimagining business and human rights". In *A Research Agenda for Business and Human Rights*, J. Schrempf-Stirling, T. Olsen & J. Van Harry III (eds). Cheltenham: Edward Elgar.

DFI Working Group 2017. "Summary report". Manila: Asian Development Bank. www.adb.org/sites/default/files/institutional-document/455291/blended-concessional-finance-ps.pdf.

Diaz-Bonilla, E. 2015. *Macroeconomics, Agriculture, and Food Security: A Guide to Policy Analysis in Developing Countries.* New York: International Food Policy Research Institute.

DiMaggio, P. 1994. "Culture and economy". In *The Handbook of Economic Sociology*, N. Smelser & N. Swedberg (eds), 27–57. Princeton, NJ: Princeton University Press.

Dittmar, H. 2007a. *Consumer Culture, Identity and Well-Being: The Search for the "Good Life" and the "Body Perfect".* Hove: Psychology Press.

Dittmar, H. 2007b. "The costs of consumer culture and the 'cage within': the impact of the material "good life" and "body perfect" ideals on individuals' identity and well-being". *Psychological Inquiry* 18: 23–31.

Dommen, C. 2022. *Human Rights Economics: An Enquiry*. Geneva: Friedrich Ebert Stiftung.

Donald, K. *et al.* 2020. *A Rights-Based Economy: Putting People and Planet First*. London: Christian Aid & CESR.

Donald, K. & N. Lusiani 2017. "Gendered cost of austerity: assessing the IMF's role in budget cuts which threaten women's rights". In *The IMF and Gender Equality: A Compendium of Feminist Macroeconomic Critiques*, 31–44. London: Bretton Woods Project.

Dowell-Jones, M. & D. Kinley 2011. "Minding the gap: global finance and human rights". *Ethics & International Affairs* 25: 183–210.

Dweck, E., P. Rossi & A. Oliveira (eds) 2020. *Economia pós-pandemia: Desmontando os mitos da austeridade fiscal e construindo um novo paradigma*. São Paulo: Editora Autonomia Literária.

Easterlin, R. 1995. "Will rasing the incomes of all increase the happiness of all?". *Journal of Economic Behavior & Organization* 27 (1): 35–47.

Economist, The 2021. "Chile's new president promises to bury neoliberalism". 20 December. www.economist.com/the-americas/2021/12/20/chiles-new-president-promises-to-bury-neoliberalism.

Economist, The 2022. "Stakeholder capitalism poisons democracy, argues Vivek Ramaswamy". 14 September. www.economist.com/by-invitation/2022/09/14/stakeholder-capitalism-poisons-democracy-argues-vivek-ramaswamy.

EDFI 2019. "EDFI principles for responsible financing of sustainable development". Brussels: EDFI.

Els, F. 2017. "Barrick shares crater as Tanzania troubles grow". Mining.com, 26 October.

Elsen, S. 2023. "Social services". In *Encyclopedia of the Social and Solidarity Economy*, I. Yi *et al.* (eds), 295–302. Cheltenham: Edward Elgar.

Elson, D. & N. Çagatay 2000. "The social content of macroeconomic policies". *World Development* 28 (7): 1347–64.

Elson, D. & A. Seth (eds) 2019. *Gender Equality and Inclusive Growth: Economic Policies to Achieve Sustainable Development*. New York: UN Women.

Elson, D., R. Balakrishnan & J. Heintz 2013. "Public finance, maximum available resources and human rights". In *Human Rights and Public Finance: Budgets and the Promotion of Economic and Social Rights*, A. Nolan, R. O'Connell & C. Harvey (eds), 295–302. Oxford: Hart Publishing.

Ely, J. 1980. *Democracy and Distrust: A Theory of Judicial Review*. Cambridge, MA: Harvard University Press.

Equal International 2022. "Global public investment for pandemic preparedness and response". London: Global Public Investment. https://qjz3c1.n3cdn1.secureserver.net/wp-content/uploads/2022/02/GPI-for-Pandemic-Preparedness-and-Response.pdf?time=1670515638.

Escalante, L. & H. Maisonnave 2022. "Gender and COVID-19: are women bearing the brunt? A case study for Bolivia". *Journal of International Development* 34 (4): 754–70.

Esping-Andersen, G. 1990. *The Three Worlds of Welfare Capitalism*. Princeton, NJ: Princeton University Press.

Espósito, C., Y. Li & J. Bohoslavsky 2013. "Introduction: the search for common principles". In *Sovereign Financing and International Law: The UNCTAD Principles on Responsible Sovereign Lending and Borrowing*, C. Espósito, Y. Li & J. Bohoslavsky (eds), 3–12. Oxford: Oxford University Press.

ETO Consortium 2013. "Maastricht Principles on Extraterritorial Obligations of States in the area of Economic, Social and Cultural Rights". Heidelberg: FIAN International.

Etter-Phoya, R. 2022. "African ministers call for UN tax convention to protect against financial secrecy supplied by the richest nations". TJN, 27 May.

Eucken, W. 2017 [1937]. "Structural transformations of the state and the crisis of capitalism". In *The Birth of Austerity: German Ordoliberalism and Contemporary Neoliberalism*, T. Biebricher & F. Vogelmann (eds), 51–69. London: Rowman & Littlefield International.

European Coalition for Corporate Justice 2022. "Comparative table: corporate due diligence laws and legislative proposals in Europe". 21 March.

European Parliament 2022. "Proposal for a Directive of the European Parliament and of the Council on Corporate Sustainability Due Diligence and amending Directive (EU) 2019/1937", A9-0184/2023. Strasbourg: European Parliament.

Expert Working Group on Global Public Investment 2022. "Building a better system: making global public investment a reality". London: Global Public Investment. https://qjz3c1.n3cdn1.secureserver.net/wp-content/uploads/2022/07/Building-a-better-system-Making-GPI-a-reality.pdf.

FACTI Panel 2021. *Financial Integrity for Sustainable Development*. New York: UN.

FAO 1999. *Implications of Economic Policy for Food Security: A Training Manual*. Rome: FAO.

Feiveson, L. & J. Sabelhaus 2018. "How does intergenerational wealth transmission affect wealth concentration?". Federal Reserve System, 1 June.

Ferraz, O. 2011. "Harming the poor through social rights litigation: lessons from Brazil". *Texas Law Review* 8 (7): 1643–68.

Fine, B., C. Lapavitsas & J. Pincus 2021. *Development Policy in the Twenty-First Century: Beyond the Post-Washington Consensus*. Abingdon: Routledge.

Fitch Ratings 2022. "Colombia tax reform does not affect fiscal forecasts". 16 November.

Forstater, M. & A. Readhead 2017. "A brutal lesson for multinationals: golden tax deals can come back and bite you". *The Guardian*, 6 July.

Foucault, M. 2004 [1979]. *The Birth of Biopolitics: Lectures at the Collège de France, 1978–79*, M. Senellart (ed.), P. Burchell (trans.). London: Macmillan.

Fraser, N. 2022. *Cannibal Capitalism: How Our System Is Devouring Democracy, Care, and the Planet and What We Can Do about It*. London: Verso.

Freeman, D. 2017. "De-democratisation and rising inequality: the underlying cause of a worrying trend", Working Paper 12. London: Department of Anthropology and International Inequalities Institute, London School of Economics and Political Science.

FTC 2017. "Who makes the rules on illicit financial flows?", policy brief. Boston: FTC.

FTC 2022. "Recovery at a crossroads: how countries spent Covid-19 funds in the Global South". Boston: FTC.

Furtado, C. 1961. *Desenvolvimento e subdesenvolvimento*. Rio de Janeiro: Fondo de Cultura.

Furtado, C. 1971. *Teoria e política do desenvolvimento*. São Paulo: Nacional.

Gadelha, C. (ed.) 2022. *Saúde é desenvolvimento: O complex econômico-industrial da saúde como opção estratégica nacional*. Rio de Janeiro: CEE/Fiocruz.

Galbraith, J. 1958. *The Affluent Society*. Boston: Houghton Mifflin.

Galeano, E. 1971. *Las venas abiertas de America Latina*. Mexico City: Siglo XXI.

Gabor, D. 2021. "The Wall Street consensus". *Development & Change* 52 (3): 429–59.

General Confederation of Greek Workers (GSEE) v Greece [2017]. Complaint no. 111/ 2014 ECSR (23 March).

Gerstenberg, O. 2014. "The justiciability of socio-economic rights, European solidarity, and the role of the Court of Justice of the EU". *Yearbook of European Law* 33: 245–76.

Getachew, A. 2019. *Worldmaking after Empire: The Rise and Fall of Self-Determination*. Princeton, NJ: Princeton University Press.

Gianella, C., J. Gideon & M. Romero 2021. "What does Covid-19 tell us about the Peruvian health system?". *Canadian Journal of Economics/Revue canadienne d'économique* 42 (1/2): 55–67.

Gideon, J. (ed.) 2016. *Handbook on Gender and Health*. Cheltenham: Edward Elgar.

GI-ESCR 2021. "Compendium of United Nations human rights treaty bodies' statements on private actors in healthcare", synthesis paper, version 4. Duluth, MN: GI-ESCR.

GI-ESCR 2022. "The failure of commercialized healthcare in Nigeria during the COVID-19 pandemic: discrimination and inequality in the enjoyment of the right to health". Duluth, MN: GI-ESCR.

Gill, I. 2022. "It's time to end the slow-motion tragedy in debt restructurings". Brookings, 25 February.

Giovanella, L. *et al.* 2018. "Universal health system and universal health coverage: assumptions and strategies". *Ciência & Saúde Coletiva* 23 (6): 1763–76.

Global Alliance for Tax Justice 2020. "Submission to the public consultation on the reports on the Pillar One and Pillar Two blueprints". 14 December.

Gobierno de Chile 2023. "Royalty minero: president promulga ley que entrega millonarios recursos para el desarrollo de las regiones". 3 August. www.gob.cl/ noticias/royalty-minero-presidente-promulga-ley-que-entrega-millonarios-recursos-para-el-desarrollo-de-las-regiones.

Gordon-Nembhard, J. & I. Ajowa Nzinga 2023. "African American social and solidarity economy and distributive justice". In *Encyclopedia of the Social and Solidarity Economy*, I. Yi *et al.* (eds), 105–12. Cheltenham: Edward Elgar.

Government of Canada 1985. "Bretton Woods and Related Agreements Act", R.S.C. 1985, c. B-7. Ottawa: Government of Canada. https://laws-lois.justice.gc.ca/PDF/ B-7.pdf.

Government of Canada 2008. "Official Development Assistance Accountability Act", S.C. 2008, c. 17. Ottawa: Government of Canada. https://laws-lois.justice.gc.ca/PDF/O-2.8.pdf.

Granovetter, M. 1985. *Economic Action and Social Structure: The Problem of Embeddedness*. Chicago: University of Chicago Press.

Guardian, The 2022a. "Serco's annual profits surge 21% to £216m on back of Covid contracts". 24 February.

Guardian, The 2022b. "Revealed: Tory peer Michelle Mone secretly received £2.9m from VIP lane PPE firm". 23 November.

Gudynas, E. 2011. "Debates sobre el desarrollo y sus alternativas en América Latina: una breve guía heterodoxa". *Más allá del Desarrollo* 1: 21–54.

Guerra Martins, A. 2015. "Constitutional judge, social rights and public debt crisis: the Portuguese constitutional case law". *Maastricht Journal of European and Comparative Law* 22 (5): 678–705.

Guidolin, A. 2019. "Crise, austeridade e o financiamento da saúde no Brasil", dissertation. Universidade de Campinas.

Hall, S., D. Massey & M. Rustin 2013. "After neoliberalism: analysing the present". *Soundings: A Journal of Politics and Culture* 53: 8–22.

Hamilton, D. 2022. "A race-conscious economic rights approach to providing economic security for all". In *The Great Polarization: How Ideas, Power, and Policies Drive Inequality*, R. von Arnim & J. Stiglitz (eds), 333–47. New York: Columbia University Press.

Hamilton, D. & W. Darity 2017. "The political economy of education, financial literacy, and the racial wealth gap". *Federal Reserve Bank of St. Louis Review* 99 (1): 59–76.

Harrington, J. & A. Manji 2018. "Judicial review and the future of UK development assistance: on the Application of O v Secretary of State for International Development (2014)". *Legal Studies* 38 (2): 320–35.

Hart, K. 1973. "Informal income opportunities and urban employment in Ghana". *Journal of Modern African Studies* 11 (1): 61–89.

Harvey, D. 2005. *A Brief History of Neoliberalism*. Oxford: Oxford University Press.

Harvey, D. 2006. *Spaces of Global Capitalism: Towards a Theory of Uneven Geographical Development*. London: Verso.

Hausknost, D. 2020. "The environmental state and the glass ceiling of transformation". *Environmental Politics* 29 (1): 17–37.

Hayek, F. 1993 [1978]. "The containment of power and the dethronement of politics". In *Law, Legislation and Liberty*, vol. 3, *The Political Order of a Free People*, 128–52. Chicago: University of Chicago Press.

Head, J. 2008. "Law and policy in international financial institutions: the changing role of law and the IMF and the multilateral development banks". *Kansas Journal of Law and Public Policy* 17: 194–229.

Healy, S. 2009. "Economies, alternative". In *International Encyclopedia of Human Geography*, R. Kitchin & N. Thrift (eds), 338–44. Oxford: Elsevier.

Heilbroner, R. 1985. *The Nature and Logic of Capitalism*. London: Norton.

Heintz, J. & R. Balakrishnan 2014. "Towards a human rights-centered macroeconomic and financial policy in the US: revisited". Amherst, MA: Political Economy Research Institute, University of Massachusetts – Amherst.

Hellowell, M. *et al.* 2020. "Covid-19 and the collapse of the private health sector: a threat to countries' response efforts and the future of health systems strengthening?". Global Health Policy Unit, 27 May.

Heyns, C. (ed.) 2002. *Human Rights Law in Africa 1999*. The Hague: Kluwer Law International.

Hickel, J. 2019. "Is it possible to achieve a good life for all within planetary boundaries?". *Third World Quarterly* 40 (1): 18–35.

Hickel, J. 2020. *Less Is More: How Degrowth Will Change the World*. London: Penguin Books.

Hickel, J. & G. Kallis 2019. "Is green growth possible?". *New Political Economy* 25 (4): 469–86.

Hillenkamp, I. & F. Wanderley 2015. "Social enterprise in Bolivia: solidarity economy in context of high informality and labour precariousness", International Comparative Social Enterprise Models Working Paper 21. Liège: HEC Management School, Université de Liège.

Hirsch, F. 1977. *Social Limits to Growth*. London: Routledge.

Hirschman, A. & M. Rothschild 1973. "The changing tolerance for income inequality in the course of economic development". *Quarterly Journal of Economics* 87 (4): 544–66.

Homedes, N. & A. Ugalde 2005. "Why neoliberal health reforms have failed in Latin America". *Health Policy* 71 (1): 83–96.

Human Rights Campaign Foundation n.d. "The lives and livelihoods of many in the LGBTQ community are at risk amidst COVID-19 crisis".

Human Rights Law Centre 2020. "Submission to the Joint Standing Committee on Northern Australia into the destruction of 46,000 year old caves at the Juukan Gorge in the Pilbara region of Western Australia". Melbourne: Human Rights Law Centre. https://static1.squarespace.com/static/580025f66b8f5b2dabbe4291/t/5f4476220957283d534efd6c/1598322222760/Sub+102_Human+Rights+Law+Centre_Published_Inquiry+into+the+destruction+of+46000+year+old+caves+at+the+Juukan+Gorge+%282%29.pdf.

Human Rights Watch 2019a. "AU: uphold rights body's independence strengthen, not weaken African Commission mandate". 26 April. www.hrw.org/news/2019/04/26/au-uphold-rights-bodys-independence.

Human Rights Watch 2019b. "'No year without deaths': a decade of deregulation puts Georgian miners at risk". 22 August.

Hunt, P. 2006. "The human right to the highest attainable standard of health: new opportunities and challenges". *Transactions of the Royal Society of Tropical Medicine and Hygiene* 100 (7): 603–7.

IEO 2014. "IMF Response to the Financial and Economic Crisis", evaluation report, Washington, DC: IMF.

Ignatieff, M. 2000. *The Rights Revolution*. Toronto: House of Anansi Press.

ILC 2001. "Draft articles on responsibility of states for internationally wrongful acts, with commentaries". In *Yearbook of the International Law Commission*, vol. 2, part 2, 31–143. New York: UN.

ILC 2007. "Responsibility of international organizations: comments and observations received from international organizations", A/CN.4/582. New York: UN.

ILC 2011a. "Draft articles on the responsibility of international organizations, with commentaries". In *Yearbook of the International Law Commission*, vol. 2, part 2, 40–105. New York: UN.

ILC 2011b. "Responsibility of international organizations: comments and observations received from international organizations", A/CN.4/637. New York: UN.

Illich, I. 1971. *Deschooling Society*. London: Calder & Boyars.

Illich, I. 1975. *Medical Nemesis: The Expropriation of Health*. London: Calder & Boyars.

ILO 2017. *Indigenous Peoples and Climate Change: From Victims to Change Agents through Decent Work*. Geneva: ILO.

ILO 2020. "COVID-19 and the world of work: updated estimates and analysis", 5th edn. Geneva: ILO.

ILO 2022a. "Partnerships between trade unions and the social and solidarity economy to support informal economy workers", Cooperatives and the World of Work Brief 15. Geneva: ILO.

ILO 2022b. "Legal compendium on the social and solidarity economy", Cooperatives and the World of Work Brief 16. Geneva: ILO.

ILO 2022c. "The ten year (2023–2032) Social and Solidarity Economy (SSE) strategy for Africa validated at African Union Tripartite Meeting". 15 November.

ILO 2022d. "Resolution concerning decent work and the social and solidarity economy", ILC.110/Resolution II. Geneva: ILO.

IMF 2021. "Questions and answers on sovereign debt issues". 8 April.

IMF 2022a. "World economic outlook update: gloomy and more uncertain". 26 July.

IMF 2022b. "Gender: IMF strategy toward mainstreaming gender", policy paper. Washington, DC: IMF.

Independent Commission for the Reform of International Corporate Taxation 2021. "ICRICT open letter to G20 leaders: a global tax deal for the rich". 12 October.

Independent expert on the promotion of a democratic and equitable international order 2017. "Promotion of a democratic and equitable international order", A/72/187. New York: UN.

INESC 2022. *Illustrated Guide to Inflation, Monetary Policy and Human Rights*. Brasília: INESC.

INESC, Oxfam & CESR 2018. *Human Rights in Times of Austerity: Visualizing Rights*. Brasília: INESC, OXFAM & CESR.

Initiative for Human Rights Principles in Fiscal Policy 2021. *Principles for Human Rights in Fiscal Policy*. New York: CESR.

Institute for Economic Justice, CESR & SECTION27 2021. "The impact of public debt on human rights during COVID-19", COVID-19 Economics and Human Rights Fact Sheet 4. Johannesburg: Institute for Economic Justice.

International Commission of Jurists 1985. "Human and peoples' rights in Africa and the African Charter": report of a conference held in Nairobi from 2 to 4 December 1985". Geneva: International Commission of Jurists.

International Court of Justice 1949. "Reparation for injuries suffered in the service of the United Nations". *ICJ Reports*: 174–220.

IPCC 2018. "Global warming of 1.5°C: summary for policymakers", special report. Geneva: IPCC.

ISER 2021. "Profiteering off a pandemic: private sector and health services in Uganda during COVID-19". Kampala: ISER.

Isham, A., B. Gatersleben & T. Jackson 2019. "Flow activities as a route to living well with less". *Environment and Behavior* 5 (4): 431–61.

Jackson, B. 2008. "How to talk about redistribution: a historical perspective". History & Policy, 19 September.

Jackson, T. 2017. *Prosperity without Growth: Foundations for the Economy of Tomorrow*. Abingdon: Routledge.

Jamasmie, C. 2021. "Vale indicted for environmental crimes in deadly dam disaster". Mining.com, 26 November.

James, C. *et al.* 2006. "To retain or remove user fees?". *Applied Health Economics and Health Policy* 5 (3): 137–53.

Jenkins, H. *et al.* 2021. "Guidelines for local governments on policies for social and solidarity economy", research report. Geneva: UNRISD.

Jensen, N., A. Kelly & M. Avendano 2022. "Health equity and health system strengthening: time for a WHO re-think". *Global Public Health* 17 (3): 377–90.

Johanisova, N. & M. Vinkjelhoferová 2019. "Social solidarity economy". In *Pluriverse: A Post-Development Dictionary*, A. Kothari *et al.* (eds), 311–13. New Delhi: Tulika Books.

Kallis, G. 2017. "Radical dematerialization and degrowth". *Philosophical Transactions of the Royal Society A* 375. DOI: 10.1098/rsta.2016.0383.

Kallis, G., F. Demaria & G. D'Alisa 2015. "Introduction: degrowth". In *Degrowth: A Vocabulary for a New Era*, G. D'Alisa, F. Demaria & G. Kallis (eds), 1–17. Abingdon: Routledge.

Kar, D. & J. Spanjers 2015. *Illicit Financial Flows from Developing Countries: 2004–2013*. Washington, DC: Global Financial Integrity.

Kataneksza, J., L. Ling & S. Shroff 2018. "Decoloniality: (re)making worlds". In *International Organization and Global Governance*, 2nd edn, T. Weiss & R. Wilkinson (eds), 205–17. Abingdon: Routledge.

Kelleher, F. 2021. "The African Continental Free Trade Area (AfCFTA) and women: a pan African feminist analysis", policy paper. Nairobi: FEMNET.

Kenert, D. *et al.* 2018. "Making carbon pricing work for citizens". *Nature Climate Change* 8 (8): 669–77.

Kentikelenis, A. 2017. "Structural adjustment and health: a conceptual framework and evidence on pathways". *Social Science & Medicine* 187: 296–305.

Kentikelenis, A. & T. Stubbs 2022. "Austerity redux: the post-pandemic wave of budget cuts and the future of global public health". *Global Policy* 13 (1): 5–17.

Keynes, J. 1932. "Economic possibilities for our grandchildren". In *Essays in Persuasion*, 321–32. New York: Harcourt Brace.

Khosla, R., P. Allotey & S. Gruskin 2022. "Reimagining human rights in global health: what will it take?". *BMJ Global Health* 7 (8). DOI: 10.1136/bmjgh-2022-010373.

Kilpatrick, C. 2017. "Constitutions, social rights and sovereign debt states in Europe: a challenging new area of constitutional inquiry". In *Constitutional Change through Euro-Crisis Law*, T. Beukers, B. de Witte & C. Kilpatrick (eds), 279–326. Cambridge: Cambridge University Press.

King, J. 2012. *Judging Social Rights*. Cambridge: Cambridge University Press.

Klare, K. 1989. "Workplace democracy and market reconstruction: an agenda for legal reform". *Catholic University Law Review* 38 (1): 1–44.

Koch, M. 2021. "Social policy without growth: moving towards sustainable welfare states". *Social Policy & Society* 21 (3): 1–13.

Kohonen, M., A. Waris & J. Christensen 2011. "Pathways towards tax justice". In *Global Civil Society Yearbook*, 78–87. London: Palgrave Macmillan.

Kothari, A. 2018. "Eco-Swaraj vs. ecocatastrophe". *Asia Pacific Perspectives* 15 (2): 49–54.

Kothari, A. *et al.* (eds) 2019. *Pluriverse: A Post-Development Dictionary*. New Delhi: Tulika Books.

Koufaki & ADEDY v Greece [2013]. ECtHR, App. no. 57665/12 (7 May).

Krajnc v Slovenia [2017], ECtHR, App. no. 38775/14 (31 October).

Kvangraven, I. & S. Kesar 2021. "Standing in the way of rigor? Economics' meeting with the decolonizing agenda", Working Paper 2110. New York: Department of Economics, New School for Social Research.

Ladd, H. 1998. "Evidence on discrimination in mortgage lending". *Journal of Economic Perspectives* 12 (2): 41–62.

Landau, D. 2010. "Political institutions and judicial role in comparative constitutional law". *Harvard International Law Journal* 51 (2): 319–77.

Landau, I. 2019. "Human rights due diligence and the risk of cosmetic compliance". *Melbourne Journal of International Law* 20 (1): 1–17.

Lang, V. 2021. "The economics of the democratic deficit: the effect of IMF programs on inequality". *Review of International Organizations* 16 (3): 599–623.

Lanovoy, V. 2016. *Complicity and Its Limits in the Law of International Responsibility*. Oxford: Hart Publishing.

Laqueur, W. & B. Rubin 1990. *The Human Rights Reader*. New York: New American Library.

Latour, B. 2005. *Reassembling the Social: An Introduction to Actor–Network Theory*. Oxford: Oxford University Press.

Latvijas Republikas Satversmes Tiesa [2009]. Case no. 2009-43-01 (21 December).

Laurell, A. 2016. "Competing health policies: insurance against universal public systems". *Revista latino-americana de enfermagem* 24. DOI: 10.1590/ 1518-8345.1074.2668.

Laurent, E. & J. Le Cacheux 2015. *Un nouveau monde économique: Mesurer le bien-être et la soutenabilité au XXIème siècle*. Paris: Odile Jacob.

Laville, J.-L. 2003. "Avec Mauss et Polanyi, vers une théorie de l'économie plurielle". *Revue de MAUSS* 2003 (1): 237–49.

Laville, J.-L. 2010. "Plural economy". In *The Human Economy: A Citizen's Guide*, K. Hart, J. Laville & A. Cattani (eds), 77–83. Cambridge: Polity Press.

Laville, J.-L. 2023a. "Origins and histories". In *Encyclopedia of the Social and Solidarity Economy*, I. Yi *et al.* (eds), 73–82. Cheltenham: Edward Elgar.

Laville, J.-L. 2023b [2010]. *The Solidarity Economy*, J. Booth & J. Benson (trans.). Minneapolis: University of Minnesota Press.

Layard, R. 2005. *Happiness: Lessons from a New Science*. London: Penguin Books.

Le Quéré, C. *et al.* 2019. "Drivers of declining CO_2 emissions in 18 developed economies". *Nature Climate Change* 9 (3): 213–17.

Leite, M. & M. Kohonen 2019. "Engendering business and human rights: applying a gender lens to the UN Guiding Principles on Business and Human Rights and binding treaty negotiations". London: Christian Aid & ACT Alliance.

Li, Y. 2021. "Report of the independent expert on the effects of foreign debt and other related international financial obligations of States on the full enjoyment of all human rights, particularly economic, social and cultural rights. International debt architecture reform and human rights", A/76/167. New York: UN.

Liebenberg, S. 2019. "The participatory democratic turn in South Africa's social rights jurisprudence". In *The Future of Economic and Social Rights*, K. Young (ed.), 187–211. Cambridge: Cambridge University Press.

Liebenberg, S. & K. Young 2015. "Adjudicating social and economic rights: can democratic experimentalism help?". In *Social and Economic Rights in Theory and Practice: Critical Inquiries*, H. Alviar García, K. Klare & L. Williams (eds), 237–57. Abingdon: Routledge.

López Cabello, A. 2021. "Pandemic momentum for health systems financialisation: under the cloaks of universal health coverage". *Global Public Health* 16 (8/9): 1334–45.

Lopreite, D. & A. Rodríguez Gustá 2021. "State feminism in democratic Argentina (1983–2021): aspirational model or institutional reality?" [in Spanish]. *Revista Sociedad Argentina de Análisis Político* 15 (2): 287–311.

Lucas, K. *et al.* 2004. *Environment and Social Justice: Rapid Research and Evidence Review*. London: Sustainable Development Research Network.

Luce, S. 2014. *Labor Movements: Global Perspectives*. Cambridge: Polity Press.

McCorquodale, R. & J. Nolan 2021. "The effectiveness of human rights due diligence for preventing business human rights abuses". *Netherlands International Law Review* 68: 455–78.

McGregor, H. *et al.* 2016. "The Industrial Revolution kick-started global warming much earlier than we realized". The Conversation, 24 August.

McKenzie v Minister for Defence & Ors [2010]. IEHC 461 (30 November).

MacNaughton, G., D. Frey & C. Porter (eds) 2021. *Human Rights and Economic Inequalities*. Oxford: Oxford University Press.

McVey, M. 2022. "Untangling the authority of external experts in the corporate implementation of the UN Guiding Principles on Business and Human Rights". *Journal of Human Rights* 21 (5): 620–38.

Magalhães Teixeira, B. 2021. "The potential of degrowth and buen vivir in addressing underdevelopment and conflict in the Global South". Degrowth, 25 April.

Maher, R. 2020. "De-contextualized corporate human rights benchmarks: whose perspective counts? See disclaimer". *Business and Human Rights Journal* 5 (1): 156–63.

Mair, P. 2013. "Bini Smaghi vs the parties: representative government and institutional constraints in the age of austerity". In *Politics in the Age of Austerity*, A. Schäfer & W. Streeck (eds), 143–68. Cambridge: Polity Press.

Maldonado-Torres, N. 2007. "On the coloniality of being". *Cultural Studies* 21 (2/3): 240–70.

Malm, A. 2016. *Fossil Capital: The Rise of Steam Power and the Roots of Global Warming*. London: Verso.

Manji, A. 2016. "The International Development (Official Development Assistance Target) Act 2015: legislative spending targets, poverty alleviation and aid scrutiny". *Modern Law Review* 79: 655–77.

Mangabeira Unger, R. 2001 [1987]. *False Necessity: Anti-Necessitarian Social Theory in the Service of Radical Democracy*. London: Verso.

Marathe, S. *et al.* 2022. "Patients' voices during the pandemic: stories and analysis of rights violations and overcharging by private hospitals". Sophisticated Analytical & Technical Help Institutes, 25 March.

Marcuello, C., A. Errasti & I. Bretos 2023. "Globalization and alter-globalization". In *Encyclopedia of the Social and Solidarity Economy*, I. Yi *et al.* (eds), 44–52. Cheltenham: Edward Elgar.

Marks, S. 2011. "Human rights and root causes". *Modern Law Review* 74 (1): 57–78.

Marshall, T. 1992 [1950]. *Citizenship and Social Class and Other Essays*. Cambridge: Cambridge University Press.

Martin, M. & D. Waddock 2022. "A Nordic initiative to resolve the new debt crisis". Oslo: Norwegian Church Aid.

Martins, P. 2010. "Citizenship". In *The Human Economy: A Citizen's Guide*, K. Hart, J. Laville & A. Cattani (eds), 157–65. Cambridge: Polity Press.

Mateus & Januário v Portugal [2013]. ECtHR, App. no. 62235/12 (8 October).

Mauss, M. 1978 [1925]. "Essai sur le don". In *Sociologie et anthropologie*, 149–279. Paris: Presses Universitaires de France.

Mauss, M. 2000 [1950]. *The Gift: The Form and Reason for Exchange in Archaic Societies*, H. Walls (trans.). London: Routledge.

Mazzucato, M. 2018. "Mission-oriented research and innovation in the European Union: a problem-solving approach to fuel innovation-led growth". Luxembourg: Publications Office of the European Union.

Mazzucato, M. 2021. *Mission Economy: A Moonshot Guide to Changing Capitalism*. London: Harper Business.

Mbeki, T. 2016. "Panama Papers: High-Level Panel's warnings are not just another recommendation!". AllAfrica, 8 April.

Meadows, D. *et al.* 1972. *The Limits to Growth*. Falls Church, VA: Potomac Associates Books.

Mecon 2020a. "Administrative decision 1314/2020". 23 July.

Mecon 2020b. "Primera Mesa Interministerial de Políticas de Cuidados". 6 February. www.argentina.gob.ar/noticias/primera-mesa-interministerial-de-politicas-de-cuidados.

Meier, B. 2010. "Global health governance and the contentious politics of human rights: mainstreaming the right to health for public health advancement". *Stanford Journal of International Law* 46 (1): 1–50.

Merchant, C. 2019. *The Death of Nature: Women, Ecology, and the Scientific Revolution*, updated edn. London: HarperCollins.

Meredith, M. 2006. *The State of Africa: A History of Fifty Years of Independence*. Jeppestown: Jonathan Ball.

Meredith, M. 2014. *The Fortunes of Africa: A 5000-Year History of Wealth, Greed and Endeavour*. London: Simon & Schuster.

Mesa Interministerial de Políticas de Cuidado 2021. "1er Informe anual: 100 acciones en materias de cuidados 2020–2021". Buenos Aires: MMGyD.

Mesa Interministerial de Políticas de Cuidado 2022. "2do Informe anual: Mesa Interministerial de Políticas de Cuidado 2021–2022". Buenos Aires: MMGyD.

Mhazo, A. & C. Maponga 2022. "The political economy of health financing reforms in Zimbabwe: a scoping review". *International Journal for Equity in Health* 21 (1): 1–4.

Michalowski, S. 2007. *Unconstitutional Regimes and the Validity of Sovereign Debt: A Legal Perspective*. Aldershot: Ashgate.

Mignolo, W. 2007. "Delinking: the rhetoric of modernity, the logic of coloniality and the grammar of de-coloniality". *Cultural Studies* 21 (2/3): 449–514.

Mignolo, W. 2009. "Epistemic disobedience, independent thought and decolonial freedom". *Theory Culture & Society* 26 (7/8): 1–23.

Mihăieş & Senteş v Romania [2011]. ECtHR, App. no. 44232/11 (6 December).

Milanovic, B. 2016. *Global Inequality: A New Approach for the Age of Globalization*. Cambridge, MA: Harvard University Press.

MMGyD n.d. "Políticas de cuidado frente al COVID-19: segundo encuentro de la Mesa Interministerial de Políticas de Cuidado". www.argentina.gob.ar/sites/default/files/politicascuidadocovid19.pdf.

Mockienė v Lithuania [2017]. ECtHR, App. no. 75916/13 (4 July).

Molyneux, M. & S. Razavi (eds) 2002. *Gender Justice, Development, and Rights*. Oxford: Oxford University Press.

Mooney, G. 2012. "Neoliberalism is bad for our health". *International Journal of Health Services* 42 (3): 383–401.

Morello-Frosh, R., M. Pastor & J. Sadd 2001. "Environmental justice and southern California's 'riskscape': the distribution of air toxics exposures and health risks among diverse communities". *Urban Affairs Review* 36 (4): 551–78.

Moyn, S. 2014. "A powerless companion: human rights in the age of neoliberalism". *Law and Neoliberalism* 77 (4): 147–69.

Moyn, S. 2016. "Rights vs. duties: reclaiming civic balance". *Boston Review* 16.

Moyn, S. 2018. *Not Enough: Human Rights in an Unequal World*. Cambridge, MA: Harvard University Press.

Muchhala, B. 2021. "A feminist and decolonial global green new deal: principles, paradigms and systemic transformations", issue brief. New York: Action Nexus for Generation Equality.

Muchhala, B. & A. Guillem 2022. "Gendered austerity and embodied debt in Ecuador: channels through which women absorb and resist the shocks of public budget cuts". *Gender & Development* 30 (1/2): 283–309.

Muchlinski, P. 2010. "Limited liability and multinational enterprises: a case for reform?". *Cambridge Journal of Economics* 34 (5): 915–28.

Muheet Chowdhary, A. & S. Picciotto 2021. "Streamlining the architecture of international tax through a UN framework convention on tax cooperation", Tax Cooperation Policy Brief 21. Geneva: South Centre.

Müller-Hoff, C. 2020. "Was the Brumadinho dam failure caused by a 'normalisation of deviance'?". BHRRC, 3 June.

Murray, R. 2004. *Human Rights in Africa: From the OAU to the African Union*. Cambridge: Cambridge University Press.

Murray, R. & D. Long 2015. *The Implementation of the Findings of the African Commission on Human and Peoples' Rights*. Cambridge: Cambridge University Press.

Mutua, M. 1995. "The Banjul Charter and the African cultural fingerprint: an evaluation of the language of duties". *Virginia Journal of International Law* 35: 339–80.

Myrdal, A. 1945. *Nation and the Family: The Swedish Experiment in Democratic Family and Population Policy*. London: Paul, Trench, Trübner.

Myrdal, G. 1978. "Institutional economics". *Journal of Economic Issues* 12 (4): 771–83.

Nabuco, J. & L. Aleixo 2019. "Rights holders' participation and access to remedies: lessons learned from the Doce River dam disaster". *Business and Human Rights Journal* 4 (1): 147–53.

Nadj, D. 2019. "Deregulation, the absence of the law and the Grenfell Tower fire". *Human Rights Law Review* 5 (2): 1–18.

Nagar, A. 2021. "The Juukan Gorge incident: key lessons on free, prior and informed consent". *Business and Human Rights Journal* 6 (2): 377–83.

Naudé Fourie, A. 2016. *World Bank Accountability: In Theory and in Practice*. The Hague: Eleven International Publishing.

Neier, A. 2015. "Human rights and social justice: separate causes". In *Can Human Rights Bring Social Justice? Twelve Essays*, D. Lettinga & L. van Troost (eds), 47–52. Amsterdam: Amnesty International Netherlands.

Newfoundland (Treasury Board) v N.A.P.E. [2004]. 3 SCR 381 (28 October).

Nolan, A. 2009. "Ireland: the separation of powers doctrine vs human rights". In *Social Rights Jurisprudence: Emerging Trends in International and Comparative Law*, M. Langford (ed.), 295–320. Cambridge: Cambridge University Press.

Nolan, A., R. O'Connell & C. Harvey (eds) 2013. *Human Rights and Public Finance: Budgets and the Promotion of Economic and Social Rights*. Oxford: Hart Publishing.

Nolan, M. 2014. "Human rights and market fundamentalism", Max Weber Lecture 2014/02. Florence: European University Institute.

Nollkaemper, A. *et al*. 2020. "Guiding principles on shared responsibility in international law". *European Journal of International Law* 31 (1): 15–72.

Nussbaum, M. 1999. "Women and equality: the capabilities approach". *International Labour Review* 138 (3): 227–37.

Nussbaum, M. 2003. "Capabilities as fundamental entitlements: Sen and social justice". *Feminist Economics* 9 (2/3): 33–59.

O'Connell, P. 2011. "The death of socio-economic rights". *Modern Law Review* 74 (4): 532–54.

O'Connell, P. 2012. *Vindicating Socio-Economic Rights: International Standards and Comparative Experiences*. London: Routledge.

O'Connell, P. 2018. "On the human rights question". *Human Rights Quarterly* 40 (4): 962–88.

O'Manique, J. 1992. "Human rights and development". *Human Rights Quarterly* 14 (1): 78–103.

OECD 2005. "The Paris Declaration on aid effectiveness: five principles for smart aid". Paris: OECD Publishing.

OECD 2008a. "Are we growing unequal? New evidence on changes in poverty and incomes over the past 20 years". Paris: OECD Publishing.

OECD 2008b. "The Accra Agenda for Action (AAA)". Paris: OECD Publishing.

OECD 2011. "Divided we stand: why inequality keeps rising". Paris: OECD Publishing.

OECD 2018a. "Chile policy brief: health". Paris: OECD Publishing.

OECD 2018b. "OECD DAC blended finance principles for unlocking commercial finance for the Sustainable Development Goals". Paris: OECD Publishing.

OECD 2020. "Statement by the OECD/G20 Inclusive Framework on BEPS on the two-pillar approach to address the tax challenges arising from the digitalisation of the economy". Paris: OECD Publishing.

OECD 2021. "Inheritance taxation in OECD countries", Tax Policy Study 28. Paris: OECD Publishing.

OECD 2022. "Joint communication from UN human rights special procedures [response]", PSA/DO (2022)44. 27 April. https://spcommreports.ohchr.org/TMResultsBase/DownLoadFile?gId=36914.

Ogle, V. 2018. "Archipelago capitalism: tax havens, offshore money, and the state, 1950s–1970s". *American Historical Review* 122 (5): 1431–58.

Oguttu, A. 2011. "Exposing and curtailing secret offshore tax shelters: the tools and the enablers. A call for vigilance in South Africa". *Comparative and International Law Journal of Southern Africa* 44 (1): 30–58.

Ortiz, I. & M. Cummins 2019. "Austerity: the new normal – a renewed Washington Consensus 2010–24", working paper. New York: Initiative for Policy Dialogue.

Ortiz, I. & M. Cummins 2022. "End austerity: a global report on budget cuts and harmful social reforms in 2022–25", working paper. New York: Initiative for Policy Dialogue.

Osborne, C. 2021. *Building a Field of Economics and Human Rights: Lessons from South Africa*. Johannesburg: IEJ, CESR & Section 27.

Ostrom, E. *Governing the Commons: The Evolution of Institutions for Collective Action*. Cambridge: Cambridge University Press.

Ostrom, V. & E. Ostrom 1977. "Public goods and public choices". In *Alternatives for Delivering Public Services: Toward Improved Performance*, E. Savas (ed.), 7–49. Boulder, CO: Westview Press.

Ostry, D., P. Loungani & D. Furceri 2016. "Neoliberalism: oversold?". *Finance & Development* 53 (2): 38–41.

Oxfam International n.d. "A deadly virus: 5 shocking facts about global extreme inequality". www.oxfam.org/en/5-shocking-facts-about-extreme-global-inequality-and-how-even-it.

Oxfam International 2021. "COVID-19 recovery in west Africa is 'austerity on steroids' and sets the region on a destructive path ahead", press release. 14 October.

Oxfam International 2022a. "IMF must abandon demands for austerity as cost-of-living crisis drives up hunger and poverty worldwide", press release. 19 April.

Oxfam International 2022b. "Profiting from pain", media briefing. Oxford: Oxfam International.

Oxfam International 2023. *Survival of the Richest: How We Must Tax the Super-Rich Now to Fight Inequality*. Oxford: Oxfam International.

Paixão, M. 2017. "Acesso ao crédito produtivo pelos microempreendedores afrode-scendentes". Rio de Janeiro: Inter-American Development Bank.

Palladino, E. & R. Gunn-Wright 2021. "Care and climate: understanding the policy intersections", issue brief. New York: Feminist Green New Deal Coalition.

Parrique, T. *et al.* 2019. "Decoupling debunked: evidence and arguments against green growth as a sole strategy for sustainability". Brussels: EEB.

Peroni, L. & A. Timmer 2013. "Vulnerable groups: the promise of an emerging concept in European Human Rights Convention law". *International Journal of Constitutional Law* 11 (4): 1056–85.

Perry, K. 2020. "The 'green' new deal should not be a new imperial masterplan". *Aljazeera*, 4 June.

Petel, M. & N. Vander Putten 2021. "Economic, social and cultural rights and their dependence on the economic growth paradigm: evidence from the ICESCR system". *Netherlands Quarterly of Human Rights* 39 (1): 53–72.

Phillips, B. 2020. *How to Fight Inequality (and Why That Fight Needs You)*. Cambridge: Polity Press.

PHM 2022. *Global Health Watch 6: In the Shadow of the Pandemic*. London: Bloomsbury Academic.

Polanyi, K. 1944. *Origins of Our Time: The Great Transformation*. New York: Farrar & Rinehart.

Presidente de la Nación Argentina 2019a. "Law of ministries", Decree 7/19. 10 December.

Presidente de la Nación Argentina 2019b. "National executive power", Decree 50/19. 19 December.

Progressive International 2021. *The Red Deal: Indigenous Action to Save Our Earth*. Albuquerque, NM: Red Nation.

Quijano, A. 2000. "Coloniality of power, Eurocentrism, and Latin America". *Nepantla: Views from South* 1 (3): 533–80.

Quijano, G. & C. Lopez 2021. "Rise of mandatory human rights due diligence: a beacon of hope or a double-edge sword?". *Business and Human Rights Journal* 6 (2): 241–54.

R (on the application of DA and others) v Secretary of State for Work and Pensions [2019]. UKSC 21 (15 May).

Ragnarsson, K. 2019. "The counter-majoritarian difficulty in a neoliberal world: socio-economic rights and deference in post-2008 austerity cases". *Global Constitutionalism* 8 (3): 605–38.

Rao, S. & H. Akram-Lodhi 2021. "Feminist political economy". In *The Routledge Handbook of Feminist Economics*, G. Berik & E. Kongar (eds), 34–42. Abingdon: Routledge.

Raworth, K. 2012. "A safe and just space for humanity: can we live within the doughnut?", discussion paper. Oxford: Oxfam International.

Raworth, K. 2017. *Doughnut Economics: Seven Ways to Think Like a 21st-Century Economist*. London: Random House.

Raygorodetsky, G. 2018. "Indigenous peoples defend Earth's biodiversity – but they're in danger". National Geographic, 16 November.

Razavi, S. 2016. "The 2030 Agenda: challenges of implementation to attain gender equality and women's rights". *Gender & Development* 24 (1): 25–41.

Razavi, S. & S. Staab (eds) 2012. *Global Variations in the Political and Social Economy of Care: Worlds Apart*. Abingdon: Routledge.

Razavi, S. *et al.* 2021. "Social policy advice to countries from the International Monetary Fund during the COVID-19 crisis: continuity and change", Working Paper 42. Geneva: ILO.

Razeto, L. 2001. *Desarrollo, transformación y perfeccionamiento de la economía en el tiempo*. Santiago: Ediciones Universidad Bolivariana.

Reddy, S. 2011. "Economics and human rights: a non-conversation". *Journal of Human Development and Capabilities* 12 (1): 63–72.

Reich, R. 2012. *Beyond Outrage: What Has Gone Wrong with Our Economy and Our Democracy, and How to Fix It*. New York: Vintage.

Rigat-Pflaum, M. 2008. "Gender mainstreaming: un enfoque para la igualdad de género". *Nueva Sociedad* 218: 40–56.

Ring, D. 2008. "What's at stake in the sovereignty debate? International tax and the nation-state". *Virginia Journal of International Law* 49 (1): 55–234.

Ritchie, H. & M. Roser 2018. "Now it is possible to take stock: did the world achieve the Millennium Development Goals?". Our World in Data, 20 September.

Roca, R. & F. Manta 2010. *Values Added: The Challenge of Integrating Human Rights into the Financial Sector*. Copenhagen: Danish Institute for Human Rights.

Rockström, J. *et al.* 2009. "Planetary boundaries: exploring the safe operating space for humanity". *Ecology and Society* 14 (2): www.ecologyandsociety.org/vol14/iss2/art32.

Rodríguez-Garavito, C. 2019. "Empowered participatory jurisprudence: experimentation, deliberation and norms in socioeconomic rights adjudication". In *The Future of Economic and Social Rights*, K. Young (ed.), 233–58. Cambridge: Cambridge University Press.

Rodríguez-Garavito, C. & D. Rodríguez-Franco 2015. *Radical Deprivation on Trial: The Impact of Judicial Activism on Socioeconomic Rights in the Global South*. Cambridge: Cambridge University Press.

Roos, J. 2019. *Why Not Default? The Political Economy of Sovereign Debt*. Princeton, NJ: Princeton University Press.

Rossi, P. & E. Dweck 2016. "Impacts of the new fiscal regime on health and education". *Cadernos Saúde Pública* 32 (12). DOI: 10.1590/0102-311x00194316.

Rossi, P., G. David & S. Chaparro 2021. "Política fiscal e direitos humanos: redefinindo responsabilidade fiscal", Complementary Document 3. New York: CESR.

Rossi, P., E. Dweck & A. Oliveira (eds.) 2018. *Economia para poucos: Impactos sociais da austeridade e alternativas para o Brasil*. São Paulo: Editora Autonomia Literária.

Rúa, M. 2021. "El préstamo stand by de 2018: fuga de capitales y dependencia". *Voces en el fénix* 83: 78–85.

Ruger, J. 2005. "The changing role of the World Bank in global health". *American Journal of Public Health* 95 (1): 60–70.

Ruggie, J. 1982. "International regimes, transactions, and change: embedded liberalism in the postwar economic order". *International Organization* 36 (2): 379–415.

Ruggie, J. 2013. *Just Business: Multinational Corporations and Human Rights*. New York: Norton.

Ruggie, J. 2014. "Global governance and 'new governance theory': lessons from business and human rights". *Global Governance* 20 (5): 5–17.

Ruggie, J. 2020. "The social construction of the UN Guiding Principles on Business and Human Rights". In *Research Handbook on Human Rights and Business*, S. Deva & D. Birchall (eds), 63–86. Cheltenham: Edward Elgar.

Ruggie, J. & J. Sherman III 2017. "The concept of 'due diligence' in the UN Guiding Principles on Business and Human Rights: a reply to Jonathan Bonnitcha and Robert McCorquodale". *European Journal of International Law* 28 (3): 921–8.

Ruggie, J., C. Rees & R. Davis 2021. "Ten years after: from UN guiding principles to multi-fiduciary obligations". *Business and Human Rights Journal* 6 (2): 1–19.

Ruling no. 187/13 [2013]. Tribunal Constitucional de Portugal (5 April).

Ryding, T. 2022. "Proposal for a United Nations convention on tax". Brussels: European Network on Debt and Development.

Sabel, C. & W. Simon 2004. "Destabilization rights: how public law litigation succeeds". *Harvard Law Review* 117 (4): 1016–101.

Sadiq, K. & H. du Preez 2021. "The case for a universal basic income in South Africa: a conceptual approach". *South African Journal of Accounting Research* 35 (3): 167–90.

Saiz, I. 2021. "Freeing fiscal space: a human rights imperative in response to COVID-19", Global Trends: Analysis 01|2021. Bonn: Stiftung Entwicklung und Frieden.

Sanders, D. *et al.* 2019. "From primary health care to universal health coverage: one step forward and two steps back". *The Lancet* 394: 619–21.

Sandwell, K. *et al.* 2019. *A View from the Countryside: Contesting and Constructing Human Rights in an Age of Converging Crises.* Geneva: FIAN International.

Savourey, E. & S. Brabant 2021. "The French law on the duty of vigilance: theoretical and practical challenges since its adoption". *Business and Human Rights Journal* 6 (1): 141–52.

Scali, E. 2022. *Sovereign Debt and Socio-Economic Rights beyond Crisis: The Neoliberalisation of International Law.* Cambridge: Cambridge University Press.

Schwab, K. & P. Vanham 2021. *Stakeholder Capitalism: A Global Economy that Works for Progress, People and Planet.* Chichester: Wiley.

Schweitzer, L. & J. Zhou 2010. "Neighborhood air quality, respiratory health, and vulnerable populations in compact and sprawled regions". *Journal of the American Planning Association* 76 (3): 363–71.

Scitovsky, T. 1992. *The Joyless Economy: The Psychology of Human Satisfaction*, rev. edn. Oxford: Oxford University Press.

Searson, A. & K. Gudgeon 2022. "Rio Tinto signs remedy agreement with WA traditional owners after Juukan Gorge blasts". Australian Broadcasting Corporation, 29 November.

Seguino, S. 2019. "Engendering macroeconomic theory and policy". *Feminist Economics* 26 (2): 27–61.

Sell, S. 2019. "21st-century capitalism: structural challenges for universal health care". *Globalization and Health* 15 (1): 1–9.

Sen, A. 2000. *Development as Freedom.* New York: Anchor Books.

Sen, G. & C. Grown 1987. *Development, Crises and Alternative Visions: Third World Women's Perspectives.* London: Earthscan.

Service for the Fight against Poverty, Precarity and Social Exclusion [Belgium] 2019. *Sustainability and Poverty: Biannual report 2018–2019* [in French]. Brussels: Service for the Fight against Poverty, Precarity and Social Exclusion. https://luttepauvrete.be/wp-content/uploads/sites/2/2019/12/Durabilite-et-Pauvrete-Rapport-bisannuel.pdf.

Shanafelt Wong, C. 2022. "Juukan Gorge". Sacred Land Film Project, 21 September. https://sacredland.org/juukan-gorge.

Shaxson, N. 2005. "New approaches to volatility: dealing with the 'resource curse' in sub-Saharan Africa". *International Affairs* 81 (2): 311–24.

Sherpa, D. 2020. "Estimating impact of austerity policies in COVID-19 fatality rates: examining the dynamics of economic policy and case fatality rates (CFR) of COVID-19 in OECD countries". *MedRxiv.* DOI: 10.1101/2020.04.03.20047530.

Sibeko, B. 2022. "A feminist approach to debt". Nairobi: Nawi Afrifem Macroeconomics Collective & African Forum and Network on Debt and Development.

Šimleša, D. 2023. "Ecological economics". In *Encyclopedia of the Social and Solidarity Economy*, I. Yi *et al.* (eds). Cheltenham: Edward Elgar.

Singer, P. 2001. "Economia solidária versus economia capitalista". *Sociedade e estado* 16: 100–12.

Skidelsky, R. 2021. *What's Wrong with Economics? A Primer for the Perplexed.* New Haven, CT: Yale University Press.

Slater, D. & F. Tonkiss 2001. *Market Society: Markets and Modern Social Theory*. Cambridge: Polity Press.

Slobodian, Q. 2019. "Democracy doesn't matter to the defenders of 'economic freedom'". *The Guardian*, 11 November.

Smithers, D. & H. Waitzkin 2022. "Universal health coverage as hegemonic health policy in low- and middle-income countries: a mixed-methods analysis". *Social Science and Medicine* 302. DOI: 10.1016/j.socscimed.2022.114961.

Social and Economic Rights Action Centre and Another v Nigeria [2001]. AHRLR 60 (27 October).

Solow, R. 1956. "A contribution to the theory of economic growth". *Quarterly Journal of Economics* 70 (1): 65–94.

Sousa Santos, B. 2014. *Epistemologies of the South: Justice against Epistemicide*. New York: Routledge.

South Centre 2021. "Statement by the South Centre on the two pillar solution to address the tax challenges arising from the digitalisation of economy". Geneva: South Centre.

Spangenberg, J. 2014. "Institutional change for strong sustainable consumption: sustainable consumption and the degrowth economy". *Sustainability: Science, Practice and Policy* 10 (1): 62–77.

Special rapporteur on the human rights to safe drinking water and sanitation 2020. "Human rights and the privatization of water and sanitation services", A/75/208. New York: UN.

Steffen, W. *et al.* 2015. "The trajectory of the Anthropocene: the Great Acceleration". *Anthropocene Review* 2 (1): 81–98.

Stiglitz, J. 2009. "Moving beyond market fundamentalism to a more balanced economy". *Annals of Public and Cooperative Economics* 80 (3): 345–60.

Stiglitz, J. 2013. *The Price of Inequality*. London: Penguin Books.

Stiglitz, J., A. Sen & J. Fitoussi 2009. *Report by the Commission on the Measurement of Economic Performance and Social Progress*. Paris: Commission on the Measurement of Economic Performance and Social Progress.

Streeck, W. 2017 [2014]. *Buying Time: The Delayed Crisis of Democratic Capitalism*, P. Camiller & D. Fernbach (trans.). London: Verso.

Stubbs, T. *et al.* 2017. "The impact of IMF conditionality on government health expenditure: a cross-national analysis of 16 west African nations". *Social Science & Medicine* 174: 220–7.

Stubbs, T. *et al.* 2021. "Poverty, inequality, and the International Monetary Fund: how austerity hurts the poor and widens inequality", Global Economic Governance Initiative Working Paper 046. Boston: Global Development Policy Center, Boston University.

Suich, H., C. Howe & G. Mace 2015. "Ecosystem services and poverty alleviation: a review of the empirical links". *Ecosystem Services* 12: 137–47.

Sukarieh, M. & S. Tannock 2008. "In the best interests of youth or neoliberalism? The World Bank and the New Global Youth Empowerment Project". *Journal of Youth Studies* 11 (3): 301–12.

Sulcs v Latvia [2011]. ECtHR, App. no. 42923/10 (6 December).

Suzuki, E. 2010. "Responsibility of international financial institutions under international law". In *International Financial Institutions and International Law*, D. Bradlow & D. Hunter (eds), 63–102. The Hague: Wolters Kluwer.

Táíwò, O. & P. Bigger 2022. "Debt justice for climate reparations". Climate and Community Project, 22 April.

Tamale, N. 2021. "Adding fuel to the fire: how IMF demands for austerity will drive up inequality worldwide", briefing paper. Oxford: Oxfam International.

Tan, C. 2008. "Mandating rights and limiting mission creep: holding the World Bank and the International Monetary Fund accountable for human rights violations". *Human Rights and International Legal Discourse* 2 (1): 79–116.

Tan, C. 2013. "Life, debt, and human rights: contextualizing the international regime for sovereign debt relief". In *Poverty and the International Economic Legal System: Duties to the World's Poor*, K. Nadakavukaren Schefer (ed.), 307–24. Cambridge: Cambridge University Press.

Tan, C. 2014. "Reframing the debate: the debt relief initiative and new normative values in the governance of third world debt". *International Journal of Law in Context* 10 (2): 249–72.

Tan, C. 2019. "Creative cocktails or toxic brews? Blended finance and the regulatory framework for sustainable development". In *Sustainable Trade, Investment and Finance: Toward Responsible and Coherent Regulatory Frameworks*, C. Gammage & T. Novitz (eds), 300–30. Cheltenham: Edward Elgar.

Tan, C. & L. Cotula 2018. "Regulating development partnerships: PPPs, blended finance and responsible investment provisions". UNCTAD, 23 March.

Tang, F. 2021. "What is the G7's global minimum tax, and how could it affect China?". *South China Morning Post*, 20 June.

Tansy, R. 2021. "When the market becomes deadly: how pressures towards privatisation of health and long-term care put Europe on a poor footing for a pandemic". Brussels: Corporate Europe Observatory.

Tapia Maella, L. 2010. "Tiempo, historia y sociedad abrigada". In *La producción del conocimiento local: Historia y política en la obra de René Zavaleta*, 305–23. La Paz: CIDES-UMSA.

Titmuss, R. 2019. *Essays on the Welfare State*. Bristol: Policy Press.

TJN 2021. *The State of Tax Justice 2021*. Bristol: TJN.

Tooze, A. 2022. "Chartbook #130: defining polycrisis – from crisis pictures to the crisis matrix". Adamtooze.com, 24 June.

Toscano, N. 2021. "'I am ultimately accountable': Rio Tinto chairman to stand down after cave blast disaster". *Sydney Morning Herald*, 3 March.

Tuhiwai Smith, L. 2012. *Decolonizing Methodologies: Research and Indigenous Peoples*, 2nd edn. Otago: Otago University Press.

Tushnet, M. 2009. *Weak Courts, Strong Rights: Judicial Review and Social Welfare Rights in Comparative Constitutional Law*. Princeton, NJ: Princeton University Press.

Tyberg, J. 2020. *Unlearning: From Degrowth to Decolonization*. New York: Rosa Luxemburg Stiftung.

Tyson, B. & A. Said 1993. "Human rights: a forgotten victim of the Cold War". *Human Rights Quarterly* 15 (3): 589–604.

UEHP 2021. "UEHP writes to the EU institutions presidents on the role of the private sector in the COVID-19 pandemic and the future of health". 31 August.

Umozurike, O. 1997. *The African Charter on Human and Peoples' Rights*. The Hague. Kluwer.

UN 2003. "Monterrey Consensus of financing for development: Monterrey, Mexico, 18–22 March 2002", A/CONF.198/11. New York: UN.

UN 2009. "Doha Declaration on financing for development". New York: UN.

UN 2012. "Report of the United Nations Conference on Sustainable Development: Rio de Janeiro, Brazil, 20–22 June 2012", A/CONF.216/16. New York: UN.

UN CEDAW 2016. "Concluding observations on the seventh periodic report of Argentina", CEDAW/C/ARG/CO/7. New York: UN.

UN ECLAC 2016. "Montevideo Strategy for implementation of the regional gender agenda within the Sustainable Development Framework by 2030". Santiago: UN ECLAC.

UN ECLAC 2021. "Reform on the multilateral tax debate is needed in the framework of the United Nations", press release. 1 June.

UN Economic and Social Council 1990. "CESCR general comment no. 3: the nature of states parties' obligations", E/1991/23. New York: UN.

UN Economic and Social Council 2008. "General comment no. 19", E/C.12/GC/19. New York: UN.

UN Economic and Social Council 2018. "Concluding observations on the fourth periodic report of Argentina", E/C.12/ARG/CO/4. New York: UN.

UN Economic and Social Council 2019. "Addressing inequalities and challenges to social inclusion through fiscal, wage and social protection policies", E/RES/2019/6. New York: UN.

UN Economic and Social Council 2021. "Summary by the president of the Economic and Social Council of the forum on financing for development follow-up, including the special high-level meeting with the Bretton Woods institutions, the World Trade Organization and the United Nations Conference on Trade and Development", A/76/79–E/2021/68. New York: UN.

UN Economic and Social Council 2022. "Report on the meeting of the Committee of Experts", E/ECA/CM/54/4/Rev.1. New York: UN.

UN Global Crisis Response Group on Food, Energy and Finance 2022. "Global impact of war in Ukraine on food, energy and finance systems", Brief 1. New York: UN.

UN HRC 2011. "Guiding principles on foreign debt and human rights", A/HRC/20/23. New York: UN.

UN HRC 2011b. "Guiding Principles on Business and Human Rights: implementing the United Nations 'Protect, Respect and Remedy' framework", A/HRC/17/31. New York: UN.

UN HRC 2014a. "Report of the special rapporteur on extreme poverty and human rights", A/HRC/26/28. New York: UN.

UN HRC 2014b. "Report on financial complicity: lending to states engaged in gross human rights violations", A/HRC/28/59. New York: UN.

UN HRC 2018. "Guiding principles on human rights impact assessments of economic reforms", A/HRC/40/57. New York: UN.

UN HRC 2021. "Effects of foreign debt and other related international financial obligations of states on the full enjoyment of all human rights, particularly economic, social and cultural rights", A/HRC/RES/46/8. New York: UN.

UN Inter-Agency Task Force on Financing for Development 2022. *Financing for Sustainable Development Report 2022: Bridging the Finance Divide*. New York: UN.

UN OHCHR 2020. "Guidance note on CEDAW and COVID-19". Geneva: UN OHCHR.

UN OHCHR 2016. "Bahamas leaks: what else do we need to know to take action? UN rights experts ask", press release. 6 October.

UN OHCHR 2017. "The business and human rights dimension of sustainable development: embedding 'Protect, Respect and Remedy' in SDGs implementation", information note. Geneva: UN OHCHR.

UN OHCHR 2020. "What is the impact of COVID-19 on gender-based violence?". Geneva: UN OHCHR.

UN OHCHR 2022. "Killings and other attacks against human rights defenders, journalists and trade unionists". Geneva: UN OHCHR.

UN Secretary-General 2020. "Trends and progress in international development cooperation", E/2020/10. New York: UN.

UN Secretary-General 2021. "Our common agenda", A/75/982. New York: UN.

UN Statistics Division 2021. "System of national accounts: Wellbeing and Sustainability Task Team".

UN Women 2020a. "Impact of COVID-19 on violence against women and girls and service provision: UN Women rapid assessment and findings". New York: UN Women.

UN Women 2020b. "COVID-19: only one in eight countries worldwide have measures in place to protect women against social and economic impacts, new data shows", press release. 28 September. www.unwomen.org/en/news/stories/2020/9/press-release-launch-of-covid-19-global-gender-response-tracker.

UN Women & UNDP 2020. "COVID-19 global gender response tracker: factsheet: Latin America and the Caribbean (version 1: September 28, 2020)". New York: UN Women & UNDP.

UNCTAD 2012. "Principles on promoting responsible sovereign lending and borrowing". Geneva: UNCTAD.

UNCTAD 2015. *Sovereign Debt Workouts: Going Forward: Roadmap and Guide*. Geneva: UNCTAD.

UNCTAD 2020. *Economic and Development in Africa: Tackling Illicit Financial Flows for Sustainable Development in Africa*. Geneva: UNCTAD.

UNCTAD 2022. *Trade and Development Report 2022: Development Prospects in a Fractured World: Global Disorder and Regional Responses*. Geneva: UNCTAD.

UNCTAD 2023. "Trade and development report update: global trends and prospects", UNCTAD/GDS/INF/2023/1. Geneva: UNCTAD.

UNDP & UN Women 2022. "COVID-19 Global Gender Response Tracker: methodological note". New York: UN Women.

UNDP & UN Working Group on Business and Human Rights 2019. "Gender dimensions of the Guiding Principles on Business and Human Rights". New York: UNDP.

UNECA 2015. "Illicit financial flows: why Africa needs to 'track it, stop it and get it'". Addis Ababa: UNECA.

UNGA 1966. "International Covenant on Economic Social and Cultural Rights", Resolution 2200A (XXI). 16 December.

UNGA 1979. "Convention on the Elimination of All Forms of Discrimination against Women", Resolution 34/180. 18 December.

UNGA 1986. "Declaration on the Right to Development", A/RES/41/128. New York: UN.

UNGA 1992. "Report of the United Nations Conference on Environment and Development (Rio de Janeiro, 3–14 June 1992)", Annex 1, "Rio Declaration on Environment and Development", A/CONF.151/26 (vol. 1). New York: UN.

UNGA 1995. "Beijing Declaration and Platform for Action adopted by the Fourth World Conference on Women: Action for Equality, Development and Peace", Resolution 50/203. 15 September.

UNGA 2005. "Third report on responsibility of international organizations", A/CN.4/553. New York: UN.

UNGA 2007. "United Nations Declaration on the Rights of Indigenous Peoples". New York: UN.

UNGA 2009. "Optional Protocol to the International Covenant on Economic, Social and Cultural Rights", A/RES/63/117. New York: UN.

UNGA 2011. "Guiding Principles on Business and Human Rights: implementing the United Nations 'Protect, Respect and Remedy' framework", A/HRC/17/31. New York: UN.

UNGA 2014. "Towards the establishment of a multilateral legal framework for sovereign debt restructuring processes", A/68/L.57/Rev.1. New York: UN.

UNGA 2015a. "Transforming our world: the 2030 Agenda for Sustainable Development", A/RES/70/1. New York: UN.

UNGA 2015b. "Addis Ababa Action Agenda of the Third International Conference on Financing for Development", A/RES/69/313. New York: UN.

UNGA 2019a. "Climate change and poverty", A/HRC/41/39. New York: UN.

UNGA 2019b. "International cooperation to combat illicit financial flows and strengthen good practices on asset returns". 16 May.

UNGA 2020. "Protection against violence and discrimination based on sexual orientation and gender identity", A/75/258. New York: UN.

UNGA 2021a. "Human rights-compatible international investment agreements", A/76/238. New York: UN.

UNGA 2021b. "Cooperatives in social development", A/76/209. New York: UN.

UNGA 2021c. "Promotion of international cooperation to combat illicit financial flows and strengthen good practices on asset return to foster sustainable development", A/C.2/76/L.28. New York: UN.

UNGA 2022a. "Towards a global fiscal architecture using a human rights lens", A/77/ 169. New York: UN.

UNGA 2022b. "Right of everyone to the enjoyment of the highest attainable standard of physical and mental health", A/77/197. New York: UN.

UNGA 2023a. "Promotion of inclusive and effective international tax cooperation at the United Nations", A/RES/77/244. New York: UN.

UNGA 2023b. "Promoting the social and solidarity economy for sustainable development", A/RES/77/281. New York: UN.

UNRISD 2022. *Crises of Inequality: Shifting Power for a New Eco-Social Contract*. Geneva: UNRISD.

Unruh, L. *et al.* 2022. "A comparison of 2020 health policy responses to the COVID-19 pandemic in Canada, Ireland, the United Kingdom and the United States of America". *Health Policy* 126 (5): 427–37.

UNWG 2018. "The report of the Working Group on the issue of human rights and transnational corporations and other business enterprises: corporate human rights due diligence—emerging practices, challenges and ways forward", A/73/163. Geneva: UNWG.

Uprimny Yepes, R. & S. Chaparro 2019. "Inequality, human rights and social rights: tensions and complementarities". *Humanity: An International Journal of Human Rights, Humanitarianism, and Development* 10 (3): 376–94.

Utting, P. 2023. "Public policy". In *Encyclopedia of the Social and Solidarity Economy*, I. Yi *et al.* (eds), 400–8. Cheltenham: Edward Elgar.

Vale 2019. "Clarifications on dam I of the Córrego do Feijão mine". 25 January. www.vale.com/pt/w/clarifications-on-the-dam-i-of-the-c%C3%B3rrego-do-feij%C3%A3o-mine.

Van Den Meerssche, D. 2021. "A legal black hole in the cosmos of virtue: the politics of human rights critique against the World Bank". *Human Rights Law Review* 21 (1): 80–107.

Vasquez, E., A. Perez-Brumer & R. Parker 2019. "Social inequities and contemporary struggles for collective health in Latin America". *Global Public Health* 14 (6/7): 777–90.

Vilchinskii, A. 2022. "Chile turns left: the foreign policy agenda of President Gabriel Boric". Australian Institute of International Affairs, 28 January.

Viljoen, F. 2007. *International Human Rights Law in Africa*. Oxford: Oxford University Press.

Von Bogdandy, A. & M. Goldmann 2013. "Sovereign debt restructurings as exercises of international public authority: towards a decentralized sovereign insolvency law". In *Sovereign Financing and International Law: The UNCTAD Principles on Responsible Sovereign Lending and Borrowing*, C. Espósito, Y. Li & J. Bohoslavsky (eds), 39–70. Oxford: Oxford University Press.

Wahlquist, C. 2020. "Juukan Gorge: Rio Tinto blasting of Aboriginal site prompts calls to change antiquated laws". *The Guardian*, 30 May.

Waldron, J. 2006. "The core of the case against judicial review". *Yale Law Journal* 115 (6): 1346–406.

Walker, C., A. Druckman & T. Jackson 2021. "Welfare systems without economic growth: a review of the challenges and next steps for the field". *Ecological Economics* 186. DOI: 10.1016/j.ecolecon.2021.107066.

Waris, A. 2013. *Tax and Development: Solving the Fiscal Crisis through Human Rights*. Nairobi: Law Africa.

Waris, A. 2019. *Financing Africa*. Bamenda, Cameroon: Langaa Research and Publishing Common Initiative Group.

Waris, A. & E. Oyare 2021. "Taxation systems and public policy in Kenya: unpacking the unwritten tax treaty policy". In *Governing Kenya: Public Policy in Theory and Practice*, G. Onyango & G. Hyden (eds), 203–20. London: Palgrave Macmillan.

Waris, A. & L. Seabrooke 2018. "Arrested development in Africa's global wealth chains: accountability and hierarchy among 'tax havens'". In *The Routledge Companion to Tax Avoidance Research*, N. Hashimzade & Y. Epifantseva (eds), 267–86. Abingdon: Routledge.

Watkins, J. & J. Seidelman 2019. "The last gasp of neoliberalism". *Journal of Economic Issues* 53 (2): 363–9.

WBA 2019. *Corporate Human Rights Benchmark: 2019 Key Findings*. Amsterdam: WBA.

WBA 2020. *Corporate Human Rights Benchmark: 2020 Key Findings*. Amsterdam: WBA.

WBA 2022. *Corporate Human Rights Benchmark 2022: Insights Report*. Amsterdam: WBA.

WBG 2020. *Creating a Caring Economy: A Call to Action*. London: WBG.

Wenham, C., J. Smith & R. Morgan 2020. "COVID-19 is an opportunity for gender equality within the workplace and at home". *British Medical Journal* 369. DOI: 10.1136/bmj.m1546.

Wettstein, F. 2009. *Multinational Corporations and Global Justice: Human Rights Obligations of a Quasi-Governmental Institution*. Stanford, CA: Stanford Business Books.

Wettstein, F. 2021. "Betting on the wrong (Trojan) horse: CSR and the implementation of the UN Guiding Principles on Business and Human Rights". *Business and Human Rights Journal* 6 (2): 312–25.

WHO 2020. "Engaging the private health service delivery sector through governance in mixed health systems: strategy report of the WHO Advisory Group on the Governance of the Private Sector for Universal Health Coverage". Geneva: WHO.

WHO 2021. "The WHO Council on the Economics of Health for All: manifesto". Geneva: WHO.

WHO 2022. "Towards better engagement of the private sector in health service delivery: a review of approaches to private sector engagement in Africa". Geneva: WHO.

Whyte, J. 2019. *The Morals of the Market: Human Rights and the Rise of Neoliberalism*. London: Verso.

Wiedmann, T. *et al.* 2013. "The material footprint of nations". *Proceedings of the National Academy of Sciences of the United States of America* 112 (20): 6271–6.

Wiedmann, T. *et al.* 2020. "Scientists' warning on affluence". *Nature Communications* 11 (1): 3107–17.

Wilkinson, R. & K. Pickett 2018. *The Inner Level: How More Equal Societies Reduce Stress, Restore Sanity and Improve Everyone's Well-Being*. London: Allen Lane.

Williams, D. 2020. "COVID-19 and private health: market and governance failure". *Development* [Rome] 63 (2/4): 181–90.

Williams, D., K. Chun Yung & K. Grépin 2021. "The failure of private health services: COVID-19 induced crises in low- and middle-income country (LMIC) health systems". *Global Public Health* 16 (8/9): 1320–33.

Williams, E. 2021. *Capital and Slavery*, 3rd edn. Chapel Hill, NC: University of North Carolina Press.

Wills, J. & B. Warwick 2016. "Contesting austerity: the potential and pitfalls of socio-economic rights discourse". *Indiana Journal of Global Legal Studies* 23 (2): 629–64.

Wilting, H. & K. Vringer 2009. "Carbon and land use accounting from a producer's and consumer's perspective: an empirical examination covering the world". *Economic Systems Research* 21 (3): 291–310.

Winch, A., K. Forkert & S. Davison 2019. "Neoliberalism, feminism and transnationalism: editorial". *Soundings: A Journal of Politics and Culture* 71: 4–10.

Wong, Y. 2012. *Sovereign Finance and the Poverty of Nations: Odious Debt in International Law*. Cheltenham: Edward Elgar.

Worger, W., N. Clark & E. Alpers 2010. *Africa and the West: A Documentary History*, vol. 2, *From Colonialism to Independence, 1875 to the Present*. Oxford: Oxford University Press.

World Bank 1986. "Financing Health Services in Developing Countries: an agenda for reform", Report 6563. Washington, DC: World Bank.

World Bank 1993. *World Development Report 1993: Investing in Health*. Washington, DC: World Bank.

World Bank 2022a. "Debt Service Suspension Initiative". 10 March. www.worldbank.org/en/topic/debt/brief/covid-19-debt-service-suspension-initiative.

World Bank 2022b. "Debt-service payments put biggest squeeze on poor countries since 2000", press release. 6 December.

World Bank 2022c. *World Development Report 2022: Finance for an Equitable Recovery*. Washington, DC: World Bank.

World Economic Forum 2019. "Chart of the day: these countries have the largest carbon footprints". 2 January. www.weforum.org/agenda/2019/01/chart-of-the-day-these-countries-have-the-largest-carbon-footprints.

Xiao, H. *et al.* 2019. "Changes in carbon intensity globally and in countries: attribution and decomposition analysis". *Applied Energy* 235: 1492–504.

Yamin, A. & J. Curtain 2022. "Lessons from the pandemic: building a movement for global public investment". Open Global Rights, 20 September.

Yi, I. 2023. "Social policy". In *Encyclopedia of the Social and Solidarity Economy*, I. Yi *et al.* (eds), 416–24. Cheltenham: Edward Elgar.

Yi, I. & S. Bruelisauer 2020. "Social and solidarity economy for the integration of migrants and refugees: experiences from three European cities", Research and Policy Brief 31. Geneva: UNRISD.

Yi, I., E. Koechlein & A. de Negri Filho 2017. "Introduction: the universalization of health care in emerging economies". In *Towards Universal Health Care in Emerging*

Economies: Opportunities and Challenges, I. Yi (ed.), 1–23. London: Palgrave Macmillan/UNRISD.

Yi, I. *et al.* (eds) 2023. *Encyclopedia of the Social and Solidarity Economy.* Cheltenham: Edward Elgar.

Yilmaz Vastardis, A. 2018. "Justice bubbles for the privileged: a critique of the investor-state dispute settlement proposals for the EU's investment agreements". *London Review of International Law* 6 (2): 279–97.

Young, K. 2012. *Constituting Economic and Social Rights.* Oxford: Oxford University Press.

Zavaleta, R. 1986. *Lo nacional-popular en Bolivia.* Mexico City: Siglo XXI.

Zimmermann, K. & P. Graziano 2020. "Mapping different worlds of eco-welfare states". *Sustainability* 12 (5). DOI: 10.3390/su12051819.

INDEX